# Gendering
# the European Parliament

# Gendering the European Parliament

## Structures, Policies and Practices

Edited by
Petra Ahrens and Lise Rolandsen Agustín

ROWMAN &
LITTLEFIELD
—————INTERNATIONAL
London • New York

ecpr PRESS

Published by Rowman & Littlefield International Ltd
6 Tinworth Street, London, SE11 5AL, United Kingdom
www.rowmaninternational.com

In partnership with the European Consortium for Political Research, Harbour House, 6–8 Hythe -Quay, Colchester, CO2 8JF, United Kingdom

Rowman & Littlefield International Ltd is an affiliate of Rowman & Littlefield
4501 Forbes Boulevard, Suite 200, Lanham, Maryland 20706, USA
With additional offices in Boulder, New York, Toronto (Canada), and Plymouth (UK)
www.rowman.com

**British Library Cataloguing in Publication Data**

A catalogue record for this book is available from the British Library

ISBN: HB 978-1-78552-308-3

**Library of Congress Cataloging-in-Publication Data Available**

ISBN: 978-1-78552-308-3 (cloth)
ISBN: 978-1-5381-5686-5 (pbk)
ISBN: 978-1-78552-309-0 (electronic)

# ECPR Press

ECPR Press is an imprint of the European Consortium for Political Research in partnership with Rowman & Littlefield International. It publishes original research from leading political scientists and the best among early career researchers in the discipline. Its scope extends to all fields of political science, international relations and political thought, without restriction in either approach or regional focus. It is also open to interdisciplinary work with a predominant political dimension.

## ECPR PRESS EDITORS

### Editors

**Ian O'Flynn** is Senior Lecturer in Political Theory at Newcastle University, UK.

**Laura Sudulich** is Reader in Public Policy at the University of Essex, UK. She is also affiliated to Cevipol (Centre d'Étude de la vie Politique) at the Université liber de Bruxelles, Belgium.

### Associate Editors

**Andrew Glencross** is Senior Lecturer in the Department of Politics and International Relations at Aston University, UK.

**Liam Weeks** is Lecturer in the Department of Government and Politics, University College Cork, Ireland, and Honorary Senior Research Fellow, Department of Politics and International Relations, Macquarie University, Australia.

To all those working towards making Europe a place truly respecting
core values – democracy, equality and diversity

# Contents

# Abbreviations

| | |
|---|---|
| AFCO | European Parliament's Committee on Constitutional Affairs |
| AfD | Alternative for Germany |
| AFET | European Parliament's Committee on Foreign Affairs |
| ALDE | Alliance of Liberals and Democrats for Europe |
| ARC | Abortion Rights Campaign |
| CONT | European Parliament's Committee on Budgetary Control |
| COREPER | Committee of Permanent Representatives |
| CSO | Civil Society Organisation |
| CULT | European Parliament's Committee on Culture and Education |
| DG | Directorate-General |
| DI | Discursive Institutionalism |
| DR | Descriptive Representation |
| EC | European Commission |
| ECHR | European Court of Human Rights |
| ECON | European Parliament's Committee on Economic and Monetary Affairs |
| ECR | European Conservatives and Reformists |
| ECSC | European Coal and Steel Community |
| EEC | European Economic Community |
| EFD | Europe of Freedom and Democracy |
| EFDD | Europe of Freedom and Direct Democracy |
| EIGE | European Institute for Gender Equality |
| EMPL | European Parliament's Committee on Social Affairs |
| ENF | Europe of Nations and Freedom |
| ENVI | European Parliament's Committee on Environment, Public Health and Food Safety |

| | |
|---|---|
| EP | European Parliament |
| EPP | European People's Party |
| EU | European Union |
| EWL | European Women's Lobby |
| FEMM | European Parliament's Committee on Women's Rights and Gender Equality |
| FI | Feminist Institutionalism |
| GM | Gender Mainstreaming |
| GMA | Gender Mainstreaming Amendment |
| Greens/EFA | Greens/European Free Alliance |
| GUE/NGL | European United Left/Nordic Green Left |
| IGC | Intergovernmental Conferences |
| IMCO | European Parliament's Committee on Internal Market and Consumer Protection |
| JURI | European Parliament's Committee on Legal Affairs |
| LGBTIQ | Lesbian, Gay, Bisexual, Transgender, Intersex, and Queer |
| LIBE | European Parliament's Committee on Civil Liberties, Justice and Home Affairs |
| MEP | Member of the European Parliament |
| MFF | Multiannual Financial Framework |
| NWCI | National Women's Council of Ireland |
| OLP | Ordinary Legislative Procedure |
| PECH | European Parliament's Committee on Fisheries |
| PES | Party of European Socialists |
| REGI | European Parliament's Committee on Regional Development |
| S&D | Progressive Alliance of Socialists and Democrats |
| SEA | Single European Act |
| SEDE | European Parliament's Subcommittee on Security and Defense |
| SR | Substantive Representation |
| SRHR | Sexual and Reproductive Health and Rights |
| TEU | Treaty on European Union |
| TFEU | Treaty on the Functioning of the European Union |
| TTIP | Transatlantic Trade and Investment Partnership |
| UKIP | UK Independence Party |

# Textboxes

# Figures

# Tables

# Acknowledgements

The book is rooted in an inspiring and long-lasting research exchange between the co-editors and furthermore the engaged chapter contributors. At the Fourth European Conference on Politics and Gender (Uppsala, Sweden, June 2015), we organised a panel with prospective chapter contributors on 'Gendering the EU Institutions: Structures, Policies and Practices of the European Parliament'. We are grateful for the feedback and encouragement we received from our fellow colleagues during the panel, because they clearly motivated us to pursue this research perspective further – with the result in the form of this edited volume. On the path to getting there, we are very grateful for the generous funding we received from the Humboldt-Universität zu Berlin in the form of a KOSMOS Workshop 'Gendering the European Parliament: Structures, Policies and Practices', which took place in spring 2016 at the Department of Social Sciences. We want to express our gratitude to our colleagues who acted as discussants – Diana Burlacu, Ksenia Meshkova, Katja Müller, Anita Nissen, Katharina Zimmermann – and to Martina Dietz for organising and ensuring the smooth running of the workshop.

As noted earlier, research focusing specifically on gender and the EP is rare and we editors are extremely grateful for the openness and enthusiasm of all our contributors when we approached them with ideas for chapters they could write – some of them who we never met before and who we traced through publications or hints from other colleagues. As a result, the book brings together scholars from a variety of theoretical and methodological backgrounds united by their ability to provide the puzzle pieces necessary to fully comprehend the EP from a gender perspective. While the book came into existence, we experienced the collaboration as a fruitful laboratory for exchange among different approaches. The book now investigates institutionalisation in the EP in a broad fashion, analysing the development of organisational patterns, rules, and procedures and their effect on gender equality as well as revealing operational aspects, the dynamics of the political groups and balance between legislature and executive, and their impact on this policy field.

Putting the final manuscript together would not have been possible without additional support. We received valuable and constructive advice from anonymous reviewers that helped improve the manuscript tremendously. Moreover, we would like to thank Donna Genta Permatasari for her support in technically setting up and compiling the draft manuscript. Finally, we are grateful for the guidance we received from ECPR Press and Rowman & Littlefield International, in particular from Rebecca Anastasi, Madeleine Hatfield, and Dhara Snowden.

Finally, we are blessed with families that support us in our endeavours – particularly our children that hopefully grow up in an ever better Europe.

# 1

# Gendering the European Parliament

## Introducing Structures, Policies, and Practices

*Petra Ahrens[1] and Lise Rolandsen Agustín*

Since its first direct election in 1979, the European Parliament (EP) has been considered a key promoter of social policy and a fierce supporter of gender equality policy with important implications for Member States' policies (Abels and Mushaben 2014; van der Vleuten in this volume). The EP has one of the highest percentages of female parliamentarians, and its multinational composition is unique in the world. To date, however, research on gender equality in the EP has mainly focused on equal representation in decision-making, on the recruitment of female Members of the European Parliament (MEPs), on social and family policy, on setting policy agendas, and on how the EP collaborates with other actors on gender equality policies dealing with issues such as combating violence against women. Gender scholars have also paid particular attention to the role and functions of the Committee on Women's Rights and Gender Equality (FEMM) as a main site for gender equality policy development in the EP (Ahrens 2016; Rolandsen Agustín 2012, 2013; Woodward 2004).

Despite the EP's central role in the European Union (EU) and as an agent for gender equality, neither mainstream EU-integration studies nor EU gender equality policy scholars have examined the EP's power and responsibilities regarding the broader gender policy field, including the EP's internal struggles and fluctuations regarding gender equality, and the roles of political groups, and its administration therein. Furthermore, even though feminist institutionalist approaches have proven fruitful when it comes to the European Commission (EC) – which has been well researched as regards its gender equality policies, implementation of gender mainstreaming, and also the relationships among different Directorate-General (DGs) (Jacquot 2015; MacRae and Weiner 2017; Pollack and Hafner-Burton 1999) – this approach has seldom been applied to the EP. Although the EP represents a great case study for the impact of a growing gender balance on political institutions, clearly revealing the results of gender equality policies and actions, there is little coordinated research on the EP's gendering as an institution.

Aside from the EC and the Council of the European Union, the EP is the third central supranational institution of the EU. Its role and powers have been constantly developing and changing. Enlargement to Central and Eastern Europe resulted in institutional changes, and with every new European treaty decision-making procedures have been modified and the responsibilities for many policy fields reshuffled. While the Commission has the right of initiative for legislative proposals, the Lisbon Treaty (2007) put the EP and the Council at the same level in almost all legislative procedures with the introduction of the Ordinary Legislative Procedure (Article 294 TFEU), which extended to many EU policies (Abels in this volume; Rittberger 2012). One of the consequences is that today's EP has become more political in general, the 'election' of the Commission's President (i.e. the nomination of the EC president should reflect the outcome of the EP elections) being one of the most recent changes to the supranational institutional power relations. The EP is a unique parliamentary body, since it is the only directly elected supranational Parliament with such wide-ranging competencies. Unlike in the Member States, there is no parliament-based government and therefore no opposition in the strict parliamentary sense.

The recent crises that hit the EU and its Member States have also led to changes to the EP (Walby 2015): the financial and economic crises, which severely affected gender equality (Kantola and Lombardo 2017; Karamessini and Rubery 2014); the so-called refugee crisis (Freedman 2017); the crisis of representation, with the level of citizen trust in political institutions dropping and support growing for Eurosceptic radical-right parties (Spierings and Zaslove 2017); and the threat of disintegration through the Brexit vote, which also affects gender equality (Dustin et al. 2019; Guerrina and Masselot 2018). The political landscape of Europe and the EU Member States has changed significantly in recent years, with populist, anti-EU, and right-wing parties seated in the majority of national parliaments as well as in the EP (Köttig et al. 2017). Even though such parties had been represented in the EP since the first direct elections in 1979, only in 2009 did they meet the requirements and find the ideological agreement to form a political group.[2] The results of the 2014 EP elections particularly transformed the EP's (ideological) composition and political priorities, and with it gender equality. Given the increasing power of the EP and its participation in European legislative procedures, the question of what the potential impact of right-wing political groups on gender equality will be is substantial.

Research on anti-feminist positions within the European Conservatives and Reformists (ECR), the Europe of Freedom and Direct Democracy (EFDD), and Europe of Nations and Freedom (ENF) at the supranational level is still in its infancy and limited to the legislative period 2009–2014. Although a 'grand coalition' of the European People's Party (EPP) and the Progressive Alliance of Social Democrats (S&D) is still central to legislative processes, content-related struggles over sociopolitical issues have also increased between the two groups in recent years (Kantola and Rolandsen Agustín 2016). In the FEMM Committee, as other studies have shown, there is a centre-left coalition of Progressive Alliance of Socialists and Democrats (S&D), the Alliance of Liberals and Democrats for Europe (ALDE), the United European Left/Nordic Green Left (GUE/NGL), and the Greens/European Free Alliance (Greens/EFA), allowing them to shape the position of the committee more strongly than in the EP plenary (Kantola and Rolandsen Agustín 2016, 2019; see Warasin et al. in this volume). Janssen (2013) noted that the then-non-attached right-wing MEPs, the ECR, and the EFD (2014–2019 EFDD) were equally opposed to anti-discrimination policies and pursued similar racist and nationalist positions. Krizsan and Siim (2018) show that such racist and nationalist positions are unevenly distributed, with a great deal of variation between countries. In the 2014 EP election campaign, right-wing parties pursued a 'femonationalism', and though nationalist perspectives on equality and family hardly played a role in northern European countries, they were central in Germany and Southern, Central, and Eastern Europe (Krizsan and Siim 2018). These recent changes in the political landscape should also shape current research agendas. Throughout this book, we thus combine the analysis of the EP long-term development regarding gender equality with the most recent changes in order to interpret the role and function of the EP in the light of the changing political landscape.

It becomes ever more pertinent to analyse, question, and discuss how gender equality is defined and which underlying understandings are at play. As the idea of gender equality and what we understand as a gender equal society are highly disputed, this presents a theoretical as well as an empirical challenge. Methodologically, Kantola and Verloo call for 'all researchers to be more precise in articulating the choices made in understanding or operationalising the concept' of gender equality and thereby address 'gender blindness', 'gender bias', as well as the 'political nature of gender equality' (2018, 211).[3] In addressing gender equality as an empirically contested notion, literature on representation has discussed how to interpret the notion of women's interests, including recent research on cross-party alliances and on conservative women and their role in advancing/halting gender equality. We are witnessing increased anti-feminism in Europe, such as the resistance to abortion rights, hate speech online, and the fight against gender study programmes. Opposition to gender equality and sexual rights is growing, with right-wing actors providing resistance to gender equality (Köttig et al. 2017; Kováts 2018; Kuhar and Paternotte 2017) and explicitly doing so in the national parties represented in the EP (Kemper 2014; Krizsan and Siim 2018). Feminist norms are being challenged by anti-equality and anti-diversity positions partly due to religious and ideological divides as well as to the rise of nationalism (Pajnik and Sauer 2017; Verloo 2018). In return, gender research criticises EU policies for a lack of political will to consider the gender and diversity consequences of austerity policies and immigration policies (Kantola and Lombardo 2017; Karamessini and Rubery 2014). At the same time, the literature also points to the potential of critical actors and acts to promote gender equality policies within gendered institutions such as the EP (Mushaben in this volume).

By bringing together a unique set of researchers to illuminate a multitude of aspects of this important parliament from a gender perspective, this book intends to challenge the silent assumption that the EP is a unified actor for gender equality. Given the EC's decreasing engagement for gender equality (Ahrens 2018a; Jacquot 2015), this research is even more important. We need to know where the EP stands and how stable its position is as a defender of gender equality, and we need to shed light on the complex dynamics of EP policy-making as well as on various crucial differences within the institution. The book thus provides an innovative multifaceted analysis of the EP by studying it comprehensively from a gender perspective and addressing its changes and continuities. It asks how and why the EP, as an institution, is gendered and what the gendered impacts of recent changes are when it comes to the EP's structures, policies, and practices.

## GENDERED POLITICAL REPRESENTATION

The EP is embedded in EU policy- and decision-making processes through a complicated set of rules and routines that cast it in different roles depending on the topic at hand. In general, the EC is often presented as the government of the EU because it holds the monopoly on initiating legislation and is – similar to the EP – a truly supranational institution. As the intergovernmental decision-making body representing Member-State governments, the Council, on the other hand, is usually described as the most powerful EU institution. Yet the EP has also gained considerable power and responsibilities over time, was crucial in institutionalising representative democracy, and also re-designed its own rules of procedure (Abels in this volume; Rittberger 2012). At this point, the Commission can be classified as having executive powers, the EP legislative ones, while the Council has executive as well as legislative powers (Lelieveldt and Princen 2015, 49–51).

The EU has often been criticised for its alleged democratic deficit: a majority of decisions is taken behind closed doors; citizens have no control over who becomes Commissioner; transnational business interest groups are strong and supranational civil society organisations (CSO) weak; and it is difficult to hold individual governments accountable for joint decisions taken by the Council. Often, the EP is presented as the only real democratic institution, because it is the EU's only directly elected body. In addition, the EP has undergone important institutional changes over the decades: from an indirectly to a directly elected assembly; from an advisory to a decision-making body; and from a parliament representing the population of six Member States to one representing that of twenty-eight Member States (with the concomitant increase in diversity). Nevertheless, its limited influence over the composition of the Commission is often still criticised, as are the EP elections' status as 'second-order elections' and the different roles performed by its political groups compared to those of national parties (Lelieveldt and Princen 2015, 288–91).

## Gender Gaps in European Parliament Representation

In the following, we turn to another democratic deficit, but one that is gradually closing in the EP: the gender gap in representation. Despite its quite high share of female MEPs, the EP is only slowly getting close to parity on all levels: among MEPs, in leadership positions, and in its own administration. Though EU institutions and the Council of Europe clearly emphasised the importance of parity in elected office, which has had an impact in some of the EU Member States, they themselves lag behind in terms of their formulated standards (Mac-Rae 2012).

The EP has 751 members,[4] elected for a five-year term by the citizens of the EU Member States. Figure 1.1 shows the shares of women and men in the EP since its first direct election.[5] From the direct elections of 1979 onwards, the share of female MEPs was usually higher than the EU average of all individual Member States,[6] an issue that was often explained by the low power of the EP, but has not changed despite its growing powers (see also Abels in this volume).

Compared to female representation in national parliaments, the national delegations to the EP often have a higher share. Before 2019's EP elections, twenty-one Member States had a higher share of female MEPs than of female members in their national parliament, and three with even more than 50 per cent: Finland (76.3 per cent), Croatia (54.5 per cent), and Ireland (54.5 per cent) (Shreeves et al. 2019, 2).

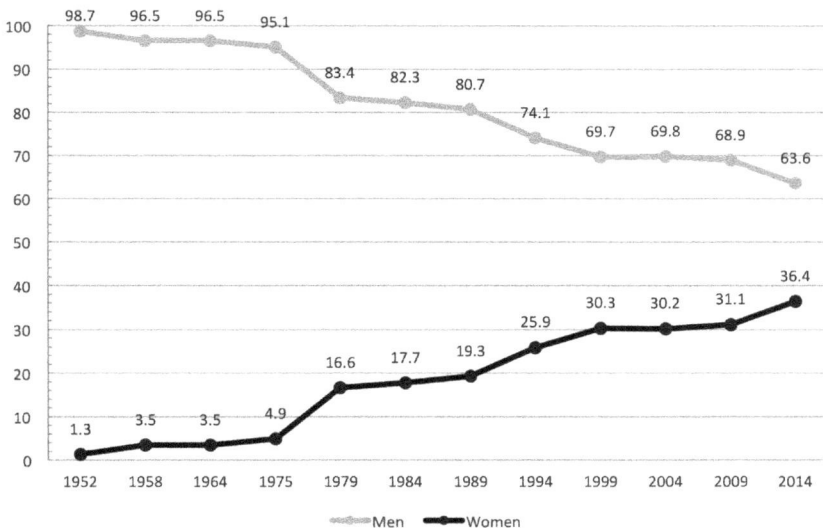

**Figure 1.1 Members of the European Parliament 1952–2014, Women and Men in Per cent.**

Source: Graph and calculation by authors. Data from European Parliament 2018a, 5.

**Table 1.1 Political Groups in the EP 2014–2019**

| Name | Seats | Seat Share % | Number of Countries | Women % | Men % |
|---|---|---|---|---|---|
| EPP | 219 | 28.8 | 27 | 30.3 | 69.7 |
| S&D | 189 | 25.3 | 28 | 45.0 | 55.0 |
| ECR | 71 | 9.9 | 18 | 21.4 | 78.6 |
| ALDE | 68 | 9.1 | 21 | 40.0 | 60.0 |
| GUE/NGL | 52 | 6.9 | 14 | 50.0 | 50.0 |
| Greens/EFA | 51 | 6.8 | 18 | 42.0 | 58.0 |
| EFDD | 44 | 6.0 | 8 | 38.6 | 61.4 |
| ENF | 36 | 4.9 | 9 | 30.5 | 69.5 |

Source: http://www.europarl.europa.eu/meps/de/hemicycle.html, as of March 2018. Share of women/men: own calculation.

EPP – European People's Party; S&D – Progressive Alliance of Socialists and Democrats; ECR – European Conservatives and Reformists; ALDE – Alliance of Liberals and Democrats for Europe; GUE/NGL – European United Left/Nordic Green Left; Greens/EFA – Greens/European Free Alliance; EFDD – Europe of Freedom and Direct Democracy; ENF – Europe of Nations and Freedom

## Gender Gaps in Political Groups

The EP is currently organised in eight political groups plus non-attached MEPs:[7] the EPP, the S&D, the ECR, the ALDE, the GUE/NGL, the Greens/EFA, EFDD, and ENF (see table 1.1).

Even though there lately have been attempts to run EU-wide election campaigns, the race is more often one between the national parties and on national issues (Lelieveldt and Princen 2015). The parties in the EP are not intergovernmentally organised along nationalities but supranationally along ideological lines. The ideological lines are also indicative of the share of women amongst MEPs (cf. table 1.1), though some right-wing national parties[8] had a fairly high proportion of women (Abels and Mushaben 2014, 144). Almost all political groups reach the so-called critical mass of 30 per cent which stipulates this threshold must be crossed to allow for women to obtain genuine influence in decision-making (Dahlerup 2006).

## Gender Gaps in Leadership Positions

EP leadership positions have been, and are still, dominated by men, even though the numbers are constantly moving towards greater gender balance (European Parliament 2014c, 2018b). Of the fifteen EP presidents elected since 1979, only two have been women: Simone Veil (1979–1982) and Nicole Fontaine (1999–2002). Since 2002, there have been seven male EP presidents in a row. The second highest leadership positions, the 14 EP vice-presidents, were before the 2019 elections taken up by nine men (64.3 per cent) and five women (35.7 per cent) (European Parliament 2018b, 7), which is better than the previous term with eleven vice-presidents of which eight were men (78.6 per cent) and only three were women (21.4 per cent) (European Parliament 2014c, 7) but worse than in 2016, when there were eight men (57.1 per cent) and six women (42.9 per cent) (European Parliament 2016b, 7).

Political group (co-)chairs are another important role, and in 2019 only two of eleven (less than 20 per cent) were taken up by women: Gabriele Zimmer chaired GUE/NGL and Ska Keller co-chaired the Greens/EFA (European Parliament 2018b, 10).[9] EP delegations are in a similar situation, as only ten of the thirty-nine (25.6 per cent) were led by women (European Parliament 2018b, 14).

Most of the work in the EP is still done by the committees covering the various policy fields. In 2018, committee chairs were shared equally among men and women, and women chairs not only covered the so-called soft (feminised) policy issues such as women's rights and gender equality, culture and education, or petitions, but also the so-called hard (masculinised) fields such as budgetary control, the internal market, security and defence, and terrorism (European Parliament 2018b, 11). However, research shows that gendered divisions of labour and stereotypes do still abound in the EP's practices, like in most other political institutions. This is, for instance, reflected in the distribution of MEPs (not chairs) in committees; policy areas such as economy and finance are considered to be masculine terrain, and female MEPs characterise the culture of the committees in these areas as being influenced by the exclusionary nature of men's networks (Kantola and Rolandsen Agustín 2019).

Apart from the national and political group distribution, we lack data on intersectional aspects such as age, (dis)abilities, and more importantly race. A 2018 newspaper article illustrated that people of colour are particularly under-represented in the EP, and the situation is likely to worsen after Brexit (Rankin 2018). Though the situation has improved over time, the EP administration also suffers from an unequal representation of women and men and a lack of data on intersectional aspects. Men are over-represented in leadership positions and middle management, and under-represented among lower staff levels – and vice versa for women (European Parliament 2018b). In 2017, the struggle to improve gender balance was bolstered by a report from the EP High Level Group on Gender Equality and Diversity, setting clear targets until 2019 and proposing measures to improve gender equality in the workplace (European Parliament 2017a).

**Gender Equality Bodies**

FEMM is considered the core EP actor for gender equality policy (Ahrens 2016; Pristed Nielsen and Rolandsen Agustín 2013; Rolandsen Agustín 2012). Aside from this important actor, several other bodies can contribute to furthering gender equality concerns in the EP. Located at the top of the institution, the High Level Group on Gender Equality and Diversity (established in 2004) is supposed to promote training and awareness-raising on gender equality and mainstreaming among the EP staff (European Parliament 2017a). Gender mainstreaming is also supported by two networks: one, established in 2003, consists of the MEPs in charge of introducing it in their respective committees, and the other network of gender mainstreaming administrators was started in 2016 (see also Ahrens in this volume). With regard to workplace harassment, including sexual harassment, the EP established the Anti-harassment Committee in 2004, which has so far been unstudied.

## PUBLIC SPHERE AND PARTICIPATION

Of the major EU institutions, the EP is generally considered to be the most open point of access for civil society actors; whereas the EC has traditionally favoured dialogue with a few selected civil society partners, the EP has been more versatile both through contacts to individual MEPs – often based on party and political-group affiliation as well as ideology – collaborations in intergroups,[10] or invitations to committee-level activities such as hearings. Most of the scholarly literature on the interaction between the EU and civil society within the sphere of gender equality policies has focused on the European Women's Lobby (EWL), the most established and dominant actor in the field (e.g. Helfferich and Kolb 2001; Strid 2009). The EWL has sought to balance providing expertise on the one hand and ensuring legitimacy by representing citizens' interests in the EU system on the other. In this regard, Holst and Seibicke (2018) find that the expertise the EWL brings to the EU can be classified not only as technical and scientific, but also as representative and moral or normative. While the EWL has a platform structure, which means that different national member organisations 'aggregate' interests, which are then channelled and represented in the EU through the Brussels-based umbrella organisations (Strid 2009), the lobby group still succeeds in speaking with one voice within the EU institutions in order to maximize its potential for influence. Though the EWL has enjoyed more stable financing from the EU than other civil society actors in the field and provided significant gender expertise, in recent years the lobby group has also been challenged by organisations and MEPs who do not share the EWL's dominant discourse of women as workers or its aim to increase women's labour-market participation, preferring instead to focus on women as carers and their 'free choice' in terms of staying at home, for instance (Rolandsen Agustín 2012). This development runs parallel to a general setback for gender equality policies in the EU, related to the economic crisis among other things. The EWL has responded to this shift by finding new sources of financing and re-strategising collaborations to offer a gendered analysis of the crisis in collaboration with other NGOs (Cullen 2015).

In an effort to enhance the share of female MEPs, the EWL has run campaigns focusing on gender balance since the 2009 EP elections. The *50/50 Women for Europe – Europe for Women* campaign aims to enhance commitment to equal representation through various actions, including a pledge for election candidates, a petition, as well as a feminist manifesto. The EP has also supported balanced representation, for instance, by actively promoting gender-balanced lists for the EP elections (European Parliament 2019a). Within the EP's political groups, attention has been raised around gender-balance-promoting measures such as internal quotas and/or gendered representation rules, and there has also been cooperation across political groups to pressure the EP to have equal representation at its executive level (see Warasin et al. in this volume). Recently, other initiatives related to the role of women in the EP have also emerged from within. Following the #MeToo movement, the EP also found itself in the spotlight, challenged to deal with its own sexual harassment issues. An EP own-initiative report was drafted in 2018 – emphasising the problem's widespread nature as well as the need for more accessible reporting measures and clear sanctions for perpetrators – and EP workers from across the administrative and political sectors created the MeTooEP webpage, providing space to share sexual-harassment testimony.

The broader context – gendered political participation and the European public sphere – collides with the consensual mode of policy-making that characterises EU politics at large (Tömmel 2014). Power relations are not always clearly detectable, particularly when it comes to normative policy issues like gender equality (Ahrens 2018a). Key questions like who has the power to push gender equality forward and where are the barriers require contextualisation to be answered. As our chapters show, power is located on different levels of the EP: with individuals, political groups, and committees and with the EP as a unique actor.

## OUTLINE OF THE CHAPTERS

The chapters in this book comprehensively study the changes and continuities of the EP's gendered structures and practices, bringing together a variety of theoretical, methodological, and disciplinary backgrounds. They are united by their ability to provide the puzzle pieces necessary to fully comprehend the EP from a gender perspective, functioning as a fruitful laboratory for exchange among different approaches.

Tackling the EP's role and history, Part I provides the necessary groundwork for understanding the connection between the EP and gender equality, looking at its changing role in the institutionalised process of EU integration, its actual activities regarding gender equality, and the construction of gender in parliamentary debates.

Chapter 2 'The Powers of the European Parliament: Implications for Gender Equality Policy' by Gabriele Abels demonstrates that the EP presents a counterexample in terms of the often-assumed decline of power when parliaments become feminised. By contrasting the EP's development with standard parliamentary functions, the chapter illustrates that the relation between 'feminisation' and parliamentarisation and between democratisation and competence transfers is a very complex one. The chapter also highlights their gendered implications for each of the different standard parliamentary functions and how these will likely influence the future of Europe due to the future parliamentarisation of the EU system.

Chapter 3 'The European Parliament as a Constant Promoter of Gender Equality: Another European Myth?' by Anna van der Vleuten reviews the historical changes to the EP and its contributions to EU gender equality policy. The chapter presents a theoretically informed historical narrative of the EP's engagement with gender equality drawing on three potential explanations: a representation hypothesis, a feminist institutionalist hypothesis, and a legitimacy hypothesis. Distinguishing four phases that in themselves each have a stable institutional setting, the chapter highlights the changes and continuities in the EP as regards the defence of gender equality over the decades.

Aside from the connection between EP gender equality policy and descriptive and substantive representation, the symbolic dimension of gender discourses also plays an important role, as confirmed in chapter 4, 'Staging Power: Constructing Gender in the Debates of the European Parliament, 1999–2014' by Julia Marie Zimmermann. She examines how femininities, masculinities, and notions of gender relations are constructed in plenary debates in relation to vertical segregation in politics and economy, particularly in the aftermath of the 2008 economic and financial crisis. The chapter deals with the representative claims, participation in debates, and what they stand for: presenting gender equality policy as a 'women's issue' (often in an essentialising way) or as a business case.

Political strategies to promote gender equality, on the one hand, and the impact of policy processes, on the other, are core features of a gendered approach to EP policy-making. Part II, on strategies and outreach beyond parliamentary affairs, comprises four chapters addressing the EP implementation of political strategies, such as gender mainstreaming and budgeting, as well as the actor constellations and collaborations that facilitate or hinder this, including civil society interaction. Together, the chapters highlight how policy-making processes are embedded in, and interact with, institutional structures and practices to create highly gendered outcomes. They seek to explain how these dynamics either facilitate or hinder progress in gender equality policies.

In chapter 5, 'Undermining Critical Mass: The Impact of Trilogues and Treaty Reforms on Gender-Sensitive Decision-Making in the European Parliament', Joyce Mushaben argues that, although women's increased descriptive representation in the EP can be explained through critical acts, the critical mass of women, once represented, is undercut by gender-blind treaty reforms and the increased use of trilogues as a mode of decision-making, which put a stop to further critical acts. As the EP as an institution became more powerful, women did not gain power apace, increasing their presence but not their impact. Shrinking the democratic gender deficit in terms of descriptive representation therefore led to widening it in terms of substantive representation.

In chapter 6, 'Working against the Tide? Institutionalising Gender Mainstreaming in the European Parliament', Petra Ahrens reviews the institutionalisation of gender mainstreaming as the main EU strategy to promote gender equality, assessing how the EP anchored it in its rules and routines. Her policy frame analysis of six EP resolutions on gender mainstreaming covering the period 2003–2019 shows that the FEMM Committee managed to make it an established practice and returning subject by taking over the reporting. Studying its institutionalisation also shows that the process became de-politicised and is less successfully institutionalised in the practices of EP committees and delegations.

The EU budget is analysed as a gender equality strategy in Firat Cengiz's 'Gendering the EU Budget: Can European Parliament Play the Role of a Gender Budgeting Advocate?' (chapter 7). Using a capability-based approach, Cengiz focuses on the EP's potential for taking up a pioneering role in gendering the EU budget as a democratisation strategy that would bring citizens and their needs into the policy-making process. At the same time, budgetary accountability is increased by evaluating whether political commitments were upheld. This should be a welcome opportunity for the EU in times of citizen distrust towards political institutions.

While the first two parts of the book address broader structures and practices inside the EP, as well as the EP as an actor itself, Part III explores the micro-level of EP policy-making by exploring MEPs' role in steering gender equality. The chapters ask how parliamentary procedures shape MEPs' ability to promote gender equality and which role the national contexts play here.

In chapter 8, 'Feminist to Its Fingertips? Gendered Divisions of Labour and the Committee on Women's Rights and Gender Equality', Mary Nugent analyses how forces of change (towards gender equality) and resistance (against gender equality) compete in the FEMM Committee. The chapter shows how a gendered division of labour persists within the structures of the EP despite general expectations of continuous progress in gender equality over time. Men remain a minority on the 'low-status' Committee and the few male members are less likely to take an active role in its work.

In chapter 9, the authors (Markus Warasin, Johanna Kantola, Lise Rolandsen Agustín, and Ciara Coughlan) argue that gender equality is becoming more and more politicised and marked by polarisation at the European level. The chapter (entitled 'Politicisation of Gender Equality in the European Parliament: Cohesion and Inter-Group Coalitions in Plenary and Committees') analyses inter-group coalitions as well as intra-group cohesion rates regarding gender equality policy issues and compares voting patterns at the level of the plenary on the one hand and the FEMM Committee on the other. At the plenary level, intra-group cohesion is high and the large political groups enter into coalitions; at the committee level, cohesion is lower in centre-right wing groups, and centre-left wing groups tend to form coalitions.

In 'The European Parliament and Irish Female MEPs: Female Political Agency for Gender Equality' (chapter 10), Pauline Cullen sheds light on the dynamics between the national and European levels. The key questions are how female politicians operate in a multilevel context and, especially, how weak opportunities for women's interests at the national level may lead to stronger mobilisation within the EP as an alternative strategy to promote gender equality. Cullen argues that the national political context, including party-political discipline, limits female political agency in the Irish case. The EP to some extent provides opportunities for gendered mobilisation, but centrist and right-wing MEPs have especially still been constrained in the EP context, for instance, by refusing membership in the FEMM Committee.

An integrated analysis of the descriptive and substantive representation of women shows the different 'rules of the game' at the national and the European levels. In chapter 11, 'Overcoming Male Dominance? The Representation of Women in the European Parliament Delegations of the Postcommunist EU Member States', Christina Chiva focuses on women MEPs from Postcommunist Member States. Descriptively, women are better represented in the EP than at the national level and, substantively, gender equality issues are less contested at the EP level, which enhances the possibilities to act in favour of women's interests. These findings lead Chiva to suggest a 'socialisation-effect hypothesis' whereby MEPs from Postcommunist Member States are socialised into a gender equality mindset rather than influencing the EP in a conservative direction.

Finally, chapter 12, '*Gender*Power*? On the Multiple Relations between Gender and Power in the European Parliament' (co-authored by Petra Meier, Petra Ahrens, and Lise Rolandsen Agustín) synthesises the findings of the other chapters by asking what kind of power relations can be detected. Building on Allen's (1999) concept of power, the chapter highlights the ongoing power struggles surrounding gender equality in the EP, arguing that these are less a result of domination than of the overall decision-making process. The chapter ultimately emphasises that the way in which power plays out largely depends on the mode of consensual decision-making, which can either support or hinder promoting gender equality.

## PERSPECTIVES FOR FUTURE RESEARCH

This edited volume provides fertile material to extend research in multiple directions on how the EP and gender equality are intertwined on micro-, meso-, and macro-levels and the role of power in all of them. While there is a growing literature on the EP and women's descriptive representation (Stockemer 2007), the impact of the number of women in the EP as well as the roles that they play deserves more fine-tuned interrogation from multiple perspectives.

With regard to the *micro-level*, we will need more analysis of the role individual MEPs play in certain functions such as (shadow) rapporteurs, committee chairs, and coordinators, and in important leadership positions, be it of a political group or as EP (vice) president, quaestor, or in the *Spitzenkandidatur* or as Commission president with Ursula von der Leyen as first woman in this position in 2019.[10] Who will become critical actors in favour or against gender equality? Mushaben (in this volume) demonstrates that such critical actors have been a driving force, yet we do not know whether critical actors will mobilise against gender equality receive similar chances to turn back the complex understanding of gender equality. Also, when it comes to those acting for gender equality, we should ask the following questions: what is their understanding of gender equality and does this include an intersectional understanding of gender equality giving space to those who have been invisible and silenced so far? Will they be heard, and can such alliances overcome the absenteeism demonstrated by the majority in plenary debates (Zimmermann in this volume)? Overall, we must examine who gains influence and who can (re)act within this policy field, and who is isolated by whom. As the chapters by Cullen and by Chiva show, national origin and parliamentary culture play key roles in this and require more attention to better understand how this impacts supranational gender equality policy (see also Cullen 2015; Kantola and Rolandsen Agustín 2016, 2019).

The EP as an organisation with formal and informal rules constitutes the *meso-level*, which deals with the political and administrative organisation and their linkages. The chapters by Warasin and colleagues (in this volume) and Nugent (in this volume) explore this level of the political organisation, specifically the role of political groups and of core gender equality bodies like the FEMM Committee in the policy field. This raises more questions too: how do political group formation and the distribution of core positions affect gender equality policy in a supranational body? Who can join forces and exert power to advance gender equality, for instance, by turning gender budgeting into practice and making the EP more relatable for citizens (Cengiz in this volume)? We can already see that the electoral gains of right-wing and populist parties have resulted in new political groups challenging the EP as an engine for gender equality, as verified by van der Vleuten and also Musha-ben (both in this volume; Ahrens 2018b). And how do political groups deal with national delegations that may challenge a common position, either by attacking its promotion as 'gender ideology' (like the Hungarian party Fidesz in the EPP) or by consistently voting against other EFDD MEPs (as Cinque Stelle does in the FEMM Committee) (Ahrens 2018b)? Both these positions lower political group coherence (Warasin et al. in this volume). Likewise, informal EP intergroups such as 'Anti-Racism and Diversity', 'Lesbian, Gay, Bisexual, Transgender and Intersex rights', 'Active Ageing, Intergenerational Solidarity & Family Policies' or 'Children's Rights' have received almost no attention in terms of their involvement and impact in this policy field. They crosscut political groups and could be fruitful to further explore coalition formation, be it in favour of gender equality or against.

Furthermore, the EP's internal organisation, its administration, and the services that keep it running regardless of election results have received no attention at all, despite their core function for the institution, prompting the following questions: how do the EP's back-office and its secretariats steer political processes? And does this affect the positioning of the EP in gender equality? Administrative support is sup-posed to neutrally organise EP work, but whether this holds true in normative and conflictual policy fields is an open question. When it comes to the linkages between the EP's political and administrative organisation, gender mainstreaming plays an important role. And despite its formal institutionalisation (Ahrens in this volume), we need to further explore whether this – together with other recent developments such as the #MeTooEP campaign – results in the EP becoming a gender-sensitive parliament (Childs 2016; Wängnerud 2015), and one that not only favours but actu-ally fosters parity in political and administrative organisation (MacRae 2012). Yet we also need to look at the different equality bodies in charge at the EP, such as the FEMM Committee, the High Level Group on Gender Equality and Diversity, the gender mainstreaming network, the Equality and Diversity Coordination Group of the EP administration, the Anti-harassment Committee, and those who participate in them, that is, whether they are actors promoting or undermining gender equality.

Finally, the EP is just one of the core EU actors, and with regard to the *macro-level*, future research can offer much to further illuminate the effects on gender equality originating from the inter-institutional triangle of EP, Commission, and Council, keeping in mind the EP's heritage in this field (van der Vleuten in this volume) and the growing number of populist right-leaning governments in the Council that reject outright core equality issues like the Council of Europe Convention on preventing and combating violence against women and domestic violence (Istanbul Convention), want to limit marriage to heterosexual couples and hence constitutionally forbid same-sex marriage (Bulgaria, Croatia, Hungary, Latvia, Lithuania, and Slovakia), and speak up against EU equality norms (Kuhar and Paternotte 2017; Roggeband and Krizsan 2018; Verloo 2018). How will decisions be made concerning gender equality? Moreover, we need more analysis of how the EP and its units interact with civil society mobilisations pro- and anti-gender equality. Do we see the latter gaining influence via political groups or in committee hearings? And what are the oppositions and cooperations in the landscape of European civil society organisations mobilising within the field of gender equality? And after the 2019 elections, will the EP still promote gender equality or will we witness a backlash and dismantling of the policy field similar to what seems to have happened in the EC and the Council (Ahrens 2019a; Ahrens and van der Vleuten 2019; Jacquot 2015)?

Against this background, we as editors wish to thank all contributors to this volume for their hard work in exploring unknown territory and adding to a better understanding of the structures, policies and practices that characterise the EP and gender equality.

## NOTES

1 Petra Ahrens' work received funding from the European Research Council (ERC) under grant agreement No 771676 of the European Union's Horizon 2020 research and innovation programme.

2 From 1984 to 1989, there was the Group of the European Right containing MEPs from France, Greece, and Italy.

3 Kantola and Verloo (2018) identify four common strategies of gender equality research: escaping equality, when gender equality as a term is ignored in order to avoid controversies; fixing equality, when the meaning of gender equality is decided a priori through explicit operationalisation; deconstructing equality, relying completely on empirical openness towards different meanings of equality without critical reflection; and delegating equality, maintaining the discussion on a theoretical and normative basis without empirical translation.

4 The number of seats per country depends on Member State populations and a digressive proportional formula that, for instance, guarantees Malta one seat per 70,000 inhabitants and Germany one per 840,000 inhabitants (Lelieveldt and Princen 2015).

5 Until 1979, MEPs were appointed by Member States. The first woman appointed to the EP was Marga Klompé (the Netherlands) in 1952. From 1952 to 1972, only ten women were appointed as MEP. Cf. https://epthinktank.eu/2014/03/05/europes-first-women/ (last accessed on 31 March 2019).

6 Without question, Member States vary greatly regarding their share of women parliamentarians in national assemblies, with almost parity in Sweden (45.4 per cent), more than 40 per cent in Spain (41.4 per cent) and Finland (41.5 per cent), and very low shares in Lithuania (12.0 per cent), Hungary (12.6 per cent) and Malta (14.9 per cent) (Data for 2018; cf. Gender

Statistics Database of the European Institute for Gender Equality (EIGE) at https://eige.europa. eu/gender-statistics/dgs; accessed 25 March 2019). See Stockemer (2007) for a cross-national analysis of the factors influencing the differences in women representation, and Praud (2012) for an overview of quota and parity reforms in Europe and their impact on women's representation.

7 Setting up political groups requires a minimum of twenty-five MEPs and seven Member States. For details, see http://www.europarl.europa.eu/aboutparliament/en/20150201PVL00010/ (last accessed on 11 January 2018). The share of men among non-attached MEPs is above 80 per cent (European Parliament 2018b).

8 It is still a new development that women are taking up important positions in right-wing parties and also contribute to their success as members and voters (Hentges and Nott-bohm 2017; Mudde 2007).

9 The Greens/EFA and ECR have co-chairs. Until 2017, there have been three female (co-)chairs, with Marine Le Pen leading the ENF.

10 Intergroups are informal networks of MEPs with the aim of promoting contact between the EP and civil society and boosting informal exchange among MEPs. They can be formed by MEPs from any political group and committee (formal support is needed from three political groups), and setting them up follows the EP rules of procedure. They are not considered organs of the EP (see also Landorff 2019).

# Part I

## FUNCTION AND HISTORY

Gender Equality and the European Parliament

# 2

# The Powers of
# the European Parliament

## Implications for Gender Equality Policy

*Gabriele Abels*

Does the empowerment of political institutions correlate (in one way or another) to its feminisation? Do growing numbers of female parliamentarians have an effect on parliamentary powers? Do powers 'move' to more extra-parliamentary fora to ensure male dominance and patriarchal politics at the expense of parliaments? Some theorising – for example, the post-democracy hypothesis or feminist interpretations of the state as an inherently patriarchal structure – could be interpreted along these lines. The question is: Does a negative correlation between parliamentary and female empowerment (in terms of descriptive representation) might also play out in the European Union (EU) as a new political system – given that for the past twenty years over 30 of the Members of the European Parliament (MEP) have been women and that during this time the powers of the European Parliament (EP) increased dramatically? The first study ever on women in the EP has argued that women's higher share among MEPs relates to the lack of legislative powers (Vallance and Davies 1986, 6), which in turn is linked to the so-called second-order[1] character of EP elections – leading to less competition from male candidates in the intra-party recruitment process.

In this contribution, I demonstrate that the EP, in fact, challenges assumptions about feminisation versus parliamentarisation. I illustrate the *co-evolution* of growing numbers of female MEPs on the one hand and the development of the EP into an 'almost normal' parliament since the 1979 direct elections on the other hand. The share of female MEPs has been higher than in most Member States' parliaments since the first direct elections, rising to 16.6 in 1979. The EP crossed the magic 'critical mass' threshold with the 1999 EP elections (31) well before many national parliaments. The ninth EP will have a record number of 40.5 female MEPs. I argue that linkages between feminisation and parliamentarisation, between democratisation and power transfers, are highly complex. My argument employs a functional power perspective,

19

grounded in the comparative analysis of parliaments. I first outline the standard 'catalogue' of parliamentary functions, then trace gradual increases in the various EP powers. I argue that the EP 'was not born as a "parliament"' (Ripoll Servent 2018, 3), but has grown up into a 'not yet completely normal' (ibid., 5) parliament. Compared to national parliaments, important functional deficiencies still exist – affecting the democratic quality of the EU in general. Drawing on ongoing debates regarding the future of European integration, I conclude with reflections on the gendered implications of further parliamentarisation efforts.

## A FUNCTIONAL PERSPECTIVE
## ON PARLIAMENTARY POWERS

Scholars have developed catalogues of parliamentary functions. There is a wide consensus regarding the key tasks of parliaments in democracies. Werner Patzelt (2003) has proposed a useful typology grouping functions according to their addressee: (1) the electorate, (2) the government. Furthermore, (3) also polity-shaping can be important.

(1) In representative democracies, it is paramount how parliaments, and their members (MPs), relate to the electorate. Two functions are significant: parliaments embody the principle of self-rule, thus raising the question as to whether and to what extent parliaments 'mirror' the population. Feminists derive claims for women's descriptive representation (actual numbers of MEPs) from this *representative function*. Parliaments moreover need to *articulate* citizen preferences related to substantive representation, that is, ensuring that parliaments are responsive to gender interests. These two functions comprise the *raison d'etre* of parliaments, justifying their existence. Parliaments thus ensure the legitimacy of a polity.

Parliaments must further *communicate* with the electorate, the media, and interest groups, not only concerning their internal functioning but also in regard to their external environment. The primary channel must address citizens because they hold parliaments accountable through elections. Parliaments also need to pursue communication with the media and interest groups, much of which is mediated via political parties. With respect to EU affairs, national parliaments increasingly have to communicate with each other as well as with parliaments at other levels, that is, with the EP or with regional parliaments found in many Member States. This inter-parliamentary communication is also called the *networking function*.

(2) The second set, addressing the government, contains four key functions shaping legislative–executive relations. The first function, which parliamentarians often perceive as their primary task, entails *legislation*: Laws must be proposed, deliberated, and adopted (or not) in parliaments before they can come into force. The precise rules defining the legislative process depend on constitutional and/or legal provisions. The presence of a second chamber usually

renders the law-making process more complex and time-consuming.[2] Parliaments use law-making to set rules for the polity, thereby ensuring legitimacy.

*Budgetary powers* comprise a legislative subset; the so-called power of the purse. Controlling the ruler's spending provided a key impetus to the parliamentarisation of monarchical systems, a century-long process with regard to the British House of Commons, for example. Today parliaments regularly engage in making decisions about state expenditures and revenues.

Parliamentary systems likewise participate, in one way or another, in *creating and/or electing the government*. In contrast to presidential systems (in which both the president and the legislature may be directly elected), parliamentary systems depend on delegation, in which the electorate determines MPs who, in turn, decide on the composition of the government (via formal investiture or other means). This mechanism ensures the government's political accountability to parliament. All EU Member States (exception: Cyprus) are parliamentary systems.[3]

Parliaments seek to *control governments* and hold them accountable based on the principle of the separation of powers. They can use various instruments, for example, questions (interpellation), inquiry committees, votes of confidence, and so forth. This right is often assumed to be a prerogative of the parliamentary opposition. Yet, governing parties can also hold their own leaders to account, albeit usually by more discrete means. This is especially the case in coalition governments, a widespread model among most EU Member States.

(3) Parliaments act as *polity-shapers*, a function possibly involving a 'para-constitutional' dimension, allowing parliaments to influence the overall development of a polity. This function is addressed to both the electorate and the government. Generally speaking, parliaments are political actors interested in their own empowerment and institutional survival; hence, they struggle to enhance their own powers. For the EP, this is most relevant (Ripoll Servent 2018, 5ff.).[4]

Finally, in the context of the complex EU polity, parliaments need to pursue a *networking function*. The EU's multilevel parliamentary system makes it especially important for parliaments to counter their informational asymmetry vis-à-vis their own governments; networking and information exchanges help to meliorate the information-gap problem, in order to improve their control capacities with respect to their home governments or vis-à-vis the European Commission (Abels 2013; Crum and Fossum 2013).

## TRACING THE EVOLUTION OF EP PARLIAMENTARY FUNCTIONS

Although researchers developed this catalogue in relation to national parliaments, recent adaptations enable them to include the EP (see below). In fact, the 'Europeanisation' of national parliaments has emerged as a prime research topic in parliamentary studies (Hefftler et al. 2015), just as the growing competencies of the EP has become as a prominent issue in EU studies (Corbett et al. 2016; Rittberger 2005). This raises the question, whether and to what extent the standard catalogue of functions also pertains to the EP. Has the EP become a *bona fide* parliament in functional terms, despite its *sui generis* features? This requires us to consider how its functions have evolved over time and what additional functions it might perform. Does it display structural deficits? If so, what are they, and what does this imply for the EP's role as a 'gendered actor' or for its chances of advancing gender equality? I argue that in functional terms the EP, by and large, now operates like a 'normal', fully fledged parliament. However, particular limitations exist and some of its special features and deficiencies could impact upon the EP's role in shaping gender equality policy.

Today's EP differs fundamentally from the parliamentary assembly of the 1950s, due to changes basically affecting all of its key features, ranging from its mode of selection (see later) to its concrete functions. The EP has witnessed a remarkable expansion of its powers, for which only two explanations can be briefly reviewed here. Rittberger (2005) argues that, first, a step-by-step increase in EP powers was influenced by national parliamentary models: a *copy-and-paste strategy* led to incremental increases in EP powers over time. This interpretation grants the national leaders in the Council an important role.[5] Second, the EP has acted as a strong *polity-shaper in its own right*. Conceiving itself to be part of an evolutionary process, the EP developed a strategy enabling it to make creative use of its once very limited powers in hopes of enhancing them and, in so doing, gradually changed the EU's 'constitutional order' (see Corbett et al. 2016, 434ff.). As Ripoll Servent (2018, 3) argues, 'If there is an area where the EP has shown a stable pattern of behaviour, it is in its defence of stronger parliamentary powers'.

The EP often monitors how national parliaments deal with issues such as party financing, government investitures and investigative committees, and adopts these national models. Also changes in the 'Rules of Procedure' have proven to be effective. In this sense, the EP has been very active in 'self-empowerment'; many subsequent treaty changes have codified what had already become established parliamentary practice. It has instrumentalised formal and informal rules; especially inter-institutional arrangements with the Council and the Commission have proved important to formalise and constitutionalise incrementally developed practices (Corbett et al. 2016; Ripoll Servent 2018, 7–26). These two interpretations are complementary in nature. We now turn to changes in the EP's functions over time.

The origins date back to the parliamentary *assembly* established in the 1950s. The assembly was part of the 1952 European Coal and Steel Community (ECSC). It consisted of delegates from the national parliaments of the six founding Member States: Belgium, France, Germany, Italy, Luxemburg, and the Netherlands. This delegation mode did not change when the European Economic Community and the European Atomic Energy Community were added in 1957, nor when the Assembly became responsible for all three communities under the 1965 Fusion Treaty. With respect to descriptive representation, the share of female MEPs was as low as

1.3 per cent in 1952. Because MEPs were sent by national parliaments, the EP's non-representative composition reflected the dearth of women at that level.

The 1979 introduction of direct elections by citizens from all Member States was a watershed in democratic terms. Also, the number of female MEPs tripled from 1975 to 1979 from 4.9 per cent to 16.6 per cent.[6] MEPs were very conscious of stronger descriptive female representation that could feed into substantive representation; they had a sense for the need of 'critical actors' (see Mushaben 1999; Vallance and Davies 1986), who take the initiative and champion for women's rights. Thus, it was no coincidence that the first president of the directly elected EP was a woman, Holocaust survivor Simone Veil (1927–2017), and that its first Committee of Inquiry, established shortly thereafter, addressed the status of women in Europe, followed by the EP's first proactive initiative.

The share of female MEPs increased steadily, reaching 35.8 per cent as of the 2014 elections (2018: 36.1 per cent; European Parliament 2018b, 5) and a record high (40.5 per cent) in 2019 – with a, by and large, clear left–right pattern.[7] Several rounds of enlargement occurred: In the 1980s, Mediterranean states (Greece, Spain, Portugal) entered the Community following decades of dictatorship; 1995 saw a northern accession (Austria, Finland, and Sweden), followed by three rounds of eastern enlargement (2004/2007/2013), when eleven postcommunist countries, plus Cyprus and Malta, joined the Union. While the 1995 accessions had a positive impact due to the Scandinavians' good record on gender equality (Galligan and Clavero 2012, 111), Eastern enlargements produced a 'mixed bag' regarding descriptive representation: the number of female MEPs fell below average in most national delegations from the Central East European countries (Chiva 2014). The EP's gender composition is more equal today than during previous decades, but still far from parity. Demands for gender parity in the EP are raised anew every five years, for example, by the European Women's Lobby. Yet, in recent years the growing number of right-winged populist parties in the Member States makes this aim more difficult to achieve.[8] Because national political parties function as gatekeepers during the nomination process, their impact on gendered representation is crucial (Fortin-Rittberger and Rittberger 2015).

When one compares the number of women at EU and national level, female MEPs in the national groups often outnumber their counterparts in the national parliaments. The share of female parliamentarians in some Member States is still well below the EP average (23.6 per cent in 2018), although that proportion is often higher than in their respective national legislatures. Thus, in terms of *descriptive representation*, the EP performs better than most national parliaments (cf. European Parliament 2018b, 6; Xydias 2016; see Introduction by the editors). Women have concurrently secured more decision-making positions *within* the EP, including, for example, vice-presidencies (in 2018 five of fourteen vice-presidents; i.e. 35.7 per cent), committee chairs (twelve of twenty four – a new record of 50 per cent female),[9] and chairs of standing delegations (currently ten of thirty nine; 27.3 per cent) (European Parliament 2018b). For the ninth EP this number is as of date (June 2019) not yet clear; however, gender is an important criterion in the ongoing selection process for the EU top jobs. Women's greater presence has had a positive, substantive effect on the development of gender equality, rendering the EP itself less of a male organisation; this has also contributed to the adoption of gender equality policies (see van der Vleuten and Mushaben in this volume).

The Constitutional Convention amounted to a lost opportunity for enhancing women's representation in 2002/2003. Whereas all previous treaties had derived from intergovernmental conferences (IGC), this treaty was deliberated and negotiated by a convention composed of Member States delegates (with accession countries as observers), in addition to MEPs and MPs, making the procedure more transparent to civil society. Despite its democratic ambitions, the convention included only 18 women among 105 delegates (Lombardo 2005, 422). 'For many, this symbolically and practically excluded women from the future of the European Union' (MacRae 2012, 302) and the lack of gender mainstreaming is omnipresent in the results (Lombardo 2005).

The EP's potential for transforming descriptive into substantial representation by way of a more gender-equal EP (compared to most national parliaments) – becoming more attentive to gender interests and promoting gender equality policies – strongly depends on its legislative powers. These have been expanded over the past decades, as illustrated in the next section.

## EXPANDING THE EP'S DECISION-MAKING POWERS AND CONTROL FUNCTIONS

Assessing the gradual legislative empowerment of the EP requires us to consider that the EU rests on the delegation of authority. The principles of subsidiarity and delegated authorities limit the EU's competences to those ceded by the Member States and codified in the treaties, with repercussions for the legal competencies of the EP. Unlike a national parliament, it cannot simply grant itself new legal responsibilities; this depends on Member States' willingness to empower the EP by, first, uploading competencies to the EU level, and, second, by applying the supranational 'Community method', which foresees EP involvement in the legislative process.

One feature that clearly distinguishes the EP from national legislatures is that the former does *not* possess the formal right to initiate legislation; this remains the monopoly of the Commission. Under the Lisbon Treaty, however, the EP can ask the Commission to submit a legislative proposal, something it does frequently. Thus, its right to initiate legislation continues to be weak and indirect, a trait seen by many as evidence of a persisting democratic deficit. Nevertheless, the gradual increase in its legislative powers since 1979 has been striking (see in detail Corbett et al. 2016; Ripoll Servent 2018)

Until the mid-1980s the EP was still very much a 'talking shop', exercising merely an advisory role. Under the initial *consultation procedure* installed in 1957, the Commission proposed legislation, the EP provided an opinion, and the Council ultimately decided. Today this procedure applies only to a limited number of legislative and non-legislative areas (table 2.1).

**Table 2.1 Legislative empowerment of the European Parliament 1957–2009**

| Procedure | Year of introduction | Legal basis | Key feature with regards to EP powers | Legislative and non-legislative areas of application today |
|---|---|---|---|---|
| Consultation | 1957 | EEC Treaty | Advisory role of EP; EP provides opinion; Council must wait for EP opinion | internal market exemptions and competition laws; international agreements under the Common Foreign and Security Policy |
| Assent (now consent) | 1986 | SEA | EP consent is required; no final decision possible without EP consent | association agreements, agreements on accession to and withdrawal from the EU, Article 7 TEU procedure, legislation on combating discrimination |
| Cooperation | 1986 | SEA | Second reading in EP | No longer in place |
| Co-decision | 1992 | TEU (Maastricht Treaty) | Third reading and conciliation committee; actual veto power for the EP (since 1996 first reading agreements possible) | Limited to a number of legislative sectors, extended with treaty modifications in the 1990s (Amsterdam, Nice) |
| Trilogues | 1992 | Inter-institutional | Direct negotiation between EP and Council, plus Commission | All co-decision, today OLP; possible in all stages of legislation |
| Ordinary Legislative Procedure (OLP) | 2009 | TEU (Lisbon Treaty) | Same as co-decision; both co-legislators have to approve an identical legal text | Applies to 85 defined legislative policy areas; some exceptions, e.g. CFSP/CSDP, taxation |

EEC: European Economic Community; SEA: Single European Act; TEU: Treaty on European Union; TFEU: Treaty on the Functioning of the EU

Source: European Parliament 2018b; compiled by the author.

Acquiring more direct legitimacy as of the 1979 elections whet the EP's appetite for enhanced legislative powers and increased the Council's willingness to empower the EP. Its powers evolved in a gradual and sectoral fashion over several decades. The Single European Act (SEA) of 1986 paved the way for the single market project, accompanied by a stronger role for the EP: (1) It introduced the *assent procedure* (now called *consent* procedure), with all subsequent treaty modifications extending the scope of its legislative and non-legislative application. It empowered the EP with regard to EU enlargement, accession and withdrawal agreements. Significant for women's and human rights, EP consent is further required for using Article 7 (Treaty on European Union, TEU) in cases of serious breaches of fundamental rights and for legislation combating discrimination. (2) The SEA moreover introduced the *cooperation procedure* between EP and Council, effectively adding a second EP reading and granting it stronger amendment powers (a procedure no longer in place today).

In 1992, the Maastricht Treaty on the European Union introduced the *co-decision procedure*, placing the Council and the EP on equal footing. It introduced a 'third reading' and optional use of a conciliation committee when the Council and the EP lack agreement. This procedure comprised a major breakthrough: now both institutions must approve a legislative proposal, granting the EP real veto power. During the early days, co-decision was restricted to only a few sectors (mainly the internal market); procedural rules, moreover, still worked to the Council's advantage, insofar as the Council could still overrule the EP. Further treaty changes (Amsterdam Treaty 1999; Nice Treaty 2003) improved the situation, following a path of gradual expansion for co-decision making. Co-decision became the legal basis for about forty defined policy areas, including employment, social affairs justice and home affairs. In addition, certain procedural changes increased its effectiveness by allowing the Council and the EP to adopt legislative proposals at the first-reading stage. This change held fundamental implications for inter-institutional negotiations, facilitating widespread use of 'trilogues' to speed up decision-making.

Adopted by the European Council in 2004 in anticipation of imminent Eastern enlargement, the Constitutional Treaty was a seminal moment. Its unique composition and the strong representation of parliaments in the convention led to changes strengthening parliamentary roles at the national and European levels. The key advantage for the EP was the introduction of the *ordinary legislative procedure* (OLP), which rests on the co-decision procedure. Rejection of the Constitutional Treaty in public referenda in France and the Netherlands in 2005 came as a shock, creating a 'constitutional crisis'. An IGC was set up to transform the 'Constitution for Europe' into a less ambitious treaty that would avoid all indicators of a 'super-state'. The outcome was the Lisbon Treaty, adopted in 2007, which entered into force (only after a few calamitous referenda) in late 2009. This Treaty rests on elements foreseen by the Constitutional Treaty, starting with codifying the OLP (Article 294 TEU), which now applies to eighty-five policy areas – among them, social policy, trafficking in persons – covering the vast majority of EU law. The EP and the Council now jointly adopt new legislation.

The Justice and Home Affairs pillar was integrated into supranational policymaking, but policy areas like external relations and defence remain exempt from

OLP and still subject to intergovernmental decision-making. Management of the 'Euro-crisis', in particular, saw a strong turn towards intergovernmentalism (called the 'Union method', in contrast to the 'Community method'). The EP's role in economic governance remains limited; it only has the right to give an opinion under Article 140 TFEU on issues involving the monetary union. In March 2013, the EP adopted a resolution on the impact of the economic crisis on gender equality and women's rights, in line with many of feminist critiques regarding the gendered impact of austerity measures, for example, with regard to child care, social policy and the like (Kantola and Lombardo 2017).

While *conciliation procedures* are common in bicameral parliamentary systems, the EU has developed a strong culture of inter-institutional negotiation under the name of trilogues. These are meetings between the EP, the Council and the Commission, which can take place any time in the legislative process. Trilogues are an informal (i.e. not constitutionalised), but widely used and effective decision-making technique. In fact, the majority of the legislative decisions in the OLP are taken today as 'first reading agreements' in the trilogue fashion (see Corbett et al. 2016, 286ff.; Ripoll Servent 2018, 242ff.; see also Mushaben in this volume).

While being very efficient in terms of speeding up the legislative process, trilogues have a democratic weakness: they take place behind closed doors. Originally, from the EP side only the chair of the competent committee and the rapporteur participated in trilogues; today 'shadow rapporteurs' also participate to allow for coalition building among political groups. The trilogue practice became more formalised since 2008 by intra-EP regulations to ensure greater transparency and internal discussions (Corbett et al. 2016, 286f.). The EP committee in charge may also decide on a mandate, priorities and time limits for trilogue negotiations. The Committee on Women's Rights and Gender Equality (FEMM) has few experiences with trilogues (only two in the 2009–2014 term; Ripoll Servent 2018, 249), due to the lack of legislative policies in its realm and its usually consultative role in legislative politics.

EP legislative powers, indeed, also expanded in the employment and social policy domains, which are especially significant for gender equality (Hubert 2012; Stratigaki 2012). Article 119 EEC famously introduced the principle of equal pay for equal work in 1957 at the time when the EP was only a 'talking shop'. While EU social policy competencies remain fairly weak, the EP's powers in this sector have grown over time. Today, issues particularly important for gender equality, such as social and employment policy, judicial affairs, migration/asylum, research, and citizenship policy, are decided under the OLP, putting the EP on equal footing with the Council and giving it substantive powers. However, the FEMM Committee is rarely assigned the role as 'competent committee', taking the lead in the legislative process.

A final procedure relevant for gender equality deserves mention here. The Maastricht Treaty introduced the idea of a social partnership to foster 'Social Dialogue' among the representatives of employers and labour organisations. Social partnership is a class-based model; employers and labour unions remain very male-dominated, whose neglect of gender interests has been broadly criticized (Eurofound 2014). These two partners are entitled to develop proposals in the employment field (e.g.

parental leave and part-time work). When they agree among themselves, they can request that their agreement be implemented by a Council decision. Before the Council decides, it refers this agreement to the responsible EP committee, which moves a resolution either to reject or adopt the social-partner request. If, however, the agreement is intended as only voluntary, the EP is informed by the Commission; the responsible committee, in turn, has the right to draw up an own-initiative report, proposing conditions for the adoption of this agreement.

In sum, looking back over the past sixty-five years, especially the past three decades, the EP's evolution 'from a toothless consultation chamber to a powerful legislative institution is a remarkable development' (Hix and Høyland 2013, 183). However, this overview also illustrates that decision-making in the EU and EP involvement is much more fragmented than seen in national systems. Legislative and non-legislative powers have evolved incrementally, and there are still some domains, such as foreign affairs and monetary union, in which the EP still is a rather toothless chamber, although these areas are shrinking. Subsidiarity remains a core EU principle and increasing Euroscepticism has raised discussions about a potential transfer of competencies back to the Member States, with repercussions for EP power. This is part of the ongoing debate over the future of the EU. The recent resurgence of the intergovernmental 'Union method' (applied in adopting the Fiscal Compact) suggests integration without 'supranationalisation', that is, without a further strengthening of the EP.[10]

For decades, EP *budgetary powers* were limited to so-called non-obligatory expenses. Not explicitly required by the treaty, these costs amounted to a small share of the budget (for details, see Corbett et al. 2016, 320ff.). EU expenditures have risen dramatically over the years, with agricultural subsidies, regional and structural funds, as well as research funding comprising major portions of the budget. The first major step expanding the EP's budgetary powers was taken in the mid-1970s. When the EC adopted its 'own resources' system, that is, creating its own revenues, national leaders felt that stronger supranational *budgetary powers* should be subject to stronger parliamentary oversight. This linkage between budgeting and representation is firmly embedded in national democratic models where the 'power of the purse' is a key legislative prerogative, offering an example of Rittberger's (2005) 'copy and paste' method.

However, EP powers were limited to non-obligatory expenditures (excluding most agricultural subsidies) until the Lisbon Treaty eliminated the distinction among different types of funding (for details, see Corbett et al. 2016, 320ff.) – thereby according to the EP equal power with the Council. Today, the EP has the final say over the budget and exercises control via its Committee on Budgetary Control. However, firstly, annual expenditures are limited by caps set in the seven-year Multiannual Financial Framework (MFF). Secondly, the EP cannot decide on revenues and taxes. Decisions regarding the MFF and revenue generation (e.g. EU taxes, national VAT contributions, tariffs) are high politics vested in the Council. Again, EP powers do not totally match those of national parliaments.

## IDENTIFYING THE EP'S GENDER GAPS

Gender equality policies are often regulatory in nature, yet, some depend on EU funding, especially projects falling under the 'Roadmap', the 'Strategy for Gender Equality' or various Action Programmes. The EP is involved in ongoing debates about gender budgeting (i.e. applying gender mainstreaming to allocations). One study for the FEMM identified substantial gaps in this area due to a lack of gender-specific indicators and data, leading another EP report (European Parliament 2015) to conclude that the EU is not living up to its equality and mainstreaming commitments.

As communicative institutions, parliaments direct their messages, above all, to voters. While national parliaments can utilise the domestic media landscape and restrict communication to a single (or limited number of) official language(s), this is not true for the EP. The few existing EU-wide media are not mass media (e.g. the EP's own TV channel), also rendered more challenging by its twenty-four official languages. Given its complicated communication environment, neither EP plenary discussions, decisions nor individual MEPs receive a lot of media coverage (Gattermann and Vasilopoulou 2015).

At the national level, election campaigns constitute highpoints in political communication, according key roles to political parties, individual candidates and parliaments as a whole. This does not hold for the EP, given that its campaigns tend to be dominated by *national* parties, often running on national issues. This effect was less visible during the 2014 EP elections, especially due to the so-called Euro-crisis, which had a somewhat politicising effect at least in some countries. Nevertheless, EP elections, including those in 2019, can still be largely classified as 'second-order elections'.

Turnout has decreased dramatically over time, from 63 per cent in 1979 to an all-time low of about 42.5 per cent in 2014. Especially in Central and Eastern Europe turnout was lower than 30 per cent (in Slovakia less than 15 per cent). This weak electoral link, especially among women, significantly affects the EP's representative function. A post-election survey found, on average, a 4 per cent gender gap in 2014, compared to 2 per cent in 2009; turnout reached 45 per cent among men but only 41 per cent among women (European Parliament 2014b, 3). The gender gap was quite striking but varied across Member States, such as Malta (79 per cent women, to 70 per cent men), Sweden (59 per cent women, 43 per cent men), France (37 per cent women, 49 per cent men) and Portugal (28 per cent women, 40 per cent men) (ibid., 12). It is a good sign that the voter turnout increased again in the 2019 'elections of fate' to 50.6 per cent – varying across Member States between 23 per cent in Slovakia and 88.5 per cent in Belgium (https://election-results.eu/turnout/). Gender-disaggregated data for 2019 are not yet available.

Explanations for lower turnout rates among women rest with their lower occupational status (European Parliament 2014b): 'homemakers/house persons', a group in which women are over-represented, are often less likely to vote. In some cases, women are more inclined to vote either out of habit (44 per cent vs. 38 per cent men) or because it is a citizen's duty (43 per cent vs. 39 per cent men). The difference was very striking in Denmark, for example, where 61 per cent of female voters considered it their duty to vote, in contrast to 47 per cent among men. Issue priorities are also gendered: 47 per cent of women (59 per cent among homemakers) labelled unemployment a key priority, compared to 42 per cent among men. In Luxembourg, only 35 per cent of women listed unemployment as their top reason, versus 45 per cent for men; the figures in Poland were 61 per cent among women, and 46 per cent for men, respectively. Gender differences were less stark involving other issues like immigration.

Further noteworthy differences emerge when it comes to trust. In Germany, for example, 30 per cent of the men and 22 per cent of the women who abstained in 2014 did so, claiming to lack trust in politics. Women are more ambivalent about the EU than men (+5 percentage points); they do not see their country's membership as either a good or bad thing (ibid., 71). In Malta, 78 per cent of women trust EU institutions as compared to 60 per cent of men (ibid., 96). More concretely, 65 per cent of Malta's female voters regard the EP as responsive to citizens' concerns as compared to 57 per cent of their male counterparts. Among homemakers, however, 59 per cent do not agree that 'the European Parliament properly takes into account the concerns of European citizens'. Moreover, 54 per cent of women generally believe that they have less access to the information they need, while 61 per cent of men think they have adequate access to election-related information (ibid., 6; see also Fortin-Rittberger 2016). The data do not reveal consistent patterns along gender lines across the twenty-eight Member States. There is certainly room for further studies, as well as for more gender- and status-sensitive communication strategies. This applies not only to national political parties but also to the EP and its political groups.

## A PARLIAMENT *SUI GENERIS*: SPECIAL FEATURES

Because it operates in a very special political environment rooted in a diffuse separation of powers, the EP lacks the right to appoint and dismiss a government – key to the accountability that rests at heart of national parliamentary powers. While it is quite clear in the national context who constitutes the executive branch (government, president), this is less obvious in the EU polity. The Commission is often viewed as the 'EU government', yet, its actual executive powers are limited; it is completely dependent on Member-State governments for policy implementation, for instance. The Council of the EU, by contrast, consists of representatives of national governments acting as a legislative high chamber at the EU level. Consisting of twenty-eight heads of state and/or government, the European Council acts as a 'motor' of integration (or lack thereof), although it has no formal legislative powers. Comprised of national ministers with sectoral responsibilities, it is the Council of the EU that exercised final decision-making power over many decades. In the supranational sectors, it can initiate policies informally by calling on the Commission to take action; it can also take formal action along these lines in the intergovernmental policy domains.

None of these organs is *directly* 'created' or elected by the EP, in contrast to the direct constitutive link that exists between parliaments and governments at the national level in the EU Member States. The Commission President and the College of Commissioners are both nominated by the Member States via the European Council. For a long time, the EP had no say in this, until the Maastricht Treaty accorded its new powers in relation to the installation of the Commission. Previously, a new Commission required the nominal support of the EP to assume office, but the latter could only vote on the slate of candidates already named by the Council. In 1995 the EP developed a new procedure, inspired by US Senate practices ('advise and consent'), introducing official hearings for would-be Commissioners *prior* to a formal EP vote, to test the candidates' competence with respect to their future dossiers. In a few cases, the EP has demanded that new candidates be named because it found the Council's nominees unsuitable. In 2004 the EP rejected one such candidate for the first time, that is, Italian conservative Rocco Buttiglione. Ultra-conservative ideas about the role of women and homophobic statements made him unsuitable for the Justice portfolio in the eyes of the MEPs (Corbett et al. 2016, 344).

Following new Lisbon Treaty provisions, the 2014 EP elections marked a turning point, requiring that the composition of the Commission reflects the outcome of EP elections (Article 17, 7 TEU). The EP decided that it would only elect a Commission President representing the winning political group – such as the conservative European People's Party (EPP) and the social-democratic S&D – whose 'top candidates' would campaign for the position. This so-called *Spitzenkandidaten* (lead candidate) strategy proved rather successful; despite strong opposition from the European Council, the EP managed to have the latter nominate Jean-Claude Juncker after the EPP secured the largest party-group vote. This strategy has strengthened the accountability link between the Commission and the EP. In addition to recasting inter-institutional dynamics, it moves the EU polity one step closer to the normal logic of 'parliamentary rule', according to which governments are set up and legitimised by their respective parliaments (Hobolt 2014). The intense conflict that has emerged over its renewed application in the May 2019 elections attests to the significance of this institutional innovation. As of today (22 June 2019) it is not likely that the strategy will be successful again; if it fails, it has repercussions on the future inter-institutional relations between EP and Council and the meaning of EP elections for the electorate.

Only the EP has the right to censure the Commission as a means of last resort, dating back to the ECSC Treaty of 1952. The EP has only sought once to make effective use of this right: In 1999 the entire Santer Commission was impelled to resign – rather than face an official EP censure vote likely to result in a majority – following an investigation into fraud, mismanagement and nepotism. Other censure motions proved less successful.

Drawing on other informal, non-codified strategies, the EP also expanded its *control powers* over the Commission. MEPs enjoy the 'normal' interpellation rights commonly seen in national parliaments, submitting written questions or requesting oral answers, debates and reports (Corbett et al. 2016, 366ff.). The EP has a long tradition of inquiry committees of various kinds (ibid., 386ff.). The EP can also use standing committee meetings and plenary sessions, including question time, to hold Commissioners accountable. Its scrutiny powers vis-à-vis the Council are much weaker, however, primarily limited to interpellation rights. Council representatives or even the ministers exercising the Council presidency are frequently invited to EP plenary sessions and committee meetings to answer questions.

Inter-parliamentary cooperation with national parliaments is another key feature of the EU's evolving, multilevel parliamentary system. The main goal of cooperation is to share information among parliaments to balance the information asymmetry that national legislatures encounter: information is a key factor in exercising control over national governments, which dominate in EU decision-making. The EP was the main driver behind new inter-parliamentary relations; it initiated stronger cooperation with national parliaments and, to some extent, among national parliaments, to enhance their scrutiny function (Buzogány 2013). There are today several venues for inter-parliamentary relations, such as Joint or Interparliamentary Committee Meetings, and so forth (Corbett et al. 2016, 419ff.).[11] There is no evidence that these have been used in the field of gender equality policy. While these inter-parliamentary relations are important, they are not always cooperative, however, because parliaments also compete with each other over influence. National parliaments sometimes use these venues to question the EP's authority, when they feel their own positions being jeopardised by EU competencies involving stronger EP powers. This is part of the overall polity-shaping struggle.

## CONCLUSION:
## THE EP – A 'NOT YET COMPLETELY NORMAL' PARLIAMENT?

The previous discussion illustrates the substantial growth of EP powers over time, allowing it now to fulfil almost all functions of 'normal' national parliaments. Furthermore, we need to consider that also national parliaments do fulfil these functions to different degrees and deficits exist. Yet some functional deficits or tensions are particular to the EP (see Ripoll Servent 2018, 270f.).

On the positive side, we can conclude that the EP represents EU citizens, enjoys budgetary and legislative powers, and participates in the installation of Commissioners. It possesses scrutiny powers vis-à-vis the Commission and, to a lesser extent, the Council. The analysis nonetheless testifies to several significant deficits regarding 'normal' powers: it displays weaknesses relating to controls over executive and other EU bodies. The analysis shows that the Commission and the Council have granted the EP more powers, based on the 'copy and paste' method, but the EP cannot constitutionally empower itself. The evolution and expansion of its powers often began informally, accompanied by follow-up inter-institutional agreements and then treaty modifications. In this sense, the EP has become a very successful polity-shaper, contributing to constitution-building. It has supported the parliamentarisation of EU politics and, therewith its democratisation. A persistent deficit is the lack of a formal right to initiate legislation. The crisis mitigation process has also left its mark on the EP; it tends to be marginalised due to the strong role assigned to intergovernmental crisis management in the so-called Union method – with gendered ramifications (Klatzer and Schlager 2017). A final obstinate quandary is the underdeveloped nature of its communicative function, which is key to representative bodies. Low voter turnout (even if stronger again in 2019), the lack of interest and knowledge among EU citizens place serious restrictions on the EP's legitimacy.

Some of these functional problems are crucial from a gender perspective. With regard to descriptive representation, the EP has clearly become a more feminised parliament over time, travelling a long way from only a few women in the first assembly of the 1950s to a 40.5 per cent share of female MEPs today; in this respect, the EP has performed better than most national parliaments. It, therefore, challenges the strong feminist belief concerning the negative correlation between the empowerment of a given political institution and women's increasing representation in that body. I argue that this owes to the specific nature of the EU polity: long perceived as a weak arena for politics, it was initially less interesting for male politicians.

Does women's 'better than average' descriptive representation situation affect their substantive and, possibly, symbolic representation? This raises the core question of whether the EP has become a more 'women-friendly' or 'gender-sensitive' parliament. In the past, the EP has often supported gender equality, gender mainstreaming and anti-discrimination (van der Vleuten and Mushaben in this volume). As in other parliaments, however, gender equality policy still requires intense lobbying, negotiations and coalition building among diverse political groups. The FEMM Committee has proven crucial for substantive representation (Ahrens 2016). Structured like national bodies along partisan lines, there is some evidence that centre-left EP coalitions are more likely to promote gender equality policies. Since the 2009 election, and exacerbated by the 2014 election, a rising number of right-wing populist MEPs have a negative impact on gender equality policies (see the contribution in this volume).

Given the complex, multilevel structure of the EU, however, EP support for equality is not enough. The Commission must first generate proposals for gender policies. The increasing influence of national parliaments may pose a second stumbling block.[12] Finally, national governments in the Council must also approve gender equality policies; too often, the vote there is equivalent to the eye of the needle. Nevertheless, the EP's growing power base in the EU has had a positive impact on gender equality, which cannot be taken for granted; the rest depends on its own partisan political composition. Celis and Lovenduski (2018) remind us that securing 'gender equality in political representation' entails a 'power struggle'. Like any power struggle, the outcome depends on the facilitating interaction of actors, actions and norms.

## NOTES

1 It is assumed that, because EP elections do not decide a future government, they generate less intense party campaigns, less media attention and, ultimately, less interest among the electorate.

2 Thirteen EU Member States have bicameral parliaments.

3 Several EU Member States are semi-presidential (e.g. Austria, France and Poland). Yet, in line with other scholars in parliamentary studies I argue that these systems essentially also follow the logic of parliamentary rule in so far as the government (and to some extent thereby also the president) depends on the confidence of the parliament and the government can be dismissed by parliament.

4 Traditionally dominated by the executive branch, involvement in EU affairs does offer evidence that this polity-shaping function exists, to some degree, in all EU Member States (see contributions in Hefftler et al. 2015).

5 In addition, many European Court of Justice decisions were supportive as well.

6 In those days the number of female national parliamentarians was between 5 per cent and 8 per cent (Vallence and Davies 1986).

7 This pattern still prevails that the left of centre political groups have a higher share of female MEPs. For the current gender breakdown in the political groups, see European Parliament (2018b, 10).

8 For the 2019 campaign '50/50 Women for Europe, Europe for Women!', see https://www.womenlobby.org/-WomenForEurope-?lang=en.

9 While in the past women often chaired committees considered as less important, this is no longer the case. Currently, for example, the Committees for International Market and Consumer Protection (IMCO), for Regional Development (REGI) and for Constitutional Affairs (AFCO) have female chairs (cf. European Parliament 2018b, 11).

10 This is the key argument of new intergovernmentalism.

11 More formalised fora are Inter-parliamentary Conferences (IPCs) such as COSAC, which brings the European Affairs Committees of national parliaments together with the EP, the so-called Article 13 conference (based on Article 13 of the Fiscal Compact) to ensure stronger parliamentary control over Eurozone affairs, or the IPC in foreign and security policy.

12 Their involvement in EU policy-making was strengthened, too, as part of a parliamentarisation strategy since the Maastricht Treaty. The Lisbon Treaty formalised their role by introducing the 'Early Warning System' of subsidiarity control (see Buzogány 2013; Corbett et al. 2016, 277ff.). This gives national parliaments a collective veto power; in several cases national parliaments have actually objected to Commission proposal's in the field of gender equality, but so far they have never yet reached the veto threshold for a 'yellow card'. For example, in 2013 the Commission issued its 'Proposal for a Directive of the European Parliament and of the Council on improving the gender balance among non-executive directors of companies listed on stock exchanges and related measures'. The UK House of Commons and the Dutch House of Representatives raised subsidiarity concerns. In 2016, for example, the Commission issued a 'Proposal for a Council Decision on the conclusion, by the European Union, of the Council of Europe Convention on preventing and combating violence against women and domestic violence' (COM (2016) 109 final). None of the national parliaments had objections based on scrutiny concerns (see http://www.ipex.eu/IPEXL-WEB/dossier/document/COM20160109.do). Yet, the Polish Senate, for example, issues a statement as part of the political dialogue with the Commission according to which joining the so-called Istanbul Convention is only 'justified by ideological reasons' and that it considers 'measures to induce change of stereotypical social and cultural roles' as problematic. In 2017, both parliamentary chambers in Poland (Senate and Sejm) raised subsidiarity concerns against the so-called work-life balance directive for parents and carers (COM (2017) 253 final).

# 3

# The European Parliament as a Constant Promoter of Gender Equality

## Another European Myth?

*Anna van der Vleuten*[1]

It seems to belong to the 'foundational myths' (Macrae 2010) of the European Union (EU) that the European Parliament (EP) is a 'real champion for gender equality' (Locher 2012, 68). In its own words, the EP 'has always been a fervent defender of the principle of equality between men and women' (Schonard 2018, 1). Scholars have confirmed this claim, stating, 'From its early days, the EP has been a strong supporter of gender justice. It has adopted many resolutions asking for new Commission initiatives. It has consistently voted in favour of amendments which aimed to strengthen European legislation on gender equality' (van der Vleuten 2012, 49). No wonder that feminist activists welcomed every strengthening of the EP's role (Kantola 2010). The EP thus enjoys a strong reputation as promoter of gender equality. Yet how can we explain this continuity, especially because gender equality is a politically sensitive issue which entails high economic, political, and ideational costs (van der Vleuten 2005)? Answering this question is especially salient as the EP has undergone important institutional changes over the past six decades. It has developed from a part-time advisory assembly to a full-time directly elected parliament with budgetary and decision-making powers, and from a parliament representing the populations of six Member States to representing those of twenty-eight, with a concomitant increase in diversity. Its political composition has also changed. The Christian Democrats have replaced the social-democrats as the largest group, and Eurosceptic and populist parties have entered the arena. Against the background of all these changes, how can we explain the EP's apparently enduring support for gender equality policies?

The first section elaborates three potential explanations: first, the high number of female MEPs; second, the EP as a new and open opportunity structure; and third, the quest for legitimacy of the EU as a whole and the EP in particular. The next section will explore the validity of these explanations through a thick narrative on the EP's engagement with gender equality over time.

# EXPLAINING THE EP'S PROMOTION OF GENDER EQUALITY

A parliament can logically be expected to show consistent support for a certain cause if it has an enduring interest in doing so. Applied to the issue at hand, this raises the question of why the EP would have an enduring interest in promoting gender equality given all its institutional, societal, and political changes. I have deduced three potential explanations from the work on representation, feminist institutionalism, and legitimacy, which I will elaborate here.

## Descriptive and Substantive Representation: A High Number of Women MEPs

In the literature, the relatively high number of female Members of the European Parliament (MEPs) is often mentioned as an explanation for the EP's positive attitude towards gender equality. As Birgit Locher argues, 'A high percentage of female members, especially since 1995, means that new equality policies fall on fruitful ground' (2012, 68). Ever since the first direct EP elections in 1979, the percentage of elected female parliamentarians has been higher than the average in the national parliaments, and it has slowly but steadily risen from 16.3 per cent in 1979 to 36.1 per cent in the 2014 elections (European Parliament 2018b). The proportion of women MEPs within political party groups varies, showing the familiar pattern of higher numbers on the left side of the spectrum (European United Left, 51.9 per cent) and lower numbers to the right (European Conservatives, 22.5 per cent).

Several explanations have been formulated for the higher proportion of women in the EP compared to many national parliaments: the electoral system, the lower degree of competitiveness, and the consensual style of parliamentary politics (for an overview, see Kantola 2010, 61–63). Clearly, women's activism and lobbying can also be said to have paid off. The European Network of Experts on Women in Decision-Making, which the European Commission created in 1992, turned the representation of women into a high-profile issue in the 1994 elections, contributing to a 6 per cent rise in the number of women MEPs. The European Women's Lobby (EWL) and the EP's Committee on Women's Rights and Gender Equality (FEMM) ran similar campaigns (Kantola 2010, 63).

Such campaigns are based on the expectation that more descriptive representation leads to more substantive representation, as parliamentarians are supposed to act 'in the interest of the represented, in a manner responsive to them' (Pitkin, quoted by Celis 2009, 97). This reasoning would imply that women MEPs would speak for women and include the perspective of women in the legislative process, which should result in legislation that meets women's needs, interests, and demands. Although some studies confirm these expectations, other studies do not find a straightforward relationship between women parliamentarians and the representation of women's interests. Celis argues that quantity matters in the sense that increasing the presence of women parliamentarians in all political factions 'fosters the articulation of different ideological positions regarding the interests of women and gender relations' (2009, 108). She finds that 'critical individuals' even seem more important for the defence of women's interests than crude quantitative representation' (ibid.). This points to the crucial roles of norm entrepreneurs as identified in research on norm diffusion (Finnemore and Sikkink 1998). Following this strand of thought, we expect to see more attention to gender equality and a more diverse understanding of it when there is a higher proportion of women MEPs that includes committed individuals.

## The Newness of the Institution as an Opportunity

Why would a novel institution be beneficial to the promotion of women's interests? Kantola suggests that men's hegemony could be less entrenched in these institutions' practices and processes (2010, 61). This resonates with feminist institutionalist arguments about institutions as structuring contexts which constrain and enable political action through the ideas and values embedded in them as well as through their incentive structures (Mackay and Meier 2003). In addition, feminist institutionalism notes issues of voice and participation and asks who has the power to make institutional design decisions (Chappell and Waylen 2013). Building on those arguments, a new institution would offer more room to voices representing non-hegemonic interests. Considering the EP as a new type of institution because of its supranational framework, in which MEPs are part of transnational party groups, it becomes plausible that traditional processes of national interest representation are side-lined by processes of transnational interest representation. This enables transnational alliance-building and therefore empowers transnational advocacy groups such as non-governmental organisations promoting the rights of Roma and Sinti, or lesbian, gay, bisexual, transgender, and intersex (LGBTI) people, but also business lobbies and sectoral interest groups. At an individual level, new institutions can offer fruitful ground to develop so-called velvet triangles (Woodward 2004), which develop between dedicated feminists (experts, trade-union leaders, femocrats, leaders of women's movements, MPs, and MEPs) who move between different positions in the policy arena (civil society – experts – the Commission – the EP – governments) and maintain close interpersonal relationships based on solidarity and a strong commitment to gender equality.

However, smooth access to the EP is only important in terms of results if the EP has formal power in the relevant policy domains. It was designed by the six founding states of the (predecessor of the) EU to hold the Supranational Authority (now the European Commission) accountable and grant the new organisation democratic legitimacy. At that time, the Parliamentary assembly was not given the power to effectively exercise the functions traditionally attributed to a parliament. From the start, the MEPs challenged the EP's weak position and, supported by some Member States, they managed to transform the institutional design of the EU. As the result of this 'remarkable process of institutional empowerment' (Rittberger 2012, 18), the EP can be said to have powers similar to domestic parliaments as regards legislative and budgetary decision-making processes since the Treaty of Lisbon came into force in 2009. There might be an interesting paradox, instead of; however, in the sense that the more the EP becomes a 'normal' parliament with concomitant powers, the more entrenchment of hegemonic interests closes the openness which was characteristic of the formerly novel institution. In the empirical sections, we will explore to what extent the EP's increase in formal power has negatively affected the access for feminist actors and the room for feminist voices in the EP.

### The Search for Legitimacy

Interestingly, the EU's search for legitimacy could constitute a factor beneficial to the power of the EP as well as the promotion of gender equality. As is widely covered in the literature on the so-called democratic deficit, the legitimacy of the EU in general and the EP in particular is contested time and again (Rittberger and Schroeder 2016). Contestation of the EU's handling of migration and the 2008 financial crisis has fuelled support for Eurosceptic parties, culminating in the British vote to leave the EU. Increasingly, the contestation of EU legitimacy has undermined its functioning. Although still contested, the EP is the only core EU institution which can credibly claim to command some democratic legitimacy, as it is the only institution whose members are directly elected by the European people. Over the years, each time when powers were moved from Member States to the supranational level, the EP has successfully used the principle of 'no integration without representation' (Rittberger 2012, 31) to strengthen its role in the inter-institutional balance of power with the Council and the Commission.

The same quest for EU legitimacy has also favoured social policy-making. Whenever the EU needed broad support for new steps in the fields of economic and monetary integration that did not seem to favour the general interest, there was a concomitant strengthening of the social dimension. The EP has also often promoted social policies as a means to increase popular support for the EU and strengthen its own reputation. Given the huge differences between Member States in terms of socioeconomic regulation, and given trade unions' and employers' fear of losing national prerogatives, such initiatives were often blocked or watered down. Promoting gender equality was perceived to be relatively easier, especially because it had a stronger treaty base. In the empirical sections, we will investigate to what extent the need to increase legitimacy is used as a lever for the promotion of gender equality.

# THE EP AND SIX DECADES OF
# PROMOTING GENDER EQUALITY

This section offers a thick historical narrative of the EP's role in promoting gender equality. I have opted for a qualitative research design, combining archival research, existing data sets, and secondary literature. Based on the EP's major institutional changes, I distinguish four periods. Keeping the institutional setting somewhat constant helps understand changes and continuities when it comes to the defence of gender equality.

### 1958–1978: A Supranational Assembly with National Parliamentarians

Article 119, the famous equal-pay article in the treaty that established the European Economic Community in 1957 (now Article 157 in the Treaty on the Functioning of the European Union (TFEU)), came about before the EP existed and arose from French concerns about the competitiveness of its industry (Hoskyns 1996; van der Vleuten 2007).[2] It firmly situated equal rights for women and men in the domain of the labour market. For lack of other binding articles in the social chapter, Article 119 became a welcome hook for parliamentary activity. In those early years, MEPs were selected members of national parliaments who went to Strasbourg to promote European integration. No wonder they insisted on developing a social dimension that could help increase support for European integration among the populations. Especially the parliamentary committee of Social Affairs[3] regularly reminded the European Commission of its duty to promote the implementation of equal pay. Almost every year, the EP adopted a report on Article 119 criticizing the Member States' poor implementation record and asked the Commission to take non-complying Member States to the Court of Justice. Rapporteur Cornelis Berkhouwer, a liberal MEP, succeeded in expanding the report beyond wage discrimination. He sought the abolishment of all other direct and indirect forms of discrimination related to women's work and their access to the labour market including prejudices in this domain. The EP tried to expand and strengthen the Commission's commitment to women's rights more than once. Rapporteur Astrid Lulling, a socialist MEP from Luxembourg, strengthened the Commission's draft recommendation concerning maternity protection in 1966 by asking for legal protection against dismissal and the extension of social-security benefits to unemployed women. The EP only had an advisory role, however, and the Commission ignored its initiatives, not daring to question Member-State prerogatives over social issues. At that time, there were only a few female MEPs. In 1958, there were four women among 142 MEPs and in 1972, five women; in 1978, there were eleven women among 198 MEPs. These pioneers, however, were powerful as chairs of committees and active as rapporteurs (European Parliamentary Research Service 2014).

In the 1970s, the Council adopted three strong directives on gender equality (pay, access to the labour market, and social security) that would earn the EEC its reputation as a champion of gender equality (Mazey 1998). Again, as with Article 119, the EP did not play an important role in bringing them about, due to its weak position in the European arena. It did indirectly contribute, however, by weaving a web between committed individuals in the EP and national parliaments, feminists in trade unions and the new women's movement, gender experts (such as lawyer Eliane Vogel-Polsky and sociologist Evelyne Sullerot), and femocrats in the Commission (Jacqueline Nonon). In sum, during the first twenty years, the EP (and especially some members of the Social Affairs committee) pushed for implementation of equal pay, tried to broaden the agenda, and developed into a node in the emerging 'velvet triangle'.

### 1979–1991: A Directly Elected Advisory Body

Starting in 1975, the European Commission and its Women Information Service had organised a campaign to inform and mobilise women as politicians and voters with the slogan 'Women for Europe'. They tried to give Europe a different, female image instead of the dominant view of bureaucracy and failed agricultural policies (Wobbe and Biermann 2009). When the first direct EP elections took place in 1979, a record number of sixty-seven women were elected. It meant that 16 per cent of MEPs were women at a time when the average in national parliaments was 7.6 per cent. Scholar Catherine Hoskyns captures the spirit when she describes how MEPs were determined to extend the EP's powers and role, and this 'was certainly the mood of many of the women MEPs, who felt not only that new things should be done but that at least some of these should directly involve women' (1996, 127). Most women MEPs were not activists from the women's movement, but they were committed to women's rights because of their own experiences with discrimination (Wobbe and Biermann 2009, 114). Social-democrats became the largest group in 1979, and female social-democratic MEPs from France and Germany persuaded their group to press for setting up an Ad Hoc Committee on Women's Rights. Their action met with success thanks to the support from the President of the EP, Simone Veil, a French liberal and feminist (Hoskyns 1996, 127).

The Ad Hoc Committee was composed of twenty-five women and ten men, representing all political groups. The Committee appointed French socialist Yvette Roudy as chair and Dutch Christian Democrat Hanja Maij-Weggen as rapporteur on 'the situation of women in the European Community'. The meetings of the Committee were public, so women's organisations could attend. Maij-Weggen drafted a report that 'caused great excitement' and was hotly debated (Hoskyns 1996, 128). Highly emotional resistance came from conservative male and female MEPs from Ireland, France, and the UK, who argued that the resolution promoted the legalization of abortion and neglected housewives. They even contended that working mothers would lead to an increase in criminal behaviour among children (Europees Parlement 1981, 195). Despite the opposition, the EP adopted the resolution with 174 votes in favour, 101 votes against, and 24 abstentions.

The Maij-Weggen report and the resolution would set the parliamentary agenda for years to come, covering issues such as the position of migrant women, women in agriculture and small and medium enterprises, the fight against trafficking, and female genital mutilation. A Committee of Inquiry was the follow-up to the Ad Hoc Committee. In an effort to do gender mainstreaming *avant-la-lettre*, its chair, Marie-Claude Vayssade, tried to persuade other parliamentary committees to deal with women's interests as well (Jacquot 2015). As her efforts failed, feminist MEPs asked for a permanent committee. After the 1984 elections, the Committee on Women's Rights was established as a regular parliamentary committee. It developed into 'an active watchdog' (Woodward 2012, 92) which made strategic use of personal links to femocrats in national and EU bureaucracies and to feminist legal experts. The Committee actively reached out to civil society by organising public hearings and agenda-setting events such as the Tribunal on Poverty in 1988, which brought marginalized women into the parliamentary hemicycle.

During the 1980s, in general, there was broad support in the EP for equal rights and opportunities. Large (65 to 70 per cent) majorities voted in favour of amendments from the Committees of Social Affairs and Women's Rights that would strengthen the Commission's draft directives, recommendations, and Action Programmes. In 1985, the EP adopted an inter-group resolution asking for annual Council meetings of ministers for women's affairs, the implementation of the directives and Action Programmes, and positive action on taxation and training. It had been jointly put forward by women MEPs from all four major political groups: socialist Ine van den Heuvel, Christian Democrat Marlene Lenz, liberal Simone Veil, and communist Vera Squarcialupi. There were two patterns of opposition. Time and again British Conservative MEPs protested whenever a proposal touched on labour conditions, such as the rights of part-time workers. Rapporteur Dame Shelagh Roberts (Conservative) even voted against her own report on parental leave (European Parliament 1984, 16). The second pattern concerned opposition against so-called moral issues, such as abortion, family, and sexual orientation. Recommendations in the Squarcialupi-report on sexual discrimination in the workplace and on equal rights for homosexuals met with indignant protests from conservative and Christian MEPs. Eventually, the resolution won overwhelming support. The same happened in 1986 with a radical resolution on violence against women based on an own-initiative report from the Committee on Women's Rights. The report and resolution, drafted by social-democrat Hedy d'Ancona, emphasised violence against women (including domestic violence, rape, forced prostitution, and trafficking of women) as a structural problem. The debate in the EP was heated and lengthy, but in the end, the resolution was adopted with 198 votes in favour, 66 against, and 50 abstentions (Locher 2007).

The attention to women's issues in the EP in the 1980s reflected the attention for the topic at the national and international levels (UN Decade for Women and World Conferences in Mexico, 1975, Copenhagen in 1980 and Nairobi in 1985). Furthermore, the EP built on policy initiatives of the European Commission, and most notably of its Women's Bureau (later Equal Opportunities Unit) at the Directorate-General V (now DG Employment, Social Affairs and Inclusion). It also helped those initiatives materialise by approving a budget line to fund the action programmes. The EP played a strong agenda-setting role by using hearings and own-initiative reports, for instance, on parental leave (1983), the rights of self-employed women and co-working spouses (1983), single-parent families (1986), and discrimination against immigrant women (1987). It depended on the Commission to turn recommendations and resolutions into regulation. The Council was obliged to consult the EP for every legislative proposal but was free to ignore its views. As a result, the EP could only exercise pressure through personal links with representatives of national governments. In the 1980s, faced with stagnation in the Council, the Commission became increasingly reluctant to develop new proposals for binding legislation on equal rights (van der Vleuten 2007). The EP also acted as watch dog in terms of implementing existing equality directives and issued monitoring reports, but it depended on the Commission to put pressure on the Member States by starting infringement procedures. In 1978, the EP for the first time managed to convince the Commission to start procedures against seven Member States which were in breach of the equal-pay directive (van der Vleuten 2007). In spite of a number of committed MEPs in the Women's Rights and Social Affairs Committees and broad support from the majority in plenary, the EP clearly had a limited influence over policy outcomes. Treaty changes in the 1990s finally strengthened its formal role and powers.

## 1992–2008:
## A Real Parliament?

The Treaty reforms in the 1990s (Treaty of Maastricht 1992; Treaty of Amsterdam 1997) strengthened the role of the EP. Its possibilities as a promoter of gender equality increased, but new obstacles and opposition also emerged. Major changes were the democratisation of decision-making; scrutiny of candidate-Commissioners; gender mainstreaming; broadening the treaty base; enlargements and the rise of Eurosceptic parties. I will discuss them each in turn.

First, the gradual democratisation of decision-making gave the EP a role as co-legislator on par with the Council of Ministers. The extension of qualified majority voting in the Council, which was deemed necessary in order to enable progress in an increasingly diverse, enlarged EU, had to be accompanied by an increase of parliamentary scrutiny. Germany and other Member States had pushed for this change to increase the legitimacy of the EU against the background of the highly technocratic development of the economic and monetary union. Thanks to the Committee of Women's Rights (hereafter FEMM), the EP had acquired a reputation for advocacy of women's rights, and its co-legislative role was hailed as good news for gender equality. However, these new powers were only useful insofar agreement with the Council could be reached. Inter-institutional negotiations continued to result in watered-down compromises, as the alternative to weak regulation often was no regulation at all. We see this mechanism at work in 2005, for instance, when the EP discussed the so-called Recast Directive (2006/54/EC) on equal opportunities and equal treatment of women and men in employment and occupation, which replaced and updated four older directives. In FEMM and the EP plenary, there was much disagreement because some MEPs wanted to finally regulate some new issues, such as parental leave and discrimination in occupational pensions, while others feared they would lose the whole directive if they would do so, given opposition in the Council. Adopting the same reasoning, the Commission was unwilling to accept amendments which aimed to expand the directive. Still, the EP managed to strengthen the directive by revising the definitions of harassment and sexual harassment, and of direct and indirect discrimination (van der Vleuten 2007).

Yet, a second change slightly qualified the EP's increased role. In the 1990s, new modes of governance were introduced that excluded the EP. The social dialogue procedure, for instance, enabled trade unions and employers to conclude collective agreements, which subsequently could be turned into directives. Although the EP had suggested this idea in the 1970s in order to circumvent Member-State opposition against social regulation, it turned out to weaken its own position. The EP was once more reduced to the role of onlooker, while the social dialogue procedure did not lead to high standards on gender issues but too weak compromises instead (van der Vleuten 2007, 154). Another innovation was the Open Method of Coordination for employment and social policy, which is based on policy coordination between the Member States through national action plans, targets, and benchmarks. While the Commission played a coordinating and monitoring role, the EP was excluded from the process (van der Vleuten and Verloo 2012).

A third change regarded scrutiny of the Commission. Given the Commission's role as drafter and gatekeeper in policy-making, the EP had an interest in seeing Commissioners appointed who would support EP initiatives and amendments. No wonder the EP was highly critical in its hearings of Commissioners-designate. This was introduced by the Maastricht treaty, which said the EP should formally approve a new Commission. The EP first used its new power in 1995, when members of the Social Affairs Committee and the Committee on Women's Rights (in that order) interrogated Pàdraig Flynn, the future Commissioner for Employment, Social Affairs and Equal Opportunities. They convinced the EP that Flynn was not acceptable for the portfolio of gender equality because of his lack of ambition in that arena, and therefore the EP could not put their faith in the Commission as a whole. Faced with this inter-institutional crisis, a compromise was negotiated: although Flynn kept the portfolio, a Group of Commissioners on Equal Opportunities was created to supervise the Commission's policy, and the Commission promised to prepare an annual report on equal opportunities.[4] In 2004, the EP heavily criticised Italian candidate Rocco Buttiglione (Justice) for his derogatory comments on women and gays, and his candidature was withdrawn.

Although there seemed to be continuous broad support in the EP for gender equality, the proof of the pudding came with a fourth change, the institutionalisation of gender mainstreaming. Mobilisation around the Fourth UN World Conference in Beijing in 1995 brought gender equality to the top of the agenda, and in 1997, the obligation to gender mainstream all EU policies and activities was included in the treaty (Article 3(2) TEC; now Article 8 TFEU). Starting in 2003, the EP would adopt a resolution on gender mainstreaming every few years. It not only reminded other EU institutions of their duties, but also pledged to gender mainstream its own activities by including a gender perspective in all policies and procedures, and creating a gender balance at all levels in its own institution. A high-level group was set up and charged with monitoring the incorporation of a gender perspective in all committee work. The first assessment in 2006 revealed that despite broad rhetorical support, most parliamentary committees had neither discussed nor adopted a gender equality strategy. They lacked expertise, had not looked for appropriate indicators or sex-disaggregated datasets, and had not analysed the allocation of budget resources. Contact with FEMM was sporadic or non-existent for 12 out of 18 committees. This sobering account showed how a majority of the MEPs continued to perceive gender equality as an add-on instead of an integral part of all policy domains, exemplified by the idea that 'incorporating gender aspects in reports and opinions will mean that the length of text will have to be revised' because of all additional stipulations (European Parliament 2006c, 8). Gender mainstreaming was perceived by some as a ground to dismantle specific policies for women, including FEMM, which instead emphasised the need for a 'dual approach' combining gender mainstreaming and positive action (Jacquot 2015).

A fifth change relates to a new Article 13 (Article 19 TFEU), which enabled policies to fight discrimination based on sex, racial or ethnic origin, religion or belief, disability, age, or sexual orientation. In the build-up to the intergovernmental negotiations in Amsterdam, Article 13 became the object of a fight between feminist actors who wanted recognition of gendered inequalities as underlying all other grounds, and others who wanted to strengthen the human rights of all groups suffering from discrimination (Jacquot 2015). Lombardo and Rolandsen Agustín (2011) have shown how including a wide range of discrimination grounds has led to a degendering of the policy content. A similar discussion developed over the budget, when in 1999 the New Opportunities for Women programme was replaced by EQUAL, which covered all Article 13 grounds of discrimination instead of maintaining a distinct programme for equal opportunities for men and women (Jacquot 2015). Article 13 required unanimity in the Council and therefore did not allow for a strong EP role. As a result, the EP could not prevent the directive on gender-based discrimination outside the labour market from being watered down by a lobby from insurance companies and media (van der Vleuten 2007).

Finally, the composition of the EP itself underwent major changes. Between 1995 and 2007, fifteen new Member States joined. In the 1994 elections, 25.3 per cent of MEPs were women, and the percentage rose to 27.6 per cent one year later, when Finland, Sweden, and Austria joined the EU (Jacquot 2015, 71). The strong Euroscepticism among women in the Nordic countries and their fear of the Nordic welfare state weakening because of EU membership contributed to putting gender equality high on the agenda. Ten years later, the 2004 enlargement with Eastern and Central European countries did not reverse the trend of increasing numbers of female MEPs at every election, though it did clearly slow down.[5]

Another change in the EP's composition was far more consequential: the increase of far-right national conservatives and Eurosceptics. In 1994, for the first time, a Eurosceptic group was created, 'Europe of Nations'. Though it collapsed after two years, there has been a Eurosceptic party group ever since.[6] Its MEPs defend anti-feminist positions, as voiced by Godfrey Bloom (UKIP), an MEP on the FEMM Committee who stated that 'I want to deal with women's issues because I just don't think they clean behind the fridge enough. . . . I am going to promote men's rights' (Wainwright 2004). Another Eurosceptic group emerged in 1995 when the right-wing European Democratic Alliance of Irish conservatives and French Gaullists was joined by Forza Italia and rebaptised Union for Europe.[7]

The presence of these groups has reinforced two trends regarding the promotion of gender equality. First, more outspoken essentialising views on women were voiced, for instance, when Polish MEP Urszula Krupa (ECR) argued that the 'equal treatment of men and women was discrimination and unfair to women, who in the vast majority of cases are mothers and. . . . should enjoy special protection' (European Parliament 2006b). Second, subsidiarity, respect for sovereignty, and cultural differences were used as arguments to undermine initiatives for the supranational promotion of gender equality. For instance, Hélène Goudin (ECR) argued that 'the EU should not have control over working time regulations, parental leave and other significant national issues. These are matters that the Member States are better dealing with independently' (European Parliament 2006b).

## Since 2009: Crises and Contestations

The Treaty of Lisbon (2009) once more strengthened the formal position of the EP. However, the post-Lisbon era has been characterised by widespread contestation of the EU. The harsh austerity policies as a response to the financial crisis and the failing management of migration have undermined trust in the EU and boosted support for Eurosceptic politicians. How has the EP fared as a promoter of gender equality in these turbulent times?

Stronger formal powers have been of limited use in the face of the Council blocking draft directives. The economic crisis was at the heart of the opposition to the proposal to revise the 1992 directive on maternity protection. In first reading, the EP used the Commission's draft to extend the minimum maternity leave to twenty weeks with full pay and add two weeks of paternity leave, also with full pay. Blocked by the opposition in the Social Affairs Council (EPSCO) for four years, the Commission withdrew the proposal against the wishes of a large EP majority (European Parliament 2019b). Two other draft directives which remain blocked in the Council (gender-balance on boards and an extension of anti-discrimination beyond the labour market) are also supported by substantive majorities in the EP, which has adopted several resolutions to push for progress. Two directives have been adopted, not in the field of gender equality but human rights, regarding human trafficking and the protection of victims of human trafficking and forced prostitution. FEMM was involved as rapporteur jointly with the Committee on Civil Liberties, Justice and Home Affairs (LIBE). The two directives and the debates concerning them took a human rights and criminal justice perspective aimed at punishing wrongdoers and protecting children and women, although the EP managed to insert references to the need for a gender perspective (European Parliament 2010).

As for the budget, since 1977 the EP has had the last word on all so-called non-compulsory expenditure (i.e. not earmarked for Common Agricultural Policy) such as the Structural Funds, research, and environment. It could reject the budget as well. The Treaty of Lisbon gave the EP an equal say with the Council over the whole budget. Already in previous periods, the EP had played an important role in ensuring and expanding funding for multiannual programmes for action on equal opportunities (NOW, EQUAL), women in development cooperation, and especially the DAPHNE programme, which dealt with combating violence against women and children. Over the past years, FEMM has time and again mobilised all MEPs to prevent further reduction of the budget for gender equality and to keep visible budget lines for projects regarding gender equality and gender-based violence, against the Commission's tendency to merge all lines into overarching programmes.[8] The budgetary struggles reflect the way in which gender mainstreaming can be used to make gender invisible.

The EP itself has continued to pay attention to gender mainstreaming efforts pushed by FEMM. FEMM started in 2009 by proposing Gender Mainstreaming Amendments (GMAs). This is even more relevant as the lack of Commission proposals on gender equality means that since 2009 FEMM has rarely had occasion to participate as a competent committee in the legislative process. It has continued to produce own-initiative reports, but they have a limited and even decreasing impact because they now are hardly ever tabled in plenary discussions due to changes in the EP procedures. Other committees mainly include FEMM's suggestions in their work when the topic is already acknowledged as gender-related, such as gender equality on the labour market, gender-based violence, gender in education, and human rights (European Parliament 2018a). Other committees and topics remain gender-blind. Research found that when it comes to attention to gender issues it does not matter whether there are many women on the committee or not (European Parliament 2018a, 45).

Within FEMM as well as in the EP plenary, the strongest opposition to feminist positions continues to come from Eurosceptics and (religious) conservatives (including members from the Christian Democrat party group). They try to replace 'gender equality' and 'LGBTI rights' with 'human rights of women, men and children' (European Parliament 2019e), and they criticise the lack of respect for state sovereignty. ECR, for instance, opposed the EP's proposed amendments to strengthen the Maternity Directive because family policies should be left to Member States. Opposition against this directive was also motivated by cost arguments 'in times of crisis' (European Parliament 2010). However, these groups continue to be outvoted by the other party groups.

## CONCLUSIONS

Looking back at more than sixty years of EP activity, it becomes clear that it indeed has acted as a staunch promoter of gender equality. Over time, the initial focus on the position of women in the labour market has been broadened to include other domains (work–life balance, education, development, gender-based violence, migration). The EP has often played an agenda-setting role, adopting resolutions on new issues at times when there was no clear treaty base yet. Since 1980, FEMM has played a key role, acting as an agenda-setter with its own-initiative reports, as (co-) rapporteur of draft directives, and as the critical committee responsible for the hearing of Commissioners-designate with gender in their portfolio. In plenary, proposals concerning gender equality have been and continue to be supported by large majorities. How to explain the remarkable commitment to gender equality of a parliament which has changed over the decades from a part-time advisory forum to a directly elected full-fledged parliament? I have formulated three hypotheses: the number of women MEPs, the newness of the institution, and EU legitimacy.

First, the number of women MEPs does not have much explanatory power on its own. There has not been a gradual increase of support for gender equality over time in parallel to the gradual increase of women MEPs, and there is no connection between parliamentary committees' number of female members and the inclusion of GMAs in their work. Also, women in right-wing Eurosceptic and Christian-conservative groups are at least as vocal as their male colleagues in opposing gender equality. Yet the presence of committed individuals clearly has played a role in getting and keeping topics on the agenda, including the establishment of a committee on women's rights. This committee subsequently developed into a node of a transnational 'velvet' network of engaged individuals, experts and femocrats, national MPs, and non-governmental organisations.

Second, though this network was influential during the 1980s and 1990s, it has lost power because the arena and the actors have changed. FEMM itself continues to be 'one of the few places at the European level where militant engagement in favour of women's rights can be fully expressed' (Jacquot 2015, 162), but it is more isolated. Ahrens (2016) contends that its niche position may have saved FEMM from being disbanded, but after each parliamentary election its raison d'être is questioned, especially since the introduction of gender mainstreaming and the lack of legislative proposals on gender equality. Even though FEMM has developed a strong feeling of togetherness and activism among its members, the changed composition of the EP is also reflected in the committee's debates. Bottom-up support through strong grassroots mobilization in favour of gender equality has weakened, while opposition against gender equality has increased (Verloo 2018). The personal connections with the Commission have changed and diversified because gender equality is now institutionalised in different places, mainly under DG Justice. In the 1970s, and especially after the first direct elections of 1979, the newness of the institution did indeed create a window of opportunity. However, the process of becoming a 'normal' parliament, especially since 2009, has offered fewer opportunities than expected. Being co-legislator gives the EP a seat at the table, but when the Council disagrees with EP amendments, it can simply block further decision-making. The EP has even been excluded from the dominant modes of economic and financial governance connected to the European Semester.

Finally, the quest for EU legitimacy has indeed enabled the EP to obtain support for gender equality. Yet, over the years, this mechanism has lost its effect and perhaps its initial 'surprise factor'. Member states have become more reluctant because they are aware that gender equality policies entail costly policy changes or because they disagree with the principle altogether. Against the backdrop of a broad contestation of EU legitimacy and the call for a return of the nation state, the Commission and the Council are also reluctant to adopt binding policies and rather look for different modes of governance to cater to the perceived demands of European citizens. Given increased contestation of gender 'ideology' and LGBTI rights, the domain of gender equality is no simple legitimacy booster anymore.

In conclusion, it is no myth that the EP is a promoter of gender equality, as is clear from the relentless commitment of a majority of the thirty-five FEMM members (usually 75 per cent) and the broad support for their initiatives in plenary. Support generally comes from the social democrat, liberal, green, and left-wing party groups (some 48 per cent of the votes in 2014–2019), and most Christian Democrats (the whole party-group commanding 29.5 per cent of the votes).[9] However, it would be a mistake to think that all MEPs are promoters of gender equality. First, there are clear patterns of opposition, generally coming from right-wing nationalists, conservatives, and Eurosceptics, supported by some Christian Democrats. These party groups have increased in numbers. Outspoken opposition follows similar lines as in national politics: liberals will criticise the costs of regulation and claim respect for individual choices; conservative Christians defend essentialist positions, the family as composed of man–woman–children and special treatment for mothers; nationalist conservatives and Eurosceptics oppose every regulation or budget line for gender equality policies as an attack on state sovereignty. These arguments have all grown louder over the past decade. Second, most MEPs continue to see gender equality as a niche affair that has little to do with other policy domains. In most parliamentary committees, commitment to gender equality remains limited to the partial inclusion of comments from FEMM. Increasing the grounds for discrimination has also resulted in degendering policy content. As a result of these two patterns, after sixty years, the EP's promotion of gender equality and gender mainstreaming continues to rest on the shoulders of committed individuals: feminists in the EP and in the broader European arena.

# NOTES

1 I am grateful to Petra Ahrens, Lise Rolandsen Agustín and Katja Müller for their comments on previous drafts.

2 This section is based on van der Vleuten (2001, 2007), as well as primary documents.

3 Composed of twenty-six male and three female members.

4 Ironically, Swedish candidate Anita Gradin, with a strong record in gender issues, wanted the portfolio but had been given Justice and Home Affairs instead (Jacquot 2015).

5 In 2014, 30.5 per cent of the MEPS elected in eleven Eastern and Central European countries were women; for the other seventeen Member States, this was 40.9 per cent. See 'Men and Women Distribution' at http://www.europarl.europa.eu/elections2014-results/en/gender-balance.html.

6 1996, Group of Independents for a Europe of Nations; 1999, Europe Democracies and Diversities (EDD); 2004, Independence/Democracy (IND/DE); 2009, Europe of Freedom and Democracy. At that time, the group was mainly composed of Danish and British Eurosceptics, Dutch religious conservatives and French agrarionists, later joined by the League of Polish Families and *Lega Norte* (Italy). After the 2014 elections, UKIP (UK) and *Movimento Cinque Stelle* (Italy) became the main components.

7 It also attracted MEPs from Latvia, Lithuania and Poland, and was rebaptised European Conservatives and Reformists (ECR) after the 2009 elections; since 2014, the German *Alternative für Deutschland*, Polish PIS (Law and Justice), and British Conservatives are the main components.

8 For 2021–2027, the EP has amended the Rights and Values programme of the Commission in first reading by a large (68 per cent) majority, proposing the title of Citizens, Equality, Rights and Values. However, its proposal for a substantial budget increase does not benefit the 'Equality, Rights and Gender Equality' and the 'Daphne' strands, but two other strands ('Union Values', on democracy and rule of law, and 'Active Citizenship') (Amendments adopted by the European Parliament on 17 January 2019 on the proposal for a regulation of the European Parliament and of the Council establishing the Rights and Values programme (COM(2018)0383 – C8–0234/2018–2018/0207(COD))).

See http://www.europarl.europa.eu/sides/getDoc.do?pubRef=-//EP//TEXT+TA+P8-TA-2019-0040+0+DOC+XML+V0//EN&language=EN.

9 See 'Seats by Political Group and Member State' at http://www.europarl.europa.eu/elections2014-results/en/seats-group-member-2014.html.

# 4

# Staging Power

## Constructing Gender in the Debates of the European Parliament, 1999–2014

*Julia Maria Zimmermann*

On 1 March 2017, during a debate on the gender pay gap, the right-wing Polish Member of the European Parliament (MEP) Janusz Korwin-Mikke stated:

> Of course women must earn less than men because they are weaker, they are smaller, they are less intelligent, and they must earn less. That is all. (NI, 1 March 2017)

While Korwin-Mikke's statement did not go uncommented on that day, only a few years earlier on such statements would have been almost unthinkable. With equal opportunities for women and men advancing and gender equality being a centrepiece of postmodern political discourses in political groups from the left to the centre-right, dissenting voices went seemingly unnoticed. That has changed since then. This change in itself is not the scope of the present chapter; I will however propose a discourse-analytical perspective on the backdrop of that evolution.[1] Taking a relatively under-researched perspective – that of EU parliamentarism – I am asking the classic question of the sociology of knowledge (Berger and Luckmann 1980): how do collective notions of society shape social reality? Thus, in my analysis, I will examine both rhetorical and discursive strategies and political topics that are relevant to this aspect of the social construction of political discourse on gender.

While the construction of gender, gender relations and gender equality serve as a case study, the underlying purpose of this chapter is to show how the discourse of a genuine 'European discourse community' is shaped in debates in the European Parliament (EP) and how they are perceived as 'unobjectionable', thus generating presentations of a social reality that introduce a specific set of gender relations as binary, elitist and neoliberal. It is this presentation of equal opportunities at the heart of EU political discourse that is increasingly refuted by many right-wing populists, while not being much supported by left-leaning feminist activists either. The aim of this chapter is, therefore, to scrutinise this rather precarious discourse and to ask how MEPs attempted to establish it as a political fact in setting it as natural and limiting it to a very small number of beneficiaries.

Debates in the EP are necessarily marked by diverse opinions. Not only is it an unusual large plenary, but it also assembles representatives from many political parties – even the spectrum of standpoints in one political group is relatively huge – and from many countries with diverse political and historical traditions.[2] Add to this the changes in political groups and fractions as well as the constituency of Member States due to the Eastern enlargement in the past fifteen years,[3] and it becomes nearly impossible to address the diversity of opinions appropriately. On the other side, many statements on gender issues, arguably with the exception of right-wing MEPs, are strikingly similar, varying only in minor differences regarding the preferred policy, or in the accentuation of the argumentation. I want to stress this similarity further by introducing the concept of the 'unobjectionable norm', a term coined by Ole Elgström (2005) describing exactly this uniformity of opinion on many value-related issues tackled on the EU level. My argument here is that the production of political discourse, albeit always manifold, may have a certain drive for normalisation, a normalisation that is necessary for political action, for it allows for coalitions across various political groups, but which also may come across as an attempt to de-normalise and de-validate competing discourses at the political margins. Against this background, increased polarisation of political discourses, as showing in the resistance against gender politics, may be interpreted as the loud manifestation of protest against a 'mainstreaming' of political discourse that is perceived as a form of 'dictatorship'.

Nevertheless, as discourses of modernity are tightly intertwined, the 'unobjectionable' discourses promoting gender equality is far from being unproblematic when looked at from a non-'neoliberal' angle, such as queer or intersectional perspectives (Crenshaw 1991).[4] Thus, non-heterosexual gender relations or the challenges non-binary gender persons may face are as invisible as are real existing differences in the experience of equal opportunities in different nation (and welfare-) states, in different socioeconomic classes, in precarious family situations such as monoparental families, and so on. As the case study will suggest, it is worthwhile to underline that, in fact, the overall notion of gender, presented in the debates by a majority of MEPs, is binary and restricted to cis-men and -women, arguably well-educated and achieving, able-bodied and reasonably young. The private relationship between genders is stereotypically heteronormative, featuring monogamous relationships with children (obviously not monoparental), with ideally both parents working. Thus, while taking on a core issue of social equality, and an issue that has become a founding myth,[5] the gender discourse in the EP is revealed as precarious, turning a blind eye on intersectional realities, and finally running a risk to enhance some of these social inequalities it ignores.

In this chapter, I present a case study based on the analysis of 11 debates on gender equality in economic and political hierarchies between 1999 and 2014. This period encompasses three complete legislative sessions. The legislative beginning in 1999 marks the 'mise en pratique' of two essential policies: it marks the first session after the 4th World Conference on Women, which took place in Beijing in 1995 and resulted in a famous declaration promoting gender mainstreaming as a political tool for equal opportunities. 1999 also marks the entrance into force of the Treaty of Amsterdam, strengthening the power of the EP.

The material selected consists of debates revolving around gender equality in hierarchic structures, such as businesses (e.g. women as CEOs), science (e.g. women as professors), and – with regard to the 2004 elections – women in politics.

Employing a discourse-analytical approach, combined with Shirin Rai's framework for performative political analyses (Rai 2015), I will not, however, ponder on the level of policies. Instead, I am examining a rather hidden, cultural, some might argue, less empirical level, that of speech acts, performances and their underlying interpretations and constructions of social reality. As this subject is still relatively under-researched in much of the political and even social sciences, and particularly when it comes to EU studies, I will elaborate in more detail on my theoretical and methodological approach before outlining three layers of a case example on the debates on women in decision-making, particularly in economic hierarchies.

Debates analysed are as follows:

- Women in the decision-making process, 1 March 2000
- Balanced participation of women and men in the decision-making process, 18 January 2001
- Election 2004: balanced representation for women and men, 6 November 2003
- Women in international politics, 15 November 2006
- Women and science, 20 May 2008
- Gender aspects of the economic downturn and financial crisis – Assessment of the results of the 2006–2010 Roadmap for Equality between women and men and forward-looking recommendations – Charter for Women's Rights – follow-up, 15 June 2010
- Female poverty – Equality between women and men – 2010, 8 March 2011
- Equality between women and men in the European Union – 2011 – Women in political decision-making, 12 March 2012
- Gender balance among non-executive directors of companies listed on stock exchanges, 19 November 2013

## ESTABLISHING THE TRUTH:
## PARLIAMENTS AS PERFORMATIVE STRUCTURES

Public expression in the plenary is not, as a certain trend in parliamentary research practice suggests, the less interesting part in parliamentary work, but fulfils a crucial task both for the manifestation of the parliament as an institution and the realisation of the discourse in debate (Rai 2012). This function is not legislative and, therefore, may be easily overlooked in the predominant political research on parliamentary work. I am following a conceptualisation of parliaments as 'performative structures', a term coined by Steven Beaudoin (2013, 111), but developed further by Shirin Rai in her framework on political performance (Rai 2010, 2012, 2015). She defines 'the term "political performance" as those performances that seek to communicate to an audience meaning related to state institutions, policies and discourses' (Rai 2015, 1179ff.). As such, political performances are a crucial mediator between the political institutions, for example, the parliament or the government, and the public. The performances, however, are not only a means to communicate or legitimise political decisions, or to mirror or represent constituencies. They serve, furthermore, to shape the discourses in debates, and thus produce new forms of political knowledge. Accordingly, talking about gender issues in the EP generates notions on 'gender', on men, women, possibly alternative genders – or not – and on gender relations, instead of simply 'governing' them. Since these public performances are central to my considerations, it is only consequent that public statements in the plenary – as the place dedicated to publicity – are my main sources. Critics may argue that these statements are, due to the restriction in the parliamentary regulations (Corbett, Jacobs and Neville 2016), overly superficial, abbreviated and shibbolethical. This is true. However, I hold that precisely because of that, they also reveal societal discourses: these statements are the discourse that MEPs would want to be heard by their audience, that is, EU citizens through the means of immediate broadcasting and publishing of minutes, and their colleagues in the plenary through simultaneous translation.

According to Rai, the Political Performance Framework deploys between two axes (Rai 2015, 1183–87). The first axis reflects social relations which become manifest and shine through performative acts of (political) representation. These are (1) the visible body, which is marked by sex/gender, colour, class, sexuality, ability/health and other traits, (2) the staging representation, such as space, place (e.g. architecture) and time, (3) auditory power of the performance, that is, of words, scripts, voices, interjections, and so forth, and (4) the performative labour which creates value, similarly to other kinds of labour. These manifestations are closely interconnected. For example, the bodily constitution allows certain occupations of space or vocal expressions and denies others. This link between body, stage, auditory (and society) has an immediate impact on the outcome of the performative labour process and its success or effectiveness. The second axis tackles the effectiveness of political performance, which is dependent on certain factors, such as the authenticity of representation (who can represent whom and whose interests?), the mode of representation (the use of cultural and/or shared narratives and symbols), the moment of liminality (in which political disruptions and the creation of new meanings are possible), and finally the resistance to claim-making (the 'opposition' through words, mockery, mimicry, etc.) to hegemonic claims through representation.

## Gender Discourses as a Discourse on Modernity: Epistemic Preconceptions

In the debates, the construction of gender is linked to a multitude of transversal discourses, for example, on cultural boundaries, on work and economy, on religion, on the political institutions of the EU, and so forth. These discourses provide a background to the specific construction of gender within a certain social formation which allows gender discourses to be consistent with other modern discourses. In this case study, I consider them insofar as they bear certain rhetorical – or performative – preconceptions that shape the way in which gender is perceived. I address several of these preconceptions, namely, the unobjectionability of certain norms and a complex connection between republican *pathos* and capitalist *logos*.

'Unobjectionable norms', a concept introduced by Ole Elgström in 2005, describes a norm or set of norms that have gained such a predominant validity within a group that objections to this norm or set of norms are either unthinkable or met with sanction:

> Some norms attain a predominant status. The become taken for granted . . . and are generally considered inviolable. They are perceived as being so morally superior that it is considered almost taboo to criticise them. (Elgström 2005, 30)

As speech acts, unobjectionable norms are, rhetorically, often introduced as facts that may or may not serve as a base for further argumentation or narratives. Wordings such as 'we all know', 'nobody denies', 'it is incontestable' set these norms as being unobjectionable, without them being necessarily dominant outside a certain discursive community (such as the EP), or aiming at persuading competing discourses. Rather, as the following quotes may illustrate, unobjectionable norms may take the rhetorical form of statements, thus setting a 'positive' fact practically ex nihilo:

> Things being what they are, nobody should dare any longer to dispute that the right of equality of men and women is a fundamental right of a democratic society, requiring equal treatment and equal opportunity be achieved by a package of active measures, including positive action. (Astrid Lulling, PPE-DE, 1 March 2000)

> It is incontestable that a democratic society must be represented in a worthy manner by both men and women. (Marie Panayotopoulos-Cassiotou, PPE-DE, 15 November 2006)

> We all know that there are important economic arguments for this proposal. (Viviane Reding, vice-president of the Commission, 19 November 2013)

On a performative level, unobjectionable norms are not seldom repeated as if in a form of ritual. This re-actualisation is an integral part of the function of unobjectionable norms, in fact, they become 'unobjectionable' only through ritualised repetition (Elgström 2005, 32).

In some regards, preconceptual speech acts make up much of the performance through which gender is constructed verbally in the EP. Some speech acts intimately connect the speaker's persona with the political statement, for example, in those cases where pregnant or parenting speakers evoke their pregnancy and motherhood (rarely fatherhood) in order to underline their interest in the promotion of gender equality. These speech acts present gender as an embodied experience, and appeal directly to similar experiences in the audience. Referring to Rai's framework, the staging of embodied social relations are used in order to enhance discursive power. Other topics, such as gender equality in hierarchies, rather refer to a neoliberal discourse, arguing both from a 'republican' perspective of values such as justice and equality, but interrelating them with capitalist discourses of 'smart business'. Other speech acts are relatively present in all areas, for example, the unobjectionable norms. Also, some rhetorical strategies are generally used across political parties, again the neoliberal nexus, while others are merely particular strategies, for example, the assessment of 'ideology', which is almost exclusively used by conservative MEPs.

From a methodological point of view, I will show that the performance of discourses, including the narratives and the setting of the debate, supports the shaping of both, the discursive co-construction of gender and European integration, and certain power relations.

## The Presence of Absence in the Performative Setting

Between 1999 and 2004, only eleven plenary debates dealt with the issue of women and gender equality in political, economic and other professional hierarchies in the EU. This sample number is relatively small, compared to the number of debates in other fields of equal rights politics, such as lesbian, gay, bisexual, transgender, and intersex (LGBTI) (fourteen debates) or women's rights in non-EU countries (twenty-one debates). This quantitative comparison itself is already telling. Obviously, questions of gender equality in the highest social ranks within the EU are far less debatable than issues of gender equality outside the EU.[6]

Additionally, when it comes to the participation in these debates, a gender bias is noticeable: while about as many men as women take part in the discussion on LGBTI rights, and about one-third of discussants on gender equality in third countries is male, the huge majority of speakers on matters of gender equality in inner-EU hierarchies is female. Admittedly, the division between 'male' and 'female' is somewhat arbitrary. The fact that the majority of speakers is female does not necessarily imply that most men were absent, and still less does it mean that the majority of female MEPs was present. Nevertheless, the lack of male participation in debates on gender equality does not go unnoted by the participants:

> Thank you very much, Mr Dover [draftsman of the opinion of the Committee on Industry, Research and Energy]. I thank you particularly in view of the fact that, apart from Commissioner Dimas, you are the only man who has signed up for this debate tonight. I have only female speakers. (The President, 20 May 2008)

It seems as though gender equality, at least in its practical manifestations, remains a 'women's issue'.

Although this question of staging representation belongs to the part of corporeal performativity that is not necessarily part of my analysis, it is inescapable to notice a material expression of gender discourse in this very performative setting (Palmieri 2011). If we take presence and non-presence as performative acts, the absence of men in these debates is as important as the presence of women, this all the more since the share of male and female MEPs throughout these years has been, despite a generally positive evolution towards parity, disadvantageous to women. This consideration alone shows how precarious gender equality is as an issue of political debate. The problematic of presence and absence in politics, debated especially in women's and minorities' representation, is not easy to discern. For instance, Anne Philipps, in her work on the 'Politics of Presence' (Phillips 1995), judged the presence of women to be necessary, albeit very problematic, and certainly not a sufficient precondition for political gender equality. Although she, and indeed many of her predecessors, rightfully claimed that the focus on descriptive representation implied a homogeneity among women that is simply non-existent, this is not the main point I want to make in this case. Rather, I underline that presence can be a marker of a relatively lower rank when it comes to discursive and performative power relations (on this point, see Lombardo and Meier 2016, 53).

It is noticeable that the presence in the political arena does not automatically imply power, while absence does not mean being excluded from it. I do not interpret the vast absence of men from the political arena in which gender issues are discussed as a sign of the empowerment of the women present. Indeed, the discussants perceive the male absence as a devaluation of gender issues:

> If I may make a personal comment, I believe that we would make rather more progress, regardless of what you may think about the contribution of the only man taking part in this debate if more men participated in debates of this kind. (The President, 15 November 2000)[7]

In this sense, absence reflects a certain power position, namely the power of retiring oneself from discursive visibility. Visibility is not, as Johanna Schaffer shows (Schaffer 2008, 51), a necessary sign of empowerment, but always also an exposure to the judgement of, and by, the more powerful discursive subjects. Usually, it is the un-normal, the particular, that is exposed and subjected to the critical and guarding eye of the 'normal'. In Schaffer's study, the deviant subject is scrutinised through observation.

Thus, absence can mean both, forced exclusion from the discourse and its opportunities for empowerment, as well as voluntary retirement from the discourse and its governance, just as presence can mean inclusion into the discourse, and hence empowerment, as well as exposure to discursive governance. It is not always distinguishable in which way the interdependence of presence and absence is operative, and presence and absence are by no means mutually exclusive binary categories. Rather, they interact with and co-construct each other. Absence not only constitutes presence but produces a kind of peculiar presence and vice versa, absence does not imply disempowerment automatically, but can refer to a complex triad between presence/absence – visibility/invisibility – power/subjection. Each position in the binary can pair which any other position in the triad, leading to permeability and ambiguousness in the binary. This issue has become crucial in the emerging perfor-mative studies and can certainly not be solved here. Therefore, I will cut short my excursion at this point.

If we take a look at the performative setting of mainly female MEPs discuss-ing issues of gender equality, both interpretations offered earlier are possible. The female discussants are by no means disempowered; in fact, they act as legislators as properly as possible. Certainly, female policy-making is not in need of approval by masculine presence. In this sense, these women are more powerful than the major-ity of Europeans, including men, and present a political elite. Meanwhile, in being absent, the male MEPs renounce their legislative power. Still, their absence gives them a discursive presence in the way that their choice makes gender equality seem like an exclusive women's issue, hence a particular interest, which is of no importance to certain groups (i.e. men), and therefore ultimately to European citizenship or humankind in general.

This is in sharp contrast to the presence of male MEPs at debates on women's (!) rights in third countries or LGBTI rights where the share of male speeches lies between one third (women's rights in third countries) and one half (LGBTI rights). It is fair to conclude that these issues, despite being far more theoretical and non-legislative than gender equality within the EU, is deemed a crucial topic for many MEPs regardless of their gender. This may be due to the importance of these debates for building a European community of values, reiterated, in this case, through a gender lens. This identity labour is less important in many inner-EU matters: as they are – allegedly – devoid of universal interest, these debates become negotiations conducted by particular 'expert' groups. This is supported by the observation that – taking into account the male-female ratio of debatants in gender-related debates, but also of member of the FEMM Committee, for instance – equal opportunities seems to be an issue for some (not all) women of nearly all political colours, thus ranging from left-wing to moderate right-wing, and a small group of men, recruiting from socialist and green political groups. I suggest that the absence of men in gender-related matters is not (necessarily) a sign of misogyny or disinterest, but rather a display of a conviction of incompetence on the side of many male MEPs when it comes to this 'women's field of expertise'.

This, however, does generate a peculiar discourse on gender: women are seen as experts when it comes to gender, while men are not. This notion is, with inverted validation, a continuation of gender discourses that treat women as 'the sex' while men are the human standard: it is still women who are considered experts on issues related to gender equality just because they are women. This suggests that 'gender' somehow is synonymous to 'woman': while men continue to be humans, women are humans with a gender.

There has been, undeniably, a shift in the interpretation of sex/gender. Not only is 'gender knowledge', or the identification of women with sex/gender no longer a stigma but expertise that can be used for profit, as I will show later on. Moreover, sex/gender is no longer defined as a purely biological fact that assigns persons to a specific social position which is deemed 'natural'. Rather, most MEPs seem to consider gender as a social relation which privileges some persons over others. This production of social inequality has to be overcome by political means, and since women are defined as being underprivileged by gender relations and norms, it is logically consistent that women are the experts when it comes to policing gender equality. Thus, gender, as it is already constructed in the performative setting of the debates is a cultural marker rather than a biological constant, although it undeniably has a biological implication (e.g. the decision on who is male or female in the first place).

## Revaluation of 'Gender Capital'

When it comes to arguing in favour of equal opportunity politics, the most prominent discursive strategy employed by many MEPs of all political colours belongs to the realm of capitalist economic discourses and consists of revaluating women, or the female gender, as an economic resource. The revaluation of women becomes manifest when MEPs expound the economic importance of women in a knowledge- and communication-based economy. In the 2011 debate, MEPs made statements such as the following:

> Research has clearly shown . . . that, when women are involved in companies' decision-making bodies, they turn in better results, perform better and are more efficient. (Rodi Kratsa-Tsagaropoulou, author)

> It is also important to recognise the link between the presence of competence and women's roles in corporate governance with a different approach to process management, optimal use of human resources, anti-discrimination rules and sustainable productivity which they often guarantee. (Silvia Costa, S&D)

And in the 2013 debate, the following was stated:[8]

> Not only is this a waste of talent, it is also a missed opportunity to make better decisions leading to better financial results in the highest bodies of our listed companies. . . . More women in management positions provide a broader insight into economic behaviour, into consumers' choices, leading to market share gains. (Viviane Reding, Vice-President of the Commission)

> It is not only synonymous with a fairer economy, it is also smart businesses [*sic*]. (Zita Gurmai, S&D)

The statements suggesting that women are an exceptionally efficient and valuable workforce in knowledge-based economies partly reflects the evolution of the 'knowledge society', which saw an expansion in high education from the 1960s, from which particularly women (and other previously marginalised groups) benefited. This evolution accompanied a general shift in post-industrial labour towards immaterial work in the service sector. It also correlates with a change in traditional gender values evolving around a single (male) breadwinner and the increasing participation of women in the labour market (Kaelble 2007, 130–33).

The latter point resonates with changes in the economic politics that actively promoted female employment – not least the EU itself, driven by the EP (Hubert 2012; Stratigaki 2012). The number of women on the labour market and the shift towards service-oriented labour, and with that, the rise of 'soft' and communication skills, however, has led to an increase of competitiveness on the labour market: not only has the number of applicants risen, their profile has become somewhat standardised through widespread and equally standardised higher education, and, additionally, applicants for positions in certain branches (very high and very low qualified) compete with rivals from different (EU) countries.

My sketch of this development is, of course, highly simplified. However, this set of various trends added to the revaluation of female workforce. This revaluation cannot, on the other hand, be understood without considering the shift of socioeconomics towards a knowledge-based and competitive service economy in which skills become crucial that have been, traditionally, ascribed to women. The class bias of this evolution is as blatant as it is (usually) silenced in the debates, as the 'flexibility' of women has mainly been exploited in precarious jobs, which, in turn, are not addressed in the debates on top positions I am analysing.

Women are, however, not only qualified through professional education, and not even through 'feminine' skills such as communication and relationship management. EP discourse takes it a little further and ascribes to women a set of values that have been shaped by experiencing discrimination in industrial, patriarchal labour structures: to some MEPs, women are a valuable human resource just because they are women.

> With an ageing population, we need women, and women mean business. Women mean life. Women mean everything positive – and we should give them a chance. (Viviane Reding, Vice-president of the Commission, 5 July 2011)

The belonging to, and upbringing according to a specific gender – not sex – ensure a set of experiences that probably make women fitter for the post-industrial economy than men:

> Mr President, Commissioner, ladies and gentlemen, as everyone knows, being a woman is already an undertaking in itself, because it means having to manage and reconcile family, professional and social life, in a context that still does not adequately recognise the high level of education, . . . professionalism and expectations of women. (Silvia Costa, S&D, 5 July 2011)

This competitive advantage that women enjoy over men can be called 'gender capital'. Indeed, this capital has constantly been operating throughout history, and the persisting gender gap in hierarchies may be read as a sign of the successful valorisation of male gender capital until now. However, in the discourse circulating in the EP, the 'gender capital' of men, discursively connected to social exclusion, unfairness and economic failure, is rejected for the sake of female 'gender capital'. Against this background, it is clear that women become a courted clientele for post-industrial, individualised economics.

However, the reasoning and involvement of the EP in this debate only partly draws on economic ideas, and partly on normative world views. The latter I call 'republican pathos', as they refer to values which are defined as universal and eternally valid, while nevertheless being subject to public democratic debate. These values comprise attitudes such as equality between genders, classes, races, nationalities, religions, and so forth; freedom; social justice; the fairness of proceedings and the principle of merit; and so on. I am broadly following Boltanski and Chiapello (2005), who argue that this republicanism, which has – sometimes – provided a critique of capitalism, has been appropriated by post-industrial capitalism. However, I want to extend this argument and claim that republicanism is in itself closely linked with capitalism and that the two share a mutual valorisation. This mutual valorisation has been hinted at, caustically, by Marx in the first volume of Capital: 'This sphere that we are deserting, within whose boundaries the sale and purchase of labour-power go on, is, in fact, a very Eden of the innate rights of man. There alone rule Freedom, Equality, Property and Bentham' (Marx 1887 (1999), 123).

Thus, just as republican values fuel capitalist accumulation, especially when a new set of values emerges (see Boltanski/Chiapello's role of critique), the accumulation process leads to developments in republicanism. I will not pursue this argumentation further here. However, the interdependence between economic/capitalist and republican values becomes manifest in various statements, for example, in the 2011 debate:

> The idea that economic and business leadership is the exclusive prerogative of men has long been untenable. (Edit Bauer, PPE, 5 July 2011)

> The established and prevailing monocultures in leading business positions are no longer acceptable, either from an economic or from a social perspective. (Andrea Češková, ECR, 5 July 2011)

While the second statement links both values as being additional, the first quote obscures in which way male business leadership is 'untenable' and suggests readings in both logics, economic and republican, as either being unfair or uneconomic.

This reading allows for the interpretation of discourses on gender and European integration as being tightly intertwined with economic ideas.[9] Gender equality within an EU society thus can be translated as an equality of chances enabling for – and enabled by – a high-profile sector of the labour market as well as economic and/

or political leadership. Not quite surprisingly (Stratigaki 2005; Hubert and Stratigaki 2016), the construction of EU integration reveals itself as driven by neoliberal logics, fostering the freedom of markets and privileging economic and political elites and employing at times utilitarist terms:

> The under-exploited pool of well-educated women represents a real untapped potential for the EU economy, especially at a time when human capital is a key factor in terms of competitiveness and when, as a society, we are ageing. (Viviane Reding, Vice-President of the Commission, 19 November 2013)

> We can simply not afford to recruit managers from only one half of the population. (Britta Thomsen, S&D, 19 November 2013)

> Because gender equality at work is not only a women's issue: it is a business issue. It is an economic imperative. (Viviane Reding, Vice-President of the Commission, 19 November 2013)

Statements like these, which treat women – and men – as 'human capital' or 'human resource' are not at odds with (feminist) struggles for liberation. Moreover, (economic) value is limited to a very specific group of women, that is, highly educated women (arguably in economics, law and similar academic fields) with access to high-ranked positions in top enterprises who willing to become part of management. In this light, the simultaneous affirmation of gender equality and social fairness may seem void.

On the other hand, EU competencies simply do not extend to the welfare state, and thus to issues such as precarious labour, the hardships single mothers may face, the class bias in education. Therefore, even if MEPs may (and do, in some statements) recognise the impact of socioeconomic inequality, such as precarious working conditions or inequalities between metropoles and the periphery, they may hesitate to question Member-State competencies and subsidiarity.

In either case, the conjunction of gender and neoliberal economics on the one hand and the EP's focus on economic elites may fuel notions of a diffuse conglomerate between gender and equal opportunities politics, neoliberal economy, elites, and the European Union.

While the exact conflation of gender discourses and capitalism discourses is certainly too bold an assertion, it is permissible, I argue, to say that specific constructions of gender and the relationship between genders are in line with certain social and economic formations, including capitalism (Zimmermann 2017, 182–200). This does not preclude the possibility for change, or diverse degrees of freedom, and certainly, neither gender nor capitalism should be perceived as uniform and/or monolithic. However, just as the housewife model was fruitful for a Fordist formation of capitalism, limiting the workforce and allowing for private consumption of former 'luxury goods', the model of gender diversity may become one pillar of postmodern capitalism.

The connection between gender and value production gains new momentum at the backdrop of the financial crisis of 2008/2009. At this point, the revaluation of women's capital becomes a historical necessity after the seeming failure of the male-dominated neoliberal economy. This aspect will be examined in the third part of this case study.

## Negative Andrology on the Backdrop of the Financial Crisis

Not quite randomly, about half of the debates take place after the financial crisis (or what was perceived its peak) in 2008/2009. This discursive event is reflected at different points in the debates and frames the discursive interpretation of gender that is generated throughout the debate. It is, however, not always present at the foreground: direct references made to the financial crisis are marginal. Still, its presence in the discursive community is somewhat palpable. Not only the fact that these debates take place after the peak of the crisis – and rarely before – shows a certain awareness of the historical opportunity. Moreover, the employment of what I refer to as unobjectionable norms, that is, the positive setting of discursive realities, may provide evidence.

In the debate on 5 July 2011, the liberal representative Siiri Oviir (Alliance of Liberals and Democrats for Europe group, ALDE) is the only speaker to draw a direct connection between the current issue, women and business leadership, and the financial crisis, quoting a wording by Ruth Sunderland published in a *Guardian/Observer* article in 2009 and gone viral in economic fora afterwards (Prügl 2012, 21): 'If Lehman Brothers had been Lehman Sisters'. The implicit discourse reflected there and voiced in several statements in 2011 and the debate on 19 November 2013 suggests that the main cause of the financial crisis was not economically induced (e.g. an intrinsic implication of capitalist accumulation), but literally 'man-made', an inevitable consequence of exclusively masculine, patriarchal structures in which, to put it in the pointed way Prügl describes it, the very biology of men, represented as testosterone, becomes the driving force behind greed, arrogance, hubris and failure (Prügl 2012, 27–29, 32). Confronted with this failure of macho economy, women represent an attractive workforce that is not only as qualified as men in economic matters, but additionally fitter to tackle the needs of a regenerated, 'chastened' (Prügl 2012) form of capitalist economy. Rodi Kratsa-Tsagaropoulou, a representative for the European People's Party group (EPP) and reporting speaker of the FEMM Committee in the 2011 debate, states:

> These [requirements] can be found in female gifts. I say 'gifts' because, apart from their knowledge and education [i.e. professional qualification on a par with men], women have special skills, which are very important to companies, to administration and to communication with the market. (Rodi Kratsa-Tsagaropoulou, reporting speaker, 5 July 2011)

A similar, even more concise statement is given by social-democratic MEP Antigoni Papadopoulou in the 2013 debate:

> Gender diversity on boards leads to more sustainable decisions and therefore to a more resistant European economy. (Antigoni Papadopoulou, S&D, 19 November 2013)

This statement suggests that a reformed economy, saved by women, is by no means 'matriarchal' (Prügl 2012, 21), but mixed-gender, in which men and women assemble their gender-related abilities (which are, as I suggested previously, not necessarily biological, but rooted in biological bodies, to say the least) in order to assure an economy which is both profitable and equitable, competitive and sustainable, thus combining 'masculine' and 'feminine' traits. As Prügl puts it slightly caustically:

> In their new togetherness, woman and man thus are envisioned to create more stable, more sustainable, less crisis-prone businesses. Man no longer sees woman as an object to be possessed, but as a partner who makes a needed contribution. She moderates where he goes for extremes, injects reason where he is driven by animal spirits, restrains where he is prone to excess. Valorised by the markets, by her ability to contribute to profit, she becomes an upgraded helpmate entering the first class to bring to it civility no longer as a stewardess toward his destination but as a competent associate in a common endeavour. A new harmony of gender foreshadows his redemption. (Prügl 2012, 31)

This shift is arguably less significant than it may seem, for it draws on several traditional branches of the gender discourse in modernity. Among others, it re-actualises modern discourses of masculinity which Christoph Kucklick qualifies as 'negative andrology' and which argue that untamed masculinity bears a source of wilderness and greed that can become harmful to society if not counterbalanced by feminine influence (Kucklick 2008).

However, in the light of experiences of crisis, the promotion of women, or, more politically, the economic valorisation of femininity, becomes a coping strategy for capitalist societies. This not only changes the emancipative outlook of feminism, and has been and continues to be deplored by feminist and/or gender theorists, such as Nancy Fraser (2013) or, more recently, Anna Elomäki (2018). It also changes the conception of women and men, of gender in general, and of gender relations.

## CONCLUSIONS:
## PRECARIOUS DISCOURSES

This case study's aim was to examine the discursive construction of gender and gender equality in the EP, starting from a relatively recent methodological approach in parliamentary performance analysis through – but very briefly – theoretical notions on gender, social construction, and diverse discourses of modernity, namely economic logics, through the performative of gender relations in presence and absence within the plenary, to, finally, a text-based analysis of concrete statements.

The most obvious, but equally least surprising, result of this analysis is certainly the fact that gender equality is understood in almost exclusively economic terms, as the enablement of women for a labour market that remains, despite its evolution towards a service-oriented knowledge economy, as liberal, as profit-oriented and as based on achievement and competitiveness as it had been before. In short: gender equality means equality of women and men in a men's world. It means further equality between the best qualified, the most flexible and most competitive members of both genders.

Gender discourses in the EP are furthermore depicted as matters of 'expertise', as an issue which is – still – supported and forwarded almost exclusively by women of nearly all political colours and a few social-liberal men. While this finding is familiar, it also reproduces traditional androcentric conceptions of masculinity being identical to what is considered as universal and all-encompassing. Presenting gender equality as a 'women's issue', affecting exclusively the social, political, economic and familial position of women, bears the risk of re-enforcing neoliberal practices of holding individuals or groups responsible for structural problems while failing to get men on board for a more encompassing vision of gender emancipation. Additionally, as this process is mainly addressing economic and political elites among both, men and women, from an intersectional perspective (Crenshaw 1991), it risks to lose out on 'the margins'.

'Gender' remains a concept that is exclusively binary, relating to heterosexual cis-men and -women that are usually considered as homogenous groups. Thus, despite the commitment of the EP to LGBTIQ rights (which is supported by MEPs usually absent in gender equality issues and vice versa), and despite the state of the art in most critical academic approaches, 'gender' lacks intersectional and gender-critical consideration. This, on the one hand, renders the gender discourse of the EP deplorably old-fashioned from a more 'postmodern' point of view that is already thriving not only in gender studies but similarly in gender activist groups. On the other hand, this relatively tame discourse is highly disputed from the economically and nationally conservative ranks.

After the 2014 elections, it seems as though this rational concept failed: still at the backdrop of the financial crisis and its various social and political deteriorations, debates on equality among CEOs give the impression of elitist unworldliness that needs to be confronted. Moreover, confronted with the rise of right-wing populist fractions within the EP – arguably another result of the financial crisis, the economic crisis as well as EU-imposed austerity politics that followed, and featuring a strange mélange of racist, sexist and anti-EU resentments – this precarious discourse may be even more in danger (Funkel and Trebesch 2017).

On the other hand, taking into account the very political and rhetorical strategies employed in order to strengthen the discourse on gender equality – the focus on a very narrow social and economic niche as to avoid conflicts with subsidiarity and, from a rhetorical perspective, the positive setting of gender equality as an unobjectionable political norm, thus dismissing conservative and/or socially weakened groups as being irrational or undemocratic – may have further fuelled resentments against both equal opportunity politics and the EU (Kováts 2018).

In the end, failing to live up to the expectations of postmodern – intersectionalised – gender discourses without gaining support from (economically) conservative groups, the EP discourse may have no other option than closing the ranks with neoliberal economics. However, this may prove adverse to a genuine politic of equal opportunity.

## NOTES

1 Since 2014, much has been written about the rise of right-wing populism in the United States and in Europe. To name but a few examples, Ruth Wodak analyses a variety of right-wing populist topics, including gender and 'mainstream' political discourse, from a linguist discourse analytical perspective, The journal Patterns of prejudices dedicated a special issue to 'Gender and Populist Radical Right Politics' in 2015. In 2016, Lazaridis, Campani and Benveniste edited a volume offering a panoramic overview of right-wing populist movements throughout Europe, and more recently, Gregor Fitzi, Juergen Mackert and Bryan S. Turner published a three-volume oeuvre on 'populism and the crisis of democracy'. For an EU perspective, see Mushaben's (this volume).

2 On this subject, see Lise Rolandsen Agustìn and Christina Chiva (this volume).

3 On the Eastern enlargement and its effects of EU equal opportunities politics, see Galligan and Clavero (2012).

4 On intersectionality in EU political discourses, see Verloo (2006), Kantola and Nousiainen (2009), and Lombardo and Agustín (2011).

5 See Anne van der Vleuten (this volume).

6 Also, among the debates on LGBTI rights, discussion revolves much around non-EU countries or the Eastern margins of the EU.

7 Note that in both quotes, the remark is made by male MEPs, but in their function as Presidents of the EP.

8 I only quote English statements as translations from other languages into English have not been available as to the publication date of this volume.

9 For this subject, see Elomäki (2015, 2018).

# Part II

## STRATEGIES AND OUTREACH BEYOND PARLIAMENTARY AFFAIRS

# 5

# Undermining Critical Mass

## The Impact of Trilogues and Treaty Reforms on Gender-Sensitive Decision-Making in the European Parliament

*Joyce Marie Mushaben*

Even before they crossed the *critical mass* threshold in the 1990s, female delegates to the European Parliament (EP) managed to generate substantial, gender-friendly changes in legislative political culture. Their proactive engagement secured greater visibility for the EP as a defender of citizen interests, human rights, environmental protection and other progressive causes. Indeed, a dramatic increase in women's presence in the EP following the introduction of direct elections in 1979 helped them to attain critical mass in most *national* parliaments within the space of a single decade. Moving beyond the symbolic politics of the 1980s, women's activism likewise contributed to the broader democratisation of European decision-making.[1] Possessing only token *advisory* rights under the Rome Treaties, the Community's only directly elected body has pushed to alleviate a chronic *democratic deficit*, first by way of enhanced *consultation* and *consent* rights, and later through the codification of *co-decision* and veto powers born of multiple treaty reforms, running from the Single European Act through the Lisbon Treaty (2009).

Women grasped the significance of *critical acts* well before they crossed the 30 per cent threshold in the EP, leading them to forge unique bonds with individual Commissioners, Directorate-General (DG) 'femocrats' and feminist academics, labelled 'velvet triangles'.[2] They established an impressive array of professional networks, cooperated with grassroots organisations and undertook systematic data collection, laying a foundation for future policy changes. Women did so during a period in which Community structures and procedures were themselves in a state of flux, due to successive enlargement waves, expanding supranational competencies, and a curious display of integration activism on the part of rotating Council presidencies.[3] Operating at the interstices of informal procedure, gender equality advocates proved very creative in carving out new spaces (European Women's Lobby) and exchange channels (Women's Summits) for injecting their expertise into crucial policy debates.

The 1980s and 1990s were also marked by the rise of Green Parties, whose EP entry strengthened the position of leftist parties pushing for gender-sensitive directives.

While mainstream democratic theorists consistently rail against the Union's 'fuzzy' competencies, its lack of procedural transparency, non-hierarchical command-and-control patterns and its under-institutionalised decision-making processes, I contend that it was exactly the *absence* of entrenched incumbents, rigidly codified procedures, hierarchical structures and official databases that opened the door to women's multi-level mobilisation and, more importantly, to their participation in EU problem defini-tion and policy formulation regarding gender issues.[4] This has given rise to a curious institutional paradox: as conventionally defined, the *democratic deficit* attributed to a lack of traditional 'representative elites' (based on male-normed parties and territorial elections) allowed new players on to the field, giving women their first chance to solve problems that entrenched male elites had considered non-existent. Commensurate with the EP's first study on women's status in Europe (Maij-Weggen Report 1981), for example, UK-MEP Dipek Nandy had insisted, 'There is no problem here and the problem that there is not is best solved by voluntary agreement' (Vallance and Davis 1986, 112). Insisting on sex-disaggregated data, feminists showed that there were actually many problems and that 'voluntary means' allowed Member States to circumvent binding elements of the acquis, starting with the Equal Pay Directive.

The 300 legislative acts needed to complete the Single Market, coupled with rising public discontent over the Community's lack of democratic legitimacy, trig-gered demands for political and institutional reforms even before the Iron Curtain collapsed, culminating in the Maastricht Treaty (Mushaben 1994, 251–75). Sub-sequent enlargements triggered an unprecedented display of treaty-activism and *institutionalisation,* marked by the Amsterdam (1997), Nice (1999) and Lisbon (2009) accords. The Lisbon Treaty attempted to remedy the formal-institutional democratic deficit by establishing EP co-decision rights as the 'ordinary legislative procedure' and by bringing national parliaments back into policy deliberations with subsidiarity controls (Abels 2013, 79–102). I argue that those mechanisms have actually undermined efforts to overcome the 'other' democratic deficit, defined in substantive-deliberative terms: ensuring the balanced participation of women and men in all facets of European life.

Now deeply rooted in primary law as a fundamental value of the European Union, gender quality has encountered many new challenges in recent years, some of which are paradoxically linked to processes that were adopted in hopes of *ameliorating* the EU's long-standing democratic deficit. The problem, affirmed by feminist scholars, is that the EU as an institution does not practice what it preaches: the biggest bar-riers to the implementation of its impressive gender acquis have been, and remain, a dearth of female decision-makers and expert monitors, a lack of political will, Member-State resistance, and the absence of effective supranational sanctions for non-compliance at the national level (Abels and Mushaben 2012, 231–34).

The Lisbon Treaty, in particular, poses new challenges for the realisation of gender equality, in conjunction with the EU's ostensible shift to neoliberal economics. The global financial crisis triggered in 2008 gave rise to new populist parties initially opposed to the EU's embrace of a single currency. Those entities have subsequently morphed into misogynistic, anti-migration and anti-EU parties. Ironically drawing on the Green template of the 1980s (using electoral 'victories' in the EP to shore up campaign funds and respectability back home), anti-EU parties like the *Front National*, the UK Independence Party (UKIP) and the Alternative for Germany (AfD) have entered the supranational legislative arena. The 2014 electoral outcomes began chipping away at the traditionally proactive, consensus-oriented EP culture, due to increasing partisan fragmentation *within* Member-State delegations as well as *across* the larger partisan spectrum. Insofar as most simultaneously oppose supranational equality initiatives, more virulent, Europhobic parties (PiS, Jobbik) pose a particular threat to the implementation of gender mainstreaming (GM), affecting the EP's ability to advance the cause across the Union.

But the threat to equality does not stop there. As Gabriele Abels infers (in this volume), there may be a negative correlation between the 'feminisation' of institutions and the amount of real power those bodies are able to exercise over time. She holds that while women's increasing presence in decision-making entities renders them more representative of society as a whole, such developments may trigger a transfer of power to informal settings that remain male dominated. This raises new questions about the relationship between descriptive and substantive representation, as well as about the presumed benefits associated with 'critical mass' in parliamentary bodies. This chapter shows, first, that the relationship between women's increasing numerical presence (descriptive representation, DR) and their ability to produce gender-equitable reforms (substantive representation, SR) is neither automatic nor linear. Secondly, I revisit the relationship between critical mass and GM in light of new co-decision powers accorded the EP under the Lisbon Treaty.

I then explore the double jeopardy that two new forces – Europhobic parties and formalised EP 'trilogues' – pose for supranational law-making in relation to gender equality. I begin with a sketch of positive changes in EP culture induced by the 'critical acts' of female MEPs throughout the 1980s and 1990s, *before* they crossed the 30 per cent threshold. Next, I consider the EP's efforts to institutionalise GM from within, followed by reflections on how representatives from anti-EU parties might undercut GM practices. I then turn to a more serious threat to gendering future EU policies: the streamlining of EP deliberation and (co)decision-making by way of 'first-reading trilogues'.

## GENDERING PARLIAMENTARY POLITICAL CULTURE

Drude Dahlerup's trail-blazing reflections on *critical mass* and its impact on Scandinavian politics led feminist scholars to turn their attention to problems of *DR*, stressing the disproportionately small number of female politicians found in most national contexts. Over the past twenty years, debates involving women's direct participation in governance have been dominated by theoretical and empirical studies involving *quotas* and other electoral mechanisms geared towards the pursuit of the magical 30 per cent – presumably the point at which women's routine ability to shape policy processes would become 'irreversible'. Revisiting 'the story of critical mass theory' in 2006, Dahlerup observed that many researchers believed 'it was unrealistic to expect major changes until women's representation had reached a critical mass'; that is, they expected to witness a qualitative shift in the policy-making environment *after* women secured 30 per cent of the legislative mandates (Dahlerup 2006, 511–22). The *critical actor* dimension did not enter their discussion until well into the new millennium, emphasizing what 'a few good women' might do to advance gender-sensitive legislation. To date there have been few detailed case studies offering positive proof of the latter.[5]

My reading of Rosabeth Moss Kantor and Dahlerup persuaded me that their best insight was that women could undertake *critical acts* to help them advance from a nearly 'invisible' minority to a 'significant' one, capable of pursuing SR even when their numerical presence fell very short of parity.[6] Women first had to change *parliamentary culture,* at least to the point where they could persuade a majority of traditionally male lawmakers and/or fellow party members to introduce electoral quotas. Drawing on a study by Elizabeth Vallance and Elizabeth Davies, and many grey-paper reports lugged back from Brussels, I engaged in 'process tracing' of the feminist whirl-wind taking place inside and outside formal chambers.[7] I concluded that by the mid-1990s the *combined effect* of women's critical acts had dramatically improved the gender climate and expanded opportunities for female legislative input as their share of EP seats rose from 19.3 per cent (1992) to 26.5 per cent (1997). *Critical acts*, in short, are what enabled women to reach the point of *critical mass*.

Elaborating on Dahlerup's six dimensions of change, I provided evidence that, first, there had been a shift away from negative reactions to women's presence in decision-making organs to gestures on the part of key officials, especially the Commission, welcoming their input (Mushaben 1999, 51–91). Secondly, the creation of *Old Girl* networks improved the 'performance' and 'efficiency' of individual politicians by accelerating the learning process for new MEPs. Third, opening the political culture (inside and outside the EP) helped to foster an acceptance of women's issues as routine agenda items. Fourth, feminist experts at all levels – voraciously consuming academic studies – contributed to a transformation of the prevailing political discourse and policy concepts (*equal treatment, positive action, balanced participation*). Fifth, this led to a proliferation of real changes in policy substance (new Directives and Action Plans), as well as in EP approaches to decision-making (e.g. FEMM's transversal interventions). Finally, there was evidence of real as well as perceived increases in the power of women working collectively, with the European Women's Lobby regularly leading the pack. By the time of the 2002 EP elections, women had also crossed the 30 per cent threshold in many Member-State parliaments, creating the 'pincer effect' noted by Anna van der Vleuten (2005, 464–88).

Although 'critical acts' did serve to transform EP culture, institutional changes that are supposed to render its decision-making processes more efficient could override its slower, more deliberative-democratic character. Commensurate with the *law of unanticipated consequences*, this could significantly impede progress towards equality, even if a radical reversal in course seems impossible. During the 2014 elections, women's share of EP mandates increased only slightly, from 35.8 per cent to 36.9 per cent (down to 36.2 per cent by 2018): at this pace, experts calculate that it will take another half-century to reach parity at the supranational level. By contrast, women in the US Congress are not expected to reach parity until 2121.[8]

In descriptive terms, women remain dismally under-represented in the Commission as well as in national governments, shaping the composition of the Council – the presence of 'the world's most powerful woman', Angela Merkel, notwithstanding. Commission President Jean-Claude Juncker called for more female inclusion at the top, but his first to-do list offered nothing of gender substance. As the Euro-crisis unfolded, gender issues were pushed onto the back burner, exactly at the point where the Commission's own Strategy for Equality between Women and Men 2010–2015 (COM (2010) 0491) should have ensured priority treatment. The same could be said of the European Council's adoption of a European Pact for Gender Equality (2011–2020). The units responsible for the European Investment Plan, the Digital Single Market, the EU Energy Union, taxation reform, an EU Migration Agenda, and Economic/Monetary Union are least inclined to practice GM, despite its 1996 inclusion in the acquis (Mlinar 2016). The six-member Governing Board of the European Central Bank did not include its first woman until 2014, six years into the crisis. Embodying DR, critical mass in the EP has not sufficed to remedy the gendered power imbalance defining the EU's other decision-making institutions.

## MAINSTREAMING GENDER IN EP DELIBERATIONS

Gender scholars presume that placing more women in positions of power is a necessary if not a sufficient condition for enhancing their ability to legislate gender-sensitive policies. The EP embodies an exception to the rule. I argue that *critical acts* undertaken by strategically placed women, rather than *critical mass* per se, laid the groundwork for the EU's embrace of GM, following the 1995 UN Beijing Conference. The Euro-Parliament as a whole has undertaken concrete efforts to operationalise GM over the past several years (see Ahrens in this volume), even if its constituent units, viz., permanent committees, have been slow to meet the basic requirements. It is precisely women's direct participation *in all stages* of the policy process that is undermined by the EP's embrace of fast-tracking trilogues (details below). GM necessitates the *ex ante* compilation of Gender Impact Assessments, utilising sex-disaggregated data analysed by 'gender-proofed' experts – all time-consuming processes. Many national leaders have used a (rhetorical) commitment to GM to eliminate women-targeted programmes or have watered-down *gender* components by shifting to (likewise rhetorical) *diversity* discourses. Europhobic parties claim to support diversity by insisting they need to secure their own 'identities' parallel to other groups. Real diversity-management would require greater resource commitment to alleviate additional dimensions of gendered inequality (Lombardo and Rolandsen Agustín 2011, 1–31).

The EP adopted five core resolutions from 2002 to 2016 (Ahrens in this volume), reflecting the EP's dual function as a law-making body *and* a workplace. The Committee of Women's Rights and Gender Equality (FEMM) played an active role in drafting three of them, then was accorded a 'reporting obligation' as the *competent committee* for subsequent GM bills. *Plenary support* for GM resolutions declined noticeably after 2009, mirroring the EP's stronger conservative composition. Follow-up reports issued in 2003, 2009, and 2011 identified implementation measures and bottlenecks. Whereas twelve of nineteen EP committees made some effort to incorporate GM into their deliberations by 2006, fourteen of nineteen *claimed* they had introduced GM by 2009, although the examples listed fell far short of its criteria.[9]

Some efforts were more surprising than others (e.g. Fisheries); Agriculture ignored the contributions and vulnerability of 'the farmer's wife', while Budget failed to respond at all. Fourteen made use of in-house expertise (FEMM), but eleven 'had neither discussed nor adopted' an equality strategy. Committees failed to meet their GM obligations even before fast-tracked negotiations with the Council rose from 15 trilogue cases in 2009, to 695 by 2013.[10] At FEMM's request, DG-Internal Policies compiled a substantive analysis of GM application in EP committees and delegations in 2013, focusing on institutional capacity, the role of actors, policy-making tools, institutional learning and contextual factors in five committees. From July 2011 to February 2013, FEMM 'finalised 33 opinions for 11 committees, including 718 suggestions/amendments on different issues', but this sounds more *ad hoc* than mainstreamed (European Parliament 2014a, 15; 13).

A potential correlation between critical mass and GM re-emerges in relation to critical committee memberships. While women's share of all EP seats exceeded 35 per cent in 2014, this did not apply across all committees. Because their presence remains limited among the political group leaders, they are unable to appoint more women to the most powerful EP committees, assigned to 'report' on the biggest number of legislative proposals. As of 2017, women accounted for five of fourteen vice-presidents, nine of thirty-nine delegation chairs, ten of twenty-four committee chairs, but only three of eleven political group chairs. They remain under-represented as regular members and as chairs of the most powerful committees (e.g. BUDG, ECON) tasked with economic regulation, resource allocation and external affairs.

If legislative processes do not *begin* with the balanced participation of women and men in all bodies, they are highly unlikely to *end* with gender-equal results – without critical acts. Given the substantive expertise they develop over time, EP committee members (especially FEMM) are best positioned to define the gender dimensions of any policy problem. They also constitute the first line of defence against Europhobe efforts to reverse elements of the gender *acquis*. Attaining critical mass in specific committees could prove more important than securing more seats in the plenary body, where equality-oriented *party* composition can compensate for inadequate DR. The EP still has a long way to go in warranting SR and countering gendered power imbalances in the Council, the Commission, the European Court of Justice and the European Central Bank.

## *STÖRENFRIEDE:*
## HOW MUCH DAMAGE CAN EUROSCEPTIC PARTIES DO?

The Euro-crisis and the austerity policies that followed 'created a veritable Petri dish for growth of populist backlash', but the 2014 elections hardly triggered a political earthquake (Birchfield and Harris 2015, 1). Vicki Birchfield and Geoffrey Harris offer persuasive evidence that even though groups ranging from moderate Eurosceptics to neo-fascist Europhobes controlled roughly 26 per cent of the EP mandates as of 2014, 72 per cent remained clearly committed to EU consensual norms and fundamental freedoms. Stemming from 18 Member States, 30 Eurosceptic parties, occupying 125 EP seats (16.6 per cent), were spread across multiple Political Groups. Radical Europhobes were aligned with sixteen parties from thirteen Member States, accounting for eighty-two delegates (10.9 per cent).[11] At best, citizens used the 2014 elections to express national discontent, mirroring *Politikverdrossenheit* [political vexation] and the importuning of populist parties at home. At worst, these parties exploited 'a mismatch between tenacious national identities and political discourses, and EU level policies operating within an ever integrated, dysfunctional global economy' (Birchfield and Harris 2015, 1).

My own approach to the disruptive potential of parties like the *Front National*, UKIP, AfD or extremist groupings like Golden Dawn is more Darwinian in nature: only the strong survive, and the party-political landscape is already quite littered with the skeletal remains of small nationalist parties that arose to protest one cause or another after 1990. Fringe parties tend to collapse quickly when they rely too heavily on a few dominant personalities, invoking a 'bonfire of the vanities'. The post-2014 period has seen a family feud chipping away at *Le Penism* (which changed its name to Rassemblement National), as well as multiple splits in the AfD, after it expelled 'founding father' Bernd Lucke, then his female arch-rival, Frauke Petry. Nigel Farage was pushed out of UKIP by a personal electoral loss, then founded a new Brexit party in 2019.

The good news is that there is no evidence that MEPs allied with Europhobic parties really participate in EP deliberations. They display little knowledge of, much less interest in pursuing committee work or reforming labyrinthian decision-rules (e.g. *Regulatory Procedure with Scrutiny vs. Delegated Acts*) (Kaeding and Hardacre. 2013, 382–40). One exception was Marine Le Pen, who briefly served on the EP International Trade Committee in order to hammer down the TTIP proposal.[12] Prior to 2019 they were largely excluded from committee leadership and rapporteur positions that would allow them to shape responses to legislative proposals. While they receive the same resources as mainstream representatives (staff, funding, office space), Frank Häge and Nils Ringe found that they 'just have no intention of playing the game. They're here by default. They were elected, they will get the money – the salary every month . . . all they're interested in is standing up in plenary when all the cameras are on and making populist speeches' (Häge and Ringe 2016, 17). One UKIP delegate admitted further: 'We make it clear when we stand for election that we will not assist the EU law-making process. We are in the opposition. In practice this means that we are never rapporteurs, we do not seek chairmanships of committees and we do not get involved in trilogues. We will vote in favour of certain amendments on a "least bad" basis but will almost always vote against the legislative reports as a whole' (ibid., 17).

Europhobe party members seem particularly incensed by the EU's long-standing commitment to gender equality as a 'fundamental value' to be actively pursued by all Member States. Adding a curious twist to intersectionality debates, they combine their fear of women's autonomy with anti-Muslim stereotypes. One UKIP candidate accused Muslim men of 'grooming children to be sex slaves', while the Danish People's Party linked Muslim migration to 'mass rapes' and 'crude violence' towards women. UKIP MEPs nonetheless voted against legislation to counteract gender-based violence and refused to enforce equal-pay requirements. Many railed against the recognition of same-sex partnerships, protected against discrimination under the Amsterdam Treaty (Lum and Renaudière 2014).

To really influence EP outcomes, anti-EU parties would have to meet several criteria. Clear decision-making structures, for instance, enabled pro-European Green parties to quickly anchor themselves in the EP landscape, reinforced by the fact that they stood FOR policies welcomed by the Commission: *ecological preservation, gender equality, non-violence* and *grassroots participation* offered the cross-cutting orientation needed to legitimate an expanding spectrum of supranational competencies and issues (Mushaben 1985, 39–66). Their links to diverse Citizen Initiatives afforded greater continuity than the politics of the street. Despite serious differences between their 'fundamentalist' and 'realist' factions, Greens mastered the art of coalition building, deriving strong support from citizens eager to take advantage of the EU's 'fundamental freedoms'.

As perennial nay-sayers, Europhobic elements meet none of these criteria. They have yet to forge the party group-coalitions necessary to block others from taking action. The EP's absolute majority requirement for plenary votes prevents the high-jacking of its consensual norms but fears of populist disruption may be driving a shift towards elite-level legislative negotiations emerging out of the EP's enhanced co-decision powers. Fast-tracking negotiations, in turn, place further constraints on efforts to embed GM in committee deliberations, even when a critical mass of MEPs at this level possesses the necessary expertise. The growing reliance on trilogues testifies to my earlier contention that efforts to mitigate the first democratic deficit, defined in institutional terms, can eliminate the space for *critical acts*, despite *critical mass*, exacerbating the SR deficit.

## CO-DECISION, AT WHOSE EXPENSE?

Accorded limited *advisory* rights under the Rome Treaties, the Community's only directly elected body has sought to counter the EU's chronic, institutional demo-cratic deficit by expanding its own powers, commensurate with the *polity-shaping function* described by Abels. Before becoming EP President in 1994, Klaus Haensch asserted, 'the Council is armed with a sword, while Parliament is armed with a kitchen knife' (Huber and Shackleton 2013, 1041). Making use of formal and infor-mal opportunities, Euro-Parliamentarians secured enhanced *consultation* and *consent* rights under the Single European Act (SEA 1987) and the Maastricht Treaty (1991). SEA consultation and cooperation opportunities applied to only 21 per cent of the legislative files, giving rise to 'a near unanimous lament' among MEPs over its 'pal-try accomplishments' (Kreppel 2010, 905). Six of twenty committees dealt almost exclusively with all dossiers between 1993 and 1999: 36 per cent were handled by Environment, 25 per cent by ECON, 18 per cent by Legal Affairs. Co-decision rules introduced under Maastricht did not permit 'first reading agreements'. Despite the existence of complex procedures for 'third reading conciliation', the Council could still impose its original 'common position' without modifications (Jacobs 2015).

The MEPs reformed their own Rules of Procedure, eventually leading to *veto* and *co-decision* powers (Kreppel 2003, 884–911). The Amsterdam Treaty (1997) simpli-fied the process, extending co-decision to 40 more areas, then 42 per cent of the legislative files under the Nice Treaty (1999). The 2009 Lisbon Treaty elevated co-decision to the level of 'ordinary legislative procedure', allowing for codecision across 85 domains, 48 of which were new. The EP gained influence regarding CAP, immi-gration-, asylum- and visa policy, select home affairs and justice measures, structural and cohesion funds, and the European Research Area. According to Francis Jacobs, 'the impact on the procedure used was immediate and profound'.

The share of proposals subject to co-decision rose from 49 per cent to 89 per cent 2009 through 2014. Equally striking was a 40 per cent decline in proposals 'deliber-ated' under normal procedures.[13] Agreements reached on a 'first reading' basis rose from 29 per cent (1999–2004) to 72 per cent (2004–2009); during the 2009–2014 session, first-reading agreements increased to 85 per cent. Only 13 per cent neces-sitated a second reading, and 2 per cent a third reading (conciliation). The time required for adoption fell from 24 to 20.7 months for co-decision; bills requiring a second Council reading can take up to 40 months.[14]

To avoid the arduous 'third-reading' conciliation process, the Council and the EP agreed on informal *trilogues*, intended to cover non-controversial dossiers where neither side anticipated a need for heavy negotiation. The aim was to reconcile their respective positions early on, creating a 'climate of predictability' (Huber and Shack-leton 2013, 1044). Trilogues quickly became more specialised, divided into 'informal bilateral contacts (EP-COUNCIL)', 'technical' (preparatory, operational) and 'full' session formats (Roederer-Rynning and Greenwood 2015, 1158). Council and EP representatives (rapporteurs, party-group leaders, committee chairs, COREPER staff) found it necessary to 'get to know each other better' in ways not foreseen by the Treaty; they began with personal 'coffee' meetings and informal letter exchanges. Over time Council-EP relations have evolved 'from a clash of cultures to smooth working relations' (Huber and Shackleton 2013, 1041). They are nonetheless problematic from a democratic standpoint, given their secretive nature, the restricted number of participants, and the expectation that both 'the Parliament' and 'the Council' will accept the results, even though intermediate outcomes are presented before either side has had time to formulate a 'common position'.

The period 2009 to 2014 saw 1,557 trilogues at all stages. Committee power has been enhanced insofar as the *competent committee* now determines who participates in the negotiating team, rather than the plenary where roll-call votes had previously been used to assess the spectrum of preferences. Rapporteurs initially gained disproportionate influence, since they were not required to share negotiating points with the committee (Costello and Thomson 2010, 219–240). The Council often depends on European People's Party (EPP) or Socialists and Democrats (S&D) power brokers (providing most rapporteurs), with the result that small parties (ALDE, Greens) lose the chance to propose amendments in committee. Intent on demonstrating 'legislative accomplishments' during its six-month reign, the presiding Member-State can present other national leaders with a 'best we could get' position reflecting its own preferences (Farrel and Héritier 2003, 24). Council dossiers adopted via early agreement call for a non-deliberative endorsement of a legislative package agreed upon by very few EP actors (Burns 2013, 990). 'Packages' may be harder to overturn when multiple committees are involved (*associated committee procedure*), due to overlapping competencies, now that eighty-five areas are subject to co-decision. This can water down 'expert' contributions, for example, from FEMM, to ensure a durable consensus among committees, before they forge a compromise with the Council. National parliaments have little time to scrutinise proposals or issue recommendations to their governments, once the trilogues have commenced.

Not all analysts welcome the efficiency and 'openness to compromise' characterizing the routinisation of trilogues. In its eagerness to prove itself a 'responsible legislative body', the EP has displayed a 'surprising lack of will' to utilise its veto power in order to protect its 'meta-norms' (Ahrens 2016, 778). Reducing open conflict, political competition and direct debate between the EP and the Council precludes transparency, accountability and external monitoring by civil society groups. Experts worry that Europe's parliamentarians might be 'prepared to sacrifice' policy content in exchange for other institutional gains. Sharing competencies among committees to facilitate first-reading decisions may 'drown out the voices of marginalised interest groups', insofar as fast-track negotiations set temporal as well as substantive limits on the degree to which all demands can be considered – behind closed doors (Burns, Rasmussen, and Reh 2013, 943). Actors 'privy to the relevant information often do not have the incentive to communicate that information to outside actors'; those who have such incentives, such as lobbyists, media specialists and MEPs from minority parties, are kept out of negotiations and thus have no access to it beyond online consultation procedures (Häge and Naurin 2013, 953). Intra- as well as inter-partygroup negotiations, that is, the ability to move a dossier 'up and down between committee and plenary level over several readings [to] facilitate exchange between specialists and generalists' have also been affected (ibid., 967). Others suggest, however, that trilogues might not have as much of an adverse effect 'on who gets what in terms of policy as previously thought' (Roger and Winzen 2015, 404).

Trilogues invoke linguistic challenges, necessitating quick translation of last minute, ad hoc amendments offered behind closed doors, thereby shutting off alternative 'framing'. This disadvantages the EP vis-à-vis the Council and its staff, dominated by professional diplomats and civil servants used to agreeing on language before leaders meet (Héritier 2013, 1074–82). Furthermore, the 'EP position' carved out by the rapporteur (whose selection reflects party-group dynamics) may not be representative of the committee itself, much less of a motley crew of supranational citizens. Reducing inter-institutional conflict will neither generate more public interest nor enable citizens to 'follow the trail' of legislation. It could increase the role of lobbyists, while fuelling citizen exasperation with Community officials who are 'high above and far away'.

EP insiders reorganised both work and resource allocations to better accommodate new co-decision demands but only gradually addressed the fast-track trade-off between *efficiency* and *transparency*. They revised 'Rule 70' (now 73) of EP Rules of Procedure on 'Interinstitutional negotiations in legislative procedures' in 2011. The revision specified the *de jure* make-up of its negotiating team (including shadow rapporteurs and political group leaders), in addition to requiring negotiators to report back to the relevant committee(s) after each trilogue session. This has led to the generation of 'joint working documents', in which the respective Commission, Council and EP positions are presented in side-by-side columns, with a fourth indicating the updated, 'agreed upon' position, for which 'the EP team holds the pen' (Roederer-Rynning and Greenwood 2015, 1158). The two bodies now coordinate decision time-tables and synchronise schedules for conciliation meetings. EP committee chairs meet with Committee of Permanent Representatives (COREPER) ambassadors (on EP turf) and attend informal Council meetings; the EP, in turn, invites Ministers to committee and plenary sessions, although MEPs complain that the Council still withholds documents.

Lacking real powers through the 1970s, MEPs who were once 'free to "demand the impossible"' now function as 'a responsible legislative actor', outlining what they want at the outset and eschewing a change in positions 'without good reason' at later stages (Huber and Shackleton 2013, 1044). The question is, at what cost to democratic deliberation, and at whose participatory expense? While critics admit that trilogues foster efficiency without ensuring the equal representation of marginal parties or stakeholders, none of the trilogue experts cited in this chapter mentions *women* as the biggest, traditionally marginalised 'interest group'. Nor do trilogue proponents consider the extent to which short-cutting the EP's internal negotiation processes reduces the time and space gender experts need to think their way through the long-term consequences of increasingly technical legislation.

Considered a 'neutral' committee based on voluntary membership, FEMM is rarely assigned a primary reporting role, although its self-selected members would be most likely to support GM. According to Petra Ahrens, FEMM was assigned only six 'ordinary legislative proposals' during the 2009–2014 legislative period (before the Europhobe onslaught), although it served in an 'opinion-giving' capacity with respect to forty-one dossiers (Ahrens 2016, 778). Generating twenty-one 'self-initiative' reports between 2014 and 2017, its best chance for influencing draft bills rests with the fact that its members serve simultaneously on other permanent committees. Although overlapping member-ships lead to more work, they can also produce a multiplier effect, provided that party and political group leaders appoint FEMM members to the more powerful committees. In one noteworthy case, the Conference of Presidents decided to assign joint responsibility for a Victims Directive to FEMM and Civil Liberties, Justice and Home Affairs (LIBE). The latter had initially rejected the associa-tion, claiming the proposal was 'not about gender', though women comprise a majority of victims.[15] The proposal to develop a 'public register' of trilogues and files, disclosing who is negotiating for each side, will not remedy the deeper democratic deficit problems created by this newly institutionalised process. The best way to ensure a regular infusion of gender expertise into 'all stages' of policy formulation would be to require every trilogue team to automatically include an FEMM rapporteur.

## CONCLUSION:
## CRITICAL MASS AND 'QUEENS WITHOUT A CROWN'

This study has gone against the feminist-theory grain by arguing that *critical mass* is neither a necessary nor sufficient condition for ensuring gender-sensitive policy-making. The correlation between DR (critical mass) and SR (GM) is more complex than assumed. Indeed, the 2019 elections raised the share of female del-egates to 40 per cent, but parity laws in France and Italy have resulted in higher numbers of women in Europhobic parties who will actively oppose further gender equality initiatives.

The 'politics of critical acts' first made it possible for women to reach an effective level of DR in the EP. Rising above the 35 per cent threshold, female MEPs helped to bring about a real expansion in EP powers by way of co-decision, but this has led to a new 'empowerment' paradox: gender-blind institutional reforms can undercut the ability of critical mass to guarantee space for further critical acts. Like 'queens without crowns', women's presence in the EP is certainly recognised, but their real power to decide remains limited, when executive actors return to the intergovern-mental paradigm during crisis periods, for example (Beveridge and Velluti 2008, 1). Trilogues have compounded women's lack of SR, given their inadequate numerical representation in key committees and EP negotiating teams.

Although malestream theorists pay regular homage to the EU's standing as a multilevel governance system *sui generis*, they continue to judge its democratic legitimacy by using the same institutional indicators they apply to gender-blind participatory processes at the national level. Thomas König observes that debates over the EU democratic deficit are 'primarily motivated by a more sceptical general attitude to the legitimacy of the EU – in terms of a supranational superstate, governance without demos, etc'. It is sooner an empirical than a normative question as to whether empowering the EP enhances or reduces EU legitimacy. Despite real gains in EP power, 'we do not find greater public support for European integration over time' (König 2008, 170). This type of assessment pays no heed to the other 'democratic deficit', rooted in the chronically imbalanced participation of women and men in all decision-making bodies. In fact, citizens have responded very positively to many EU-mandated policy changes, ranging from expanded parental leave options, to new opportunities for women in science and research, and support for same-sex partnerships. The problem is that national governments profit in electoral terms when they present these as *their own* policy accomplishments. The Merkel Government, for instance, is credited with expanding day-care guarantees for children under three, although Germany had received multiple warnings regarding its non-compliance with EU 'reconciliation' directives (parental leave, maternity protection, part-time work) under the SPD-Green government a decade earlier. EU mandates have forced many intransigent Member States to adopt regulations against pay discrimination, sexual harassment, gender violence, and LBGT rights, thanks to effective lobbying by a consensus-oriented EP prior to 2005.

The EP will continue to function as the most 'gender friendly' body in the multilevel governance system, insofar as women, with few exceptions, occupy more seats in Brussels/Strasbourg than in their respective national parliaments. The arrival of Europhobic parties could deepen the partisan gap among women MEPs, however. Subject to French parity law, the *Front National* filled 40 per cent of its seats with female MEPs, a trend that continued in 2019 (Abels and Mushaben 2014, 138–50). FEMM members moreover had to resist a bid by avowed anti-feminist Beatrix von Storch (AfD) for a vice-chair post in 2014.

While the EP's institutional powers have increased significantly since 1979, efforts to resolve one democratic deficit have had the unintended consequence of reducing women's ability to 'define' policy problems and shape negotiation outcomes through informal channels, exacerbating the other democratic deficit. Open to policy *change*, the EP's stronger supranational orientation gives it a bigger incentive to 'bargain' – to get something, rather than nothing – vis-à-vis Member States attached to sovereignty and the status quo. This means that 'the rejection costs of the final proposal are much higher for the EP than any bargaining concession'.[16] It is not the presence of Europhobic parties per se, but rather the growing reliance on trilogues that leaves less room for *femocratic* manoeuvring. Expediting negotiations among designated Council, Commission and EP actors to secure 'first reading' approval has reshaped the balance of power among these three bodies in ways that reinforce gender imbalances WITHIN each of these institutions.

A more serious problem is that despite multiple EP resolutions operationalising GM, few MEPs seem to understand what GM is and how it works. The 2014 report commissioned by FEMM on *Gender Mainstreaming in Committees and Delegations of the European Parliament* offers a damning indictment along these lines. Over a two-year period, FEMM members offered 177 GM amendments in relation to twenty-seven reports, usually seeking just to add the terms *gender, female, women*, or the *promotion of gender equality* to the legislative text. The report found that a 'high proportion of suggestions/amendments are adopted when they refer to topics already recognised and accepted inside and outside the EP as "gender related" or when they do not touch upon particularly sensitive issues'.[17] The whole point of GM, however, is to move beyond the traditional 'add women, day-care and stir' items, in order to de- and reconstruct the fundamentally gendered nature of all societal institutions, resource allocations and divisions of labour.

It is a bit puzzling as to how members of a parliamentary body known for its proactive stance on gender equality and human-rights issues could have failed to grasp even the fundamentals of GM. During a 2015 trip to Brussels, I asked two young women working for DG-Communications whether their units were practicing GM; both responded, 'Well, we do have a female Director-General'. When I asked MEP Jo Leinen (SPD) whether the Environmental Committee was practicing GM, he responded that the ratio among committee members was 'about 50–50'. Not one of them seemed to interpret GM as more than an effort to secure better *DR* in their respective units.

This brings us back to the potentially negative correlation between institutionalisation and women's empowerment, stressed by Abels (Introduction). Institutional reform per se cannot be viewed as a gender-neutral process; treaty changes, and rule revisions also require close monitoring for their potential, longer-term gender effects. As noted earlier, the mandatory inclusion of an FEMM rapporteur *in all trilogue negotiation processes* would provide at least a partial remedy to the new imbalances generated by fast-tracking. Finding ways to make all committees actually comply with *existing* GM requirements would be even better.

In 2015 Kristalina Georgieva, Commissioner for Budget and Human Resources, promised to boost women's share of top positions in the Commission and the DGs from 27 per cent to 40 per cent by 2019, but she left that post to return to the World Bank before fulfilling her promise. Though still not meeting the core requirements of GM, achieving a *critical mass* of female decision-makers in the 'other' bodies responsible for supranational governance – the Commission, the European Court of Justice and the European Central Bank – would go a long way in helping the Community to practice what it preaches to the Member States. This would amount to a *critical act*, long overdue.

## NOTES

1  For details, see Mushaben (1999, 1994). Consider the now-mandatory EP committee 'hearings' for would-be Commissioners prior to formal appointment. In 2004, this resulted

in the elimination of arch-conservative Italian nominee Rucco Buttiglione, whose views on women and gays proved unacceptable.

2 See Woodward (2004) and Abels (2011).

3 This trend began with the Swedish presidency, emphasising gender equality in 2001. Since then, Member States have sought to convey a positive integration image during each six-month rotation. Before taking charge, each presiding state 'plans' its priorities, then presents its accomplishments (Conclusions) at the end of its term. Although the German presidency of 2007 pushed hard for a Europe 20–20–20 package (recommended by Tony Blair in 2005), France was happy to adopt it in 2008, allowing it to claim the 'achievement'.

4 See Neunreither (1994) and Mushaben and Abels (2012).

5 See Mushaben (2017).

6 See Kanter (1977) and Dahlerup (2006).

7 For example, see Mushaben (1999) and Bennett and Checkel (2015).

8 See Milevska (2014) and Abels and Mushaben (2014). The Institute for Women's Policy Research (Washington, DC) calculated this probability two years prior to the 2016 presidential elections.

9 See European Parliament (2009a), Mlinar (2016) and Meier and Celis (2011).

10 See European Parliamentary Research Service (2017).

11 See Birchfield and Harris (2015) and Treib (2014).

12 Le Pen was already facing charges for fraudulent use of her EP funds by the time she returned to the French National Assembly in June 2017.

13 The EP's role in CFSP, competition, monetary policy, certain employment and social policy fields, and fiscal management remains limited to consultation. See Jacobs (2015).

14 See Jacobs (2015) and Huber and Shackleton (2013, 9). http://www.europarl.europa.eu/RegData/etudes/BRIE/2017/599256/EPRS_BRI(2017)599256_EN.pdf.

15 Roger (2016). Also, Nikoleta Yordanova makes only token references to FEMM in Yordanova (2013).

16 See König (2008). Also, Jo Leinen conceded this point in a conversation with visitors from the University of Tübingen on 25 June 2015.

17 Executive Summary, 16.

# 6

# Working against the Tide?

## Institutionalising Gender Mainstreaming in the European Parliament

*Petra Ahrens*[1]

While the Beijing Platform for Action of the UN Women's World Conference in 1995 led many governments to adopt gender mainstreaming (GM), parliaments seldom embraced GM as an official strategy. The European Parliament (EP) is one of the few parliaments worldwide that committed to implementing GM and can therefore be characterised as a vanguard. Since 2003, the EP has adopted six resolutions and several reports on GM, the most recent in January 2019.

The continuing effort to institutionalise GM in the EP is puzzling, given that GM as a tool to promote gender equality has lost considerable ground on the supranational level over the past decade (Ahrens 2018; Debusscher and van der Vleuten 2017; Jacquot 2015). It is even more astonishing given that in many Member States political parties also represented in the EP openly oppose gender equality policies and attack gender studies as 'gender ideology' (Korolczuk and Graff 2018; Verloo 2018; Verloo and Paternotte 2018). Given this background, these questions arise: how did the EP, and particularly its Committee on Women's Rights and Gender Equality (FEMM Committee), manage to work against the tide and keep GM on the EP agenda? How was pursuing GM implementation justified? Can we speak of a successful institutionalisation of GM in the EP, and if yes, to which extent?

This chapter examines the ideas and discourse used to justify the adoption of GM in the EP, conceptualising them in the form of different frames, with the aim of understanding the broader context and direction of GM implementation in the EP. I also examine how the occurrence and the political implications of the particular frames changed over time. The chapter contributes to understanding how parliaments, even with their predictable changes of politicians and staff, can institutionalise GM rules. Analysing the institutionalisation of GM also helps answer a key question about the power relations in the EP: who has the power to introduce new rules and who the power to implement, block, or ignore them in one way or another? The EP is of particular interest because, as a supranational institution, it has to develop new rules and practices due to the heritage of differently gendered national parliaments.

The first section briefly reviews studies on GM in EU institutions and elaborates how combining Discursive Institutionalism (DI) and Feminist Institutionalism (FI) offers a useful framework to understand the institutionalisation of GM in the EP. The second section presents the frames used to justify GM implementation in the EP and explores their political implications for promoting gender equality. The third section then attends to GM's implementation over time and which elements proposed in the resolutions were actually realised before concluding the chapter by discussing the main findings in a broader perspective.

## THEORISING GENDER MAINSTREAMING IN THE EP

GM as a political strategy aims to change structures causing inequalities, questions existing institutions and suggests a paradigm shift by promoting gender equality as a goal (Beveridge et al. 2000; Rees 1998; Woodward 2012). GM considerably changed the scope of EU gender equality policy by moving beyond employment policy (Mazey 2001) and attempting to change the institutional setting (Behning and Sauer 2005). A strong feminist coalition mobilised for including GM in the Treaty of Amsterdam (Hubert and Stratigaki 2016), but 'bending, stretching or shrinking' almost always led to integrating or even co-opting gender equality instead of transforming existing policies (Lombardo et al. 2009). Hence, a range of scholars have attested the Commission and the EU in general lack any clear and coherent vision of gender equality, with GM becoming an empty signifier (Lombardo and Meier 2008; Verloo 2005) and pursuing integrationist, co-optative, or toolkit approaches to GM implementation (Stratigaki 2005). Effective GM implementation also failed in the European Court of Justice (Kenney 2002), the European constitution-making process (Lombardo 2005), and the Council of Europe (Lovecy 2002), and we lack insights on any GM implementation at the European Council or the Council of the European Union. The fate of GM in EU policy-making relied less on legislation than on administrative everyday policy-making routines (Jacquot 2015). Overall, inadequate GM implementation on the supranational level de-politicised gender equality policy, weakened the original institutional gender equality structure, and undermined the previously strong cross-institutional collaboration between feminist actors (Ahrens 2018; Jacquot 2015).

Even though the role of the EP in gender equality policy in general has been investigated (Ahrens 2018; Rolandsen Agustín 2013; van der Vleuten 2012, also in this volume), researching the institutionalisation of GM in the EP as an institution almost requires starting from scratch. As the EP – like other EU institutions – is characterised by constant (institutional) change (Abels in this volume), we can expect that nesting new GM rules in everyday EP practices would be possible, especially also given the long-standing self-understanding of the EP as a gender equality promoter (Debusscher and van der Vleuten 2017; van der Vleuten in this volume). Nonetheless, the EP might face similar difficulties as the newly established Scottish Parliament, where Mackay (2014, 566) found signs of 'institutional amnesia and political drift', as 'the combination of "newness" and "gender" appears to make the institutionalisation of reforms even harder'.

Moreover, ideas and how they are discursively generated and communicated play an important role in co-constituting institutional change and empowering its actors (Mackay et al. 2010). Politics and their articulation through discourses represent the 'struggle for representation of needs, problems, and identities' (Kulawik 2009, 265). Therefore, it is useful to conceptualise EP decision-making processes as an ongoing discourse and an ongoing construction of policy problems and solutions in the form of frames (Lombardo and Forest 2012). Frames are important because they reveal how actors understand the policy field and how they fit political issues into the broader context of their institution (Lombardo et al. 2009). Despite the rich literature on GM implementation in certain policy fields or different institutions, we know little about competing ideas and frames used in justifying GM institutionalisation.

To capture the variety of frames actors' use in discourses and the resulting political change in the EP as an institution, this chapter builds on FI and DI as important recent strands of analysing European integration (Mackay et al. 2010; MacRae and Weiner 2017). Both institutionalisms emphasise actors and endogenous institutional change, allowing us to examine 'the ways in which gender norms are reproduced and gendered power dynamics are maintained within EU structures' (Haastrup and Kenny 2016, 206). With its multicultural and multinational setting, the EP provides an exceptional case to study competing ideas about how to promote best gender equality in a system defined by consensual decision-making. DI helps focus 'on the interrelations of institutional arrangement, actor constellations, and political discourse', even though 'the constitutive dimension of discourse limits the scope of statements that can be meaningfully articulated in a given society' (Kulawik 2009, 267, 269). Repeating ideas over and again prompts 'continuity through change', yet ideas and practical implementation can still become disconnected (Schmidt 2011, 109ff.), and GM in the EP is an illustrative example of disconnections and how actors in favour of GM repeatedly aim to overcome institutional barriers and push for collective action.

While DI focuses on how and why (incremental) institutional change through ideas occurs, the concept of 'nested newness' (Mackay 2014) extends that perspective to what happens with new institutions once installed. The concept of nested newness captures the fact that newly established institutions – be they organisations or policy-making practices – are created in a specific context that motivates them to design an either similar or contrasting institution (Mackay 2009, 2014). Simultaneously, the institution's context affects how a new institution develops, as the 'nestedness' means that establishing any new practices and rules might go against previous procedures and therefore meet opposition. Furthermore, EP actors arrive with knowledge from their previous (national) institutions, and when it comes to gender issues rules related to changing (new) institutions are apparently among those that are particularly easily 'forgotten' (Mackay 2009).

In this chapter, the EP self-appointed mission to implement GM is conceptualised as creating a new institution by adopting new rules that by definition shall ultimately lead to institutional change. In this context, Mackay et al. (2010) highlight the *constitutive* aspect of ideas and frames in institutions, yet there is also a *receptive* aspect of ideas at work here. The frames regarding GM implementation communicated in texts and EP plenary debates gain different levels of power at different times. Combining DI and FI allows for tracing which particular frames (as in ideologically grouped discourses and ideas) stand out in introducing and maintaining GM processes in the EP.

To analyse the discursive aspect of institutions, I draw on primary material from the EP, such as resolutions, minutes of plenary debates, committee documents, and other documents, produced in the context of the following EP resolutions:[2]

- on GM in the EP (2002/2025 (INI))
- on GM in the work of the committees (2005/2149 (INI))
- of 22 April 2009 on GM in the work of its committees and delegations (2008/2245 (INI))
- of 17 November 2011 on GM in the work of the EP (2011/2151 (INI))
- of 8 March 2016 on GM in the work of the EP (2015/2230 (INI))
- of 15 January 2019 on GM in the EP (2018/2162 (INI))

Such documents provide data in which ideas, norms, and cultures are embodied and rendered visible (Teghtsoonian 2016). Political actors, moreover, use frames to transport their norms and ideas, and connect them to a broader institutional context in parliamentary texts (Schmidt 2010, 2011). Studying the written texts and plenary debates on the EP resolutions, I first categorised the frames that were used to justify formally implementing GM in the EP. Next, I examined which frames appeared when and determined whether their composition changed over time. Finally, I assessed what the resolutions tell us about the scope of nesting GM in the everyday practices of the EP.

## EMBEDDING GM RESOLUTIONS IN PARLIAMENTARY PROCEDURES

Gaining support for the first gender mainstreaming resolution and embedding it in the formal EP procedures was crucial for all further steps of institutionalisation. It should be noted here that the Conference of Presidents does not generally authorise the EP to produce a so-called own-initiative report and a resolution, on the contrary.

According to Mamadouh and Raunio (2003), such requests are often turned down as a form of EP agenda control. EP resolutions are prepared on the request of either a motion for resolution by individual members or by a committee, in this case FEMM. The Conference of Presidents assigned the first GM resolution as an own-initiative report to FEMM as lead committee, with the Committee on Legal Affairs and the Internal Market (AFET) as opinion-giving. Passing the initial formal procedure meant automatically institutionalising all following resolutions because it included a reporting obligation in the form of own-initiative reports assigned to FEMM as the competent committee (European Parliament 2003a).

FEMM prepared all resolutions following the EP standard procedure. The political group of the different rapporteurs caused no noticeable differences regarding the process or adoption. GM resolutions have thus become a well-institutionalised new standard output of the EP, not least because FEMM, as the initiating committee, is in charge of them. All resolutions received a clear majority in FEMM, though with increases in rejection votes. In plenary, only the 2009 resolution received broad support, while the first one in 2003 and those after 2009 were more contested. Table 6.1 presents rapporteurs, adoption dates, voting outcomes, and frame distribution over time.

While institutionalising resolutions was easy, establishing new practices and rules that ensure GM's implementation in the overall environment of the EP is a different task. In this regard, the resolutions (except the first) are interesting hybrids of otherwise quite formalised EP resolutions: not only do they signal the way forward on topics as resolutions usually do, they also are themselves the reporting mechanism for GM developments since the previous resolution. Consequently, the policy process becomes inevitably intertwined with ideas and discourses about justifying the need for GM, with necessary steps for further institutionalising the strategy, and with judging the results beyond the FEMM Committee. The next section presents the particular frames that were mobilised to gain support for GM, as well the one that was used *against* GM institutionalisation.

## EP GENDER MAINSTREAMING FRAMES

The frames used in texts and plenary debates are instructive to understand internal parliamentary struggles and power relations because they function as attempts to 'nest' gender equality in all aspects of the EP. What each frame presents as the problem and what it suggests as solution also imply different implementation trajectories. Discourses about GM revolved around seven different frames justifying (and one discrediting) gender mainstreaming implementation in the EP (see table 6.1), all of which are familiar from other presentations of GM and have different underlying logics that imply different consequences for gender equality policy. Each of them is listed according to their prevalence in the different stages of the resolutions texts and in EP plenary debates.

**Table 6.1 Overview of the Votes and Frames of EP Resolutions on Gender Mainstreaming**

| Resolution | 2003 | 2007 | 2009 | 2011 | 2016 | 2019 |
|---|---|---|---|---|---|---|
| Assigned to FEMM | 14.03.2002 | 15.06.2006 | 23.09.2008 | 07.07.2011 | 10.09.2015 | 05.07.2018 |
| Adopted | 13.03.2003 | 18.01.2007 | 22.04.2009 | 17.11.2011 | 08.03.2016 | 15.01.2019 |
| Rapporteur | Lissy Gröner, S&D | Anna Záborská, PPE | Anna Záborská, PPE | Mikael Gustafsson, GUE/NGL | Angelika Mlinar, ALDE | Angelika Mlinar, ALDE |
| | + − 0 | + − 0 | + − 0 | + − 0 | + − 0 | + − 0 |
| Committee vote | 23 1 0 | 30 0 1 | 23 0 1 | 21 4 0 | 23 6 1 | 19 6 0 |
| Plenary vote | 255 186 15 | Show of hands | 603 12 64 | 378 154 40 | 453 173 79 | 492 126 75 |
| **Frame Distribution over Time** | | | | | | |
| GM as a goal in itself | +++ | ++ | ++ | ++ | +++ | ++ |
| GM as a placeholder for descriptive representation | +++ | +++ | ++ | +++ | +++ | +++ |
| GM as a trademark of a progressive EP | ++ | ++ | ++ | +++ | ++ | +++ |
| GM as a democratic necessity | ++ | ++ | + | ++ | + | + |
| GM as a tool for better reconciliation | +++ | + | ++ | + | − | + |
| GM as a safeguard of human and fundamental rights | − | ++ | − | − | + | − |
| GM as a tool to advance the economy | − | + | − | − | + | + |
| GM as an instrument to address demographic changes | − | + | − | − | − | − |
| GM as ideology and threat | − | − | − | − | + | ++ |

Compilation by author. Key: no mention = − | mentioned at least once = + | mentioned at least three times = ++ | mentioned more than four times = +++

## GM as a Goal in Itself

In this frame, not using the correct tools to promote gender equality is presented as the problem, the solution being GM as something that offers tools for all actors at all levels. The frame is characterised by references to using adequate tools and instruments, and presents GM as the only possibility to promote gender equality. GM remains unquestioned and is presented as a 'natural' step; it becomes a goal in itself, as the following quotes illustrate:

> The Committee on Women's Rights and Gender Equality stresses the need for committees and delegations to have suitable instruments at their disposal for ensuring maximum awareness of gender mainstreaming. We need indicators, data and statistics grouped according to gender, and we also need budgetary resources to be allocated from a gender equality perspective. (Plenary debate 2009)

> Secondly, Parliament – further to several resolutions on gender mainstreaming – gradually developed a gender mainstreaming structure. However, analysis shows that the system is fragmented and not particularly efficient. It is time for corrective measures, as well as an efficient feedback and evaluation mechanism, if we want to prevent this resolution from remaining a dead letter. (Plenary debate 2016)

Even though this frame implies using certain tools, it can nevertheless stop actors such as the different MEPs, rapporteurs, committee (vice) chairs or political groups from discussing gender equality policy goals and instead use GM as an 'empty signifier' (Verloo 2005) without clear targets that should be reached within a certain time span. Thus, the frame allows for GM to be de-politicised and turned it into a technical step, a toolkit approach (Lombardo et al. 2009) everyone must take without further discussing the ultimate vision of what gender equality may mean in different policy fields. In this frame, GM becomes a matter of following technical steps and nesting them into the institutional logic of the institution, but it does not address the issue that actors need to be trained and inclined to use these new tools.

## GM as a Placeholder for Descriptive Representation

The second major frame presents the low number of women in the EP as a problem and uses GM as a stand-in for pushing to improve the recruitment of women overall and particularly in leadership positions. GM here stands for increasing the quantitative representation of women in all bodies and levels of the EP – as MEPs and staff, as the quotes show:

> The European political parties must strive to promote the participation of women in public life, to put more women forward for election, and here in Parliament they should encourage and create fairer and more equal representation. (Plenary debate 2007)

> There's still huge work to be done. That is why I believe that the top hierarchy of the European Parliament should really take this into consideration, and to have more women, at least 40 per cent, at top management and top posts and positions. (Plenary debate 2016)

While reaching parity is certainly an important indicator of gender equality, as the final distribution predominantly depends on national party practices and electoral laws in Member States, it is out of the EP's scope. Using GM as a placeholder for descriptive representation might limit it to counting heads instead of questioning structures and policy content. It also uses binary categories and tends to neglect other intersectional aspects of representation like race, ethnicity, or physical abilities. Nevertheless, using this frame could help create pressure to reconsider the Rules of Procedure regarding parity rules for (vice) committee chairs, political group leaders, and administrative staff.

## GM as a Trademark of a Progressive EP

The trademark frame's main problem is that GM is not implemented well, also not in Member States' parliaments, so the solution is that the EP becomes the vanguard. Consequently, the frame highlights the role of the EP as the lead institution in promoting gender equality and mainstreaming in parliaments and beyond, and it was usually supported by utterances such as these:

> I believe that this is an excellent initiative for transferring to national parliaments the positive model offered by the EP on gender equality. (Plenary debate 2007)

> Finally, the best way to promote gender equality is to set a good example, to live its essence, and to show how it is done. Gender mainstreaming and gender equality are principles that are enshrined in the Treaties. Who, if not the EU institutions, could be the best example when it comes to implementation? (Plenary debate 2016)

Even though this trademark frame reinforces the image of a progressive EP, a notion quite widely held in EP discourses (van der Vleuten in this volume), it loses its mobilising potential if everyone thinks gender equality is accomplished in the EP (e.g. as opposed to everywhere) or if gender issues beyond traditional topics such as representation, reconciliation or equal pay are not recognised as necessary fields for intervention. Rolandsen Agustín (2013) illuminated how a form of cultural othering occurred in discourses on gender-based violence that may lead to overlooking gendered inequalities in one's 'own' setting.

## GM as a Democratic Necessity

In this frame, the problem to be solved by implementing GM is located in the broader context of various EU crises, particularly the alleged democratic deficit. The democracy frame references the necessity of promoting gender equality through GM as an indicator of the EP's credibility (globally) and EU democracy in general. It questions whether it is justified to ask other actors to promote gender equality if one's own institution fails to do so itself, as the following quotes highlight:

> Often, work begins at home, in one's own house, and for us that means in this House, our Parliament. We cannot be credible in our work and in the demands that we make

of others outside Parliament if we are not at the same time prepared to practice what we preach. (Plenary debate 2011)

It'll lead to greater democracy. (Plenary debate 2016)

Similarly to the trademark frame, the democracy frame tries to establish internal pressure to implement GM, and its appeal largely depends on whether MEPs and political groups consider the democratic deficit a problem or – as is the case for some of the newer right-wing political groups – a reason to object to GM even more as part of their strategy to further undermine the EU and its policies.

**GM as a Tool for Better Reconciliation**

While most of the frames so far concern more process- and institution-related frames, the reconciliation frame presents the unequal share of paid and unpaid work as the major barrier to reaching gender equality and casts GM implementation as the solution. Here, GM is justified as a tool to promote work-life balance and the reconciliation of private and public life, as can be seen in the following quote:

All these options must encourage the continual exchange of good practice, with the aim of implementing the integrated strategy for combining family life and work life and facilitating the career development of female employees. (Plenary debate 2009)

While the distribution of paid and unpaid work is a core question in gender equality, its use as a frame for GM implementation in the EP also presents some challenges due to its limitation to employment and social policy. If GM would rely on this frame alone, it could be limited to the committees concerned with employment and social policy, while other important policy issues such as gender-based violence, sexual rights, gender and public health, or gender identity would probably receive less attention.

**GM as a Safeguard of Human and Fundamental Rights**

The frame presenting GM as a safeguard for human and fundamental rights problematises the fact that gender equality policies were not fully accepted as a human-rights issue and that international obligations need to be taken more seriously. Overall, this frame casts women's rights and gender equality as global values:

Equality between women and men is a fundamental principle of community law – I emphasise that this fundamental principle, and thus also its advancement, is the indisputable task of the community. (Plenary debate 2007)

While the frame offers the chance to nest GM implementation in a broader political context, it might also lead to limiting gender equality to a question of legal rights, instead of taking the transformative approach that characterises GM.

## GM as a Tool to Advance the Economy

This frame relies on casting gendered inequalities as a limitation to making full use of human resources and thus presents GM as a tool to enable full economic growth through better human-resource management:

> And also, there's certainly inequality on the boards of businesses. Enormous differences there. We need changes in business, we need changes in society so that women are more involved in decision-making. Especially, I say, in businesses. And I think this [resolution] will make a contribution to the well-being of businesses as well. (Plenary debate 2016)

This economic frame ties gender equality to the promise of accomplishing economic goals, but if this frame dominates, only proposals that can be linked to economic efficiency can be justified. If a proposal lacks a clear economic advantage or would even be costly, it could be rejected.

## GM as an Instrument to Address Demographic Changes

This frame presents low birth rates across Europe as a major challenge and proposes that GM will change certain policies that would lead to women having more children. Here, changes to the age composition of the EU population function as the main justification for GM:

> The ageing of Europe will be an impossible problem to solve unless we revise our approach to gender mainstreaming. (Plenary debate 2007)

Similarly to the reconciliation and the economic frames, such a limited policy focus would most likely also limit the implementation of GM to this topic, thereby ignoring that the real problem is usually not too few children but the way the social-security system is organised.

## GM as Ideology and Threat

The last frame is fundamentally different from all previous ones, because it opposes rather than supports GM. First appearing in 2016, its problem is 'feminists gone wild' that attempt to brainwash the EU population through 'gender ideology'. The solution suggested is abandoning GM and any gender equality policies, as illustrated by the following quotes:

> But unfortunately, I cannot support this report, because it goes in the wrong direction. I never heard of a worse proposal for harmonising private- and business-lives. We cannot allow such interference. Policies in totalitarian regimes never try to do something like that, which explains quite a lot about this proposal. (Plenary debate 2016)

> We're talking about transposing gender ideology into the internal organisation of the European Parliament. . . . The Mlinar report has two advantages. It's clear how much

money is being squandered on gender ideology, and the text, seems to me, to bear out everything bad the people are saying about the European Parliament being cut off. (Plenary debate 2016)

As the range of frames illustrates, GM resolutions and plenary debates used many different issues to justify GM implementation. They refer to the EP's internal organisation, such as its committees, delegations, human-resources department, and administration, and to policy fields such as employment and demography. The frames and the resolutions themselves become more detailed and sophisticated over time, as various discourses represented in the frames find their place and are institutionalised as topics for GM implementation in the EP. Moreover, over time, the scope of resolutions also extended to intersectional aspects, for instance, LGBTQI-rights, gender identity, and transgender issues, as is clearly visible in the 2016 resolution, and additional diversity aspects and sexual harassment in the EP in the 2019 resolution.

The next section compares which frames dominated over time, how they affected the content of the political debate and how implementation changed over time. I will also examine in greater detail the specific settings of each resolution and what this tells us about the discourses that shape GM's nesting in the EP.

## NESTING GM IN PARLIAMENTARY PROCEDURES

All resolutions present information on how GM is implemented (or not) and all resolutions follow the same standardised structure of EP resolutions. They start by linking GM with the EU legislative framework, such as treaty articles on gender equality (TFEU §8), non-discrimination (TFEU §10, §19), and equal pay (TFEU §157), EP resolutions, and EP rules, and also cover the activities of other supranational actors like the European Commission. All resolutions then continue by summarising why promoting gender equality is still a necessary goal, briefly assessing GM implementation in the EP thus far and postulating necessary future steps. The function of the explanatory statement attached to the resolutions changed over time: in the first four resolutions, the rapporteurs used it to report the results of evaluating GM implementation in the EP since the previous resolution, but it disappeared in the 2016 resolution. It returned in the 2019 resolution in the form of a political statement that simultaneously summarised overall results and urgently called for more serious attempts in implementation, given the time already spent on GM's institutionalisation process. The FEMM Committee kept track of this process by compiling data on GM in the EP with surveys covering the GM implementation steps defined in the 2003 resolution. In addition, FEMM regularly invited the (vice-)chairperson in charge of GM within each committee to report in an FEMM meeting and arranged joint meetings of the GM network that was created after the first resolution. What follows is a detailed timeline of GM in the EP.

***2003*.** The first resolution was influenced by broader political discourses at the time that were concerned with transposing the Treaty of Amsterdam and its GM provisions and with the upcoming EU enlargement to Central and Eastern Europe. For the former, the resolution presented the European Commission's GM approach as a best practice and blueprint for the EP, and the suggested implementation steps quite accurately followed the specialist group report of the Council of Europe (1998), which was then considered a blueprint for GM implementation. Two core steps were nevertheless omitted: gender training and consultative measures directed at stakeholders and/or think tanks. For the latter, the rapporteur highlighted that in light of the 2004 enlargement it would be necessary to ensure a high proportion of women in parliament and also reasoned that GM and promoting gender equality would be a core EP task to support democracy 'as the European institution closest to citizens' (European Parliament 2003b, 16). Overall, GM implementation was justified by only five frames: GM as a goal in itself, descriptive representation, trademark, democratic necessity, and reconciliation; the last frame never again receiving similar attention. The resolution initially used the neutral formulation 'effective work by the competent committee' (ibid., 9) to allocate the responsibility for GM, and only in the explanatory statement was 'competent committee' specified by suggesting that all tasks mentioned in the resolution be assigned to the FEMM Committee. GM institutionalisation thus became a life insurance for the FEMM Committee by assigning it recurring tasks and reporting duties.

***2007*.** Now that the EP had committed to implement GM and report biannually, the 2004 EP elections meant that the stage had changed, resulting in a delay of the 2007 report. Constituting a new EP and returning to formal and informal rules clearly had an impact for GM. The various drafts and the final adopted version aptly illustrate the internal struggles and problems of nesting GM in the existing procedures and of establishing new ones. The frames used in the plenary debate emphasised descriptive representation and GM as a goal in itself. While some MEPs highlighted that EP committees were quite reluctant to implement GM, the written texts were much more cautious. The explanatory statement almost excused shortcomings by flagging the 'political and technical dynamic inherent in each topic' that 'determines the attention paid to the specific challenge posed by gender mainstreaming', and that 'this should not under any circumstances result in a moral condemnation of individuals' (European Parliament 2006a, 9ff.). Committees seemed to have forgotten about the requirement to mainstream gender and moreover were reluctant to adopt more decisive steps and implement stricter rules. The committee report which was adopted as a basis for the final resolution included concrete steps such as, for instance, the need for the High Level Group on Gender Equality to establish obligatory political priorities for GM in legislation, communication and information policy, gender budgeting, and staff policy. The report also suggested adopting compulsory quotas for female MEPs and, in a previous version, providing gender trainings for all MEPs. All these disappeared in the final resolution, demonstrating the difficulty of institutionalising GM in an EP composed differently after the elections.

***2009***. Adopted towards the end of the legislature, the 2009 resolution clearly resembled the previous two in terms of the drafts and adopted text. The content of the explanatory statement changed considerably though, listing details on each of the EP committees and delegations[3] in a 'name-and-shame-approach'. Instead of summarising the main findings regarding certain topics, the explanatory statement disclosed details on the (non-existent) activity of a majority of committees. While fourteen out of nineteen committees stated that they had included gender aspects in some (non-)legislative acts, the committees on constitutional (AFCO), legal (JURI), and civil liberties, justice and home affairs (LIBE), budgetary control (CONT), and the environment (ENVI) did not. Moreover, only the committees on regional development (REGI), fisheries (PECH), foreign affairs (AFET), and its Subcommittee on Security and Defense (SEDE) reported a dedicated internal equality strategy. Few committees used gender-disaggregated data, indicators, gender impact assessments, and gender budgeting. Yet, compared to 2007, where not a single committee had an internal equality strategy (European Parliament 2009b, 8), the numbers had increased. The Independence/Democracy Group opposed the resolution and proposed a number of weaker formulations such as 'reiterates *that it is possible* to adopt' instead of 'reiterates *the need* to adopt' (European Parliament 2009c, 5). The number of frames used in the plenary debate was never as large again while simultaneously being balanced in their percentage of occurrences; all frames except those of the GM as ideology and as threat were mobilised, and this was the only time when the demography frame appeared.

***2011***. As with the 2007 resolution, for the 2011 resolution we also see that the newly elected EP affected how GM implementation is reported and to what extent it faces challenges nesting in the everyday parliamentary business. It provided no details on the different committees; the results presented were rather general and useless for estimating which committees were (in)active or how things had developed since the last report. The policy process leading to the resolution was the shortest of all the studied resolutions, which might be interpreted as a sign of institutionalisation, at least regarding the level of routinisation in the FEMM Committee. The frames on descriptive representation and GM as a trademark were the ones most often used in the (brief) plenary debate, while policy-related ones – economy, demography, human rights – disappeared.

While the other resolutions focused on how to push other committees to implement GM, the 2011 resolution signalled a change of strategy on the part of the FEMM Committee. Throughout the resolution, so-called 'gender mainstreaming amendments' (GMAs) were emphasised as a useful tool. GMAs are tabled and voted in the FEMM Committee and then forwarded to the lead committee, which then can but is not required to adopt them. In other words, instead of the earlier practice of competing with other committees over gender-related (non)legislative acts (Ahrens 2016) or pushing for GM implementation, FEMM considered GMAs the most successful strategy. GMAs became the informal new GM standard rule, and the 2011 resolution suggested formally including them in the rules of procedure;

a suggestion repeated in each follow-up resolution yet not implemented to date. According to a commissioned study, 'the majority of GMAs in most cases simply add the words "gender", "female" or "women" to the respective text, be it a proposal for legislation of the Commission or an own-initiative report of a parliamentary committee' (European Parliament 2014a, 77).

***2016.*** The 2016 resolution once more signals that institutionalizing GM in the EP is a question of matching existing rules and routines with new ones. Ostensibly, the biannual GM reporting does not synchronise well with the EP's 5-year election cycle, as the previous legislature only had the 2011 report. We can assume that a second report was probably not prepared because of the change in committee chair[4] and timing problems with the 2014 election, both most likely affecting committee routines.

However, the 2016 resolution also indicates the routinisation and perseverance of FEMM Committee members, evincing their ability to detect the mismatches between long-established rules and routines and the new requirements connected to GM. Strong emphasis was placed on the frames of GM as a goal in itself and of descriptive representation, and in general a variety of frames were mobilized in support. For the first time though, the frame of GM as ideology and threat also appeared.

The resolution proposes additional measures to ensure better 'nesting' of GM in the EP, for instance, through:

- setting up an institutional coordination and monitoring mechanism for the bodies in charge of GM, such as the High Level Group on Gender Equality and Diversity, the FEMM Committee, the gender mainstreaming network, and the EP's administration services;
- staffing up the gender mainstreaming network with delegation members and additional substitutes, and co-chairing it with a representative from the FEMM Committee and someone from among the different committees on a rota basis in order to signal that GM involves all committees;
- calls for gender balance (at least 40 per cent of each sex by 2020) in chairpersons for committees and political groups, heads of (administrative) units, as well as middle and senior management, and by nominating MEPs from the under-represented gender in each committee (incl. the FEMM Committee);
- establishing a standing rapporteur on GM to coordinate with the high-level group (European Parliament 2016a, 7–8).

For the first time, the report mentioned LGBTIQ issues as a subject for GM implementation. Gender budgeting and gender training re-appeared as requested measures, and the resolution called for greater involvement of the European Institute for Gender Equality and the EP research services. Overall, the 2016 resolution demonstrates that some elements of GM implementation had been institutionalised, such as reporting, certain actors like the High-Level Group and the GM network, but also some tools like GMAs, as attention for gender aspects was growing in a number of committees. Moreover, FEMM stressed how important it is 'to establish a clear procedure, to be incorporated into Parliament's Rules of Procedure, on the adoption of a gender action plan by each committee and delegation' (European Parliament 2016a, 10).

***2019.*** The most recent resolution replicates core elements of the 2016 one and demonstrates clear advancements in institutionalising GM. Angelika Mlinar, in charge of the resolution, became the first 'Standing Rapporteur on Gender Main-streaming' in 2016 and in addition to the GM network, the EP set up another one with GM network administrators for each committee. Furthermore, nineteen out of twenty-three committees prepared a gender action plan, for the first time publicly accessible on the FEMM Committee website after the resolution's adoption.[5] The four committees not publishing a gender action plan were the FEMM Committee itself, those without a policy field – Budgetary Control and Petitions – and the 2018 special (temporary) committee on Financial Crimes, Tax Evasion and Tax Avoidance (TAX3). Also, in 2017 the EP bureau unanimously adopted the report 'Gender Equality in the European Parliament Secretariat – state of play and the way forward 2017–2019' with quantified targets for different positions.

The FEMM Committee clearly attempted to further foster GM implementation and extend its scope beyond the elements reached thus far by mobilising a variety of frames in plenary, but this was met with the growing use of the GM as ideology and threat frame. The resolution contains a stronger emphasis on diversity as an impor-tant element of promoting gender equality and refers specifically to LGBTQI and gender identity, as well as to the importance of male role models for gender equality (European Parliament 2019a, 7). Finally, the resolution proposed to add rules on sexual harassment and abuse to the EP rules of procedure and to organise measures that raise consciousness about this issue in the EP; whether or not this will actually be implemented remains to be seen.

## CONCLUSION

This chapter set out to examine the policy frames and processes leading to the adop-tion of EP gender mainstreaming resolutions that (self-)oblige the EP to implement GM on all levels, that is, committees, delegations, EP Bureau, Secretariat, and staff management. The FEMM Committee assigned itself to regularly monitor and evalu-ate implementation, and to present the results to plenary. Four frames used to justify GM implementation dominated the policy discourses surrounding all resolutions: (1) GM as a goal in itself, (2) GM as placeholder for descriptive representation, (3) GM as a trademark of a progressive EP, and (4) GM as a democratic necessity.

All frames lacked a clear definition of gender equality, and the use of the first frame de-politicised the discussion by only trying to oblige actors to adopt certain technical steps. The third and fourth frame relied on the self-representation of the EP

*Petra Ahrens*

as an equality promoter to push for institutionalisation. These frames clearly related well to the growing role of the EP in EU policy-making, but whether they will work effectively in the future depends on the composition of future EPs and the number of MEPs and political groups opposing gender equality.

The continuing repetition of the four frames over time caused institutional change by intractably linking the ideas with new rules and practices (Schmidt 2011) compatible with existing EP ones. Hence, the overall process and the use of certain ideas helped to prevent new gender rules from being 'forgotten' (Mackay 2014), although a newly elected EP posed a particular challenge to the partly institutionalized rules. Notably, the frame of GM as a goal in itself also changed: in the beginning, actors using the frame emphasized that GM tools are available and just need to be picked up, while nowadays the frame is used to stress that the EP needs to adapt tools to its own structure to implement GM. The system that the FEMM Committee set up managed over time to make it almost impossible for the EP to forget about the new GM rules because of the continuous reporting and additional elements such as GMA, gender action plans, GM networks, and a GM Standing Rapporteur that constantly require all parts of the EP to engage with the topic – even if rather unwillingly. Remarkably, using the GM resolutions the FEMM Committee managed to indirectly exert power over the different EP branches despite it usually being considered powerless and un-prestigious (Ahrens 2016). Whether the FEMM Committee will find ways to use this power in a future EP which will most probably become much more conservative, right-wing, and anti-feminist remains to be seen.

Overall, we can distinguish different, overlapping steps in institutionalizing GM in the EP:

- Making it an established practice and returning subject by institutionalizing reporting mechanisms with the responsibility clearly allocated to one institutional body, the FEMM Committee, secured the long-term survival of GM as a subject.
- De-politicising the process by presenting it as a technical process increased receptivity in the EP and allowed for stepwise interweaving new rules with existing ones. Nevertheless, the technical focus did imply slow progress with regard to the content of gender equality policies.
- Institutionalizing GM in other committees than the FEMM Committee, in delegations, and in other duties of EP took more time and was less successful, as committees remained reluctant, and inactive change only happened slowly.
- Intersectional aspects long played no role, though more attention was paid in the most recent resolutions. The same applies to the notion of gender-sensitive parliaments,[6] which appeared only in the last resolution.

When we consider the broader implications of a successful GM implementation in the EP, we could expect a considerable impact on supranational and national policies, because the increased power of the EP would allow for enforcing the mainstreaming of gender in all EU policies. This could even help to correct the omissions of an inactive European Commission in policy fields not directly associated with gender equality. Can the EP thus become a best-practice example for national parliaments? Can there be a spillover? Will the EP continue working against the tide? Future developments will hopefully answer these questions positively.

## NOTES

1 Petra Ahrens' work received funding from the European Research Council (ERC) under grant agreement No 771676 of the European Union's Horizon 2020 research and innovation programme.

2 In the following, the resolutions will be referred to by their adoption year, not their starting year.

3 The report contained no data on other EP bodies such as the Bureau.

4 At the end of 2011, Mikael Gustavsson replaced Eva-Britt Svensson as chair. Why no second GM resolution was adopted was not available on the EP website.

5 For details, see http://www.europarl.europa.eu/committees/en/femm/subject-files. html?id=20160602CDT00721, accessed 7 March 2019. Two gender action plans were adopted by subcommittees.

6 See, for example, Childs (2016), Palmieri (2011) and Wängnerud (2015).

# 7

# Gendering the EU Budget

## Can European Parliament Play the Role of a Gender Budgeting Advocate?

*Firat Cengiz*

Spending and revenue collection decisions constitute a fundamental aspect of citizens' relationship with a polity. These decisions reflect salient political preferences as to what parts of society should benefit from the monetary resources in what ways and how should different clusters of society pay for the public services. Hence, budgets comprising spending and revenue collection decisions have a fundamental impact on equality within society.

Feminist political economists have long acknowledged budgets' fundamental implications on gender equality. Accordingly, they advocate a 'gender-sensitive approach' to budgeting (Budlender et. al. 2002; Sharp and Broomhill 2007; Stotsky 2007). This has also been echoed by international organisations, such as the United Nations Beijing Platform for Action that called for a gender-sensitive approach to budgetary processes in 1995 (Council of Europe 2005, 10).

Gender-sensitive budgeting or 'gender budgeting' means gender mainstreaming of the entire budgetary process with a view to incorporating a gender equality perspective to all revenue and spending decisions. Contrary to the common belief, gender budgeting does not mean allocation of specific funds to gender equality in the budget. Accordingly, this chapter will not look into the allocation of public funds to gender equality in the European Union (hereafter EU) budget. Rather, the chapter takes a holistic approach and investigates whether and to what extent gender equality plays a role in the design and the adoption process of the EU budget as a whole.

In the light of the overall objectives of this book, specific attention is paid here to the potential role of the European Parliament (EP) in a gender-sensitive EU budgetary process. The Parliament, as the institution entrusted with the task of representing citizens in the budgetary processes, appears as the best placed institution to be the institutional advocate of gender budgeting in the EU. Accordingly, the Parliament's Women's Rights and Gender Equality (hereinafter 'FEMM') Committee as well as its plenary adopted resolutions calling for all EU institutions, and in particular the European Commission, to follow a gender-sensitive approach in the spending of EU Funds.[1] Similarly, each year during the budgetary adoption and discharge processes the FEMM Committee repeats its calls for gender budgeting with placing an increasing importance and emphasis on the subject.[2]

Nevertheless, actions of the Parliament have so far not translated into a tangible change in the EU budgetary process. It is argued here that whether the Parliament could successfully play the potential role of a gender budgeting advocate very much depends on whether or not the Parliament could play the role of a veto player within the budgetary process. The potential role of the Parliament as a veto player is subject to significant endogenous and exogenous challenges and limitations, including: the fragmented nature of the Parliament as an institution comprising of various committees and groups with varying priorities and interests (see also Abels in this volume); the limited role of the Parliament within the budgetary process vis-à-vis the Member States and the overarching neoliberal discourse of efficiency and competitiveness that leaves limited role for social priorities and equality in general (Kantola and Verloo 2018). It is argued here that in the face of these significant challenges, as potentially successful strategies the Parliament could rely on internal coalition building between its committees, external coalition building with actors with an interest in equality, most notably the national parliaments, and taking advantage of alternative political frames of calls for increased democracy and accountability in the EU. These challenges and strategies to overcome them are discussed further in section five of this chapter discussing the role of the Parliament.

Against the politics of neoliberalism, counter citizen movements calling for decentralisation of economic policy-making in the hands of citizens are also becoming increasingly strong. These movements resulted in several decentralised decision-making platforms and institutions that accommodate deliberation among citizens, including participatory budgeting initiatives (see Della Porta and Rucht 2013; Moir and Leyshon 2013; Panitch and Albo 2018). Similarly, the capability approach to equality calls for a democratic, person-centric way of measuring equality that is based on the individual needs of citizens rather than the amount of monetary resources allocated to them (Sen 1993).

Given that gender and participatory budgeting share the fundamental objective of creating a more egalitarian and democratic society, the methodology of gender budgeting should naturally be participatory. Accordingly, an original methodology for gender budgeting is proposed here that is inspired by participatory budgeting as well as the capability approach. This methodology could both be used to investigate to what extent the EU budget is gender-sensitive at present as well as to propose institutional reforms for making the EU budgetary process more participatory and democratic. This chapter confines with the former and leaves the latter for future research.

The structure of the chapter is as follows: section one discusses why gender budgeting is necessary for the EU. Section two introduces the capability-based methodology to gender budgeting. Afterwards, section three reports the findings of the screening of the EU budget in the light of the capability-based methodology. This is followed with a fourth section that discusses the EU budgetary process and politics. Section five then discusses the Parliament's role as a potential gender budgeting advocate. This is followed with conclusions.

## WHY IS GENDER BUDGETING IN THE EU NECESSARY?

Unlike nation states, the EU does not share a direct revenue and spending relationship with citizens. In other words, the EU does not redistribute wealth between citizens by directly collecting tax from them and by directly making welfare payments to them. Nevertheless, EU spending is still likely to affect equality between citizens. Thus, a gender-sensitive budgeting process at the EU level is likely to contribute towards gender equality.

First and foremost, the EU has shown a high-level political commitment to gender equality as a principle. Gender equality is recognized as a value and a key principle of EU governance, among others, in Articles 2 and 3 of the Treaty on European Union and Article 23 of the Charter of Fundamental Rights of the European Union. Nevertheless, it is not entirely clear whether this political commitment to gender equality is also reflected in tangible policy decisions. Since the emergence and increasing prevalence of neoliberal economic policies and principles in the 1990s, gender equality has gradually been overshadowed by growth and competitiveness objectives. Women's participation to economy and production remains as the only gender equality objective to which the EU remains committed (see Elomäki 2015; Elomäki and Kantola 2018; Eschle and Maiguasshca 2018; Jacquot 2015; Kantola and Verloo 2018). Similarly, the European Commission's replacing of the EU's 2010–2015 gender equality strategy with a mere 'strategic engagement' document (Commission 2016) raises concerns. Accordingly, gender budgeting would play a fundamental role as a budgetary accountability tool, as it would reveal whether and to what extent the EU's commitment to gender equality as a principle is followed on in budgetary decisions.

Secondly, spending in the context of structural EU policies and programmes, such as the European Social Fund, takes place in a multilevel governance setting in which national organisations carry out the actual investment under the monitoring of the European Commission. As a result, a gender-sensitive EU budget could rely on the power of *Europeanisation* (see for example Lombardo and Forest 2012) and make the release of EU funds conditional on the following of gender equality targets. In the light of the EU's general commitment to gender mainstreaming, all EU policies and programmes would be expected to incorporate clear gender equality targets. As a result, consistent enforcement of gender equality targets in EU spending would make a positive and significant effect on gender equality at the national and local levels. Previous research in European Social Fund and the EU Research and Innovation Policy have found that the European Commission has already been enforcing conditionalities in these areas (Abels 2012; Ahrens and Callerstig 2017).

## A CAPABILITY-BASED METHODOLOGY
## FOR GENDER BUDGETING IN THE EU

This chapter proposes a 'capability approach' to gender budgeting. The capability approach to equality shares the underlying objective of gender budgeting to contribute to the creation of a more just and democratic society. As a result, it provides a suitable analytical framework to think about the democratic effects of resource allocation decisions. The capability approach originates from Amartya Sen's ground-breaking work proposing a people-centric alternative to the utilitarian, macro-economic driven approaches to human well-being. Sen criticizes utilitarian approaches for failing to depict the true and whole picture of people's satisfaction with their lives (Sen 1993, 41). He argues that rather than income and material goods, our understating of equality should centre on people's 'capabilities', in other words, the options and freedoms available to them to engage in activities that make life an enjoyable experience. Similarly, the capabilities approach offers an alternative perspective based on experiences, issues and objects that intrinsically matter to men and women, rather than monetary values and resources (Sen 1995, 125). As a result, the capability approach fully reflects the nature of gender equality as an essential problem of disparate freedoms.

This naturally brings the question: what are those capabilities that are essential to men and women? While proposing a capability approach, Sen did not attempt to draw a list of predefined capabilities that are essential for human well-being. This was a deliberate choice, since as a people-centric approach, the capabilities approach is supposed to give men and women from different social groups and backgrounds a voice in deciding what is essential for their well-being. As a result, in an ideal world, if a capability approach is to be followed, a participatory process should be adopted with a view to giving people the opportunity to define the capabilities that are central to their own well-being. In other words, if the capability approach is followed wholeheartedly and holistically, the budgetary process should naturally be deliberative and participatory. Nevertheless, in the real-world budgetary processes and discourses prove to be overly bureaucratic and exclusionary. Budgetary process is mostly understood and perceived as an area reserved for experts to which citizens have only little, if any, to contribute.

This causes serious impediments not only to the democratic quality of the budget-making processes but also to the methodological quality of the scientific research looking into equality effects of budgets. Researchers investigating the equality implications of public spending will have to second guess citizens' preferences and needs when attempting to apply the capability approach to a specific policy context.

Accordingly, several scholars proposed lists bringing together capabilities which they perceived as essential for women's and men's well-being (see for example Nussbaum 2003; Robeyns 2005). Some of those lists were specifically designed to be used in the context of gender budgeting (see for example Addabo et al. 2010). Similarly, international organisations with an interest in gender equality adopted lists of capabilities that feed into equality indices that they use to measure gender equality. These include the United Nations Development Programme's Gender-Related Development Index, the Gender Empowerment Measure and Gender Equality Index, the World Economic Forum's Gender Gap Index and the European Institute for Gender Equality's (hereinafter EIGE) European Gender Equality Index. Among these, the latter incorporates the largest group of capabilities (see EIGE 2015).

In another, more comprehensive study we subjected a selection of EU budget chapters to gender budgeting analysis (see Cengiz and Beveridge 2015).[3] In the context of that study in order not to replicate the existing work in the field, we did not propose an entirely new and different list of capabilities. Rather, we proposed as comprehensive a list as possible bringing together capabilities perceived as essential in the lists proposed by other scholars as well as the European Gender Equality Index. As a result, our methodology faces the same limitation facing other pieces of scientific research in the field, as it is not based on a participatory methodology giving a voice to citizens to identify the capabilities. Nevertheless, as a substantial difference with other studies we paid particular attention to draw the list of capabilities as widely as possible in order to be inclusive of all capabilities that could potentially affect gender equality.

As a result, our list comprised five broad categories of capabilities (ibid., 16):

a) *Women's and men's engagement with the society*: this group of capabilities includes the capabilities to have equal shares in non-market labour and care economy, to have equal voice in family decisions, to engage in social activities, to move, and so forth.

b) *Women's and men's engagement with the political and social system*: this group includes the capabilities to have equal access to education, market, employment and politics, and so forth.

c) *Women's and men's engagement with the environment*: this group includes the capabilities to have shelter and to live in a safe, clean environment in harmony with the environment and other species, and so forth.

d) *Women's and men's engagement with their personality*: this group includes the capabilities to plan one's own time, to have hobbies, to engage in spiritual and religious activities, to choose the education and profession one desires, and so forth.

e) *Women's and men's engagement with their physicality*: this group includes the capabilities to feel safe, to live a dignified life, to be free from physical, psychological or emotional violence, to express thoughts, desires and personality in any way, including physical appearance, without the fear of violence or intimidation.

---

## Text Box 7.1
## A Methodology for Capabilities
## Approach to Gender Budgeting

**Step 1:** Identify capabilities key to women's well-being and gender equality
**Step 2:** Match those capabilities with policies, define policies' *gender spectrum* and *gender impact*
**Step 3:** Analyse policy objectives and resource allocations in light of conclusions reached at step 2
**Step 4:** Identify beneficiaries and participants
**Step 5:** Reflection and policy change

Source: Cengiz and Beveridge (2015).

---

Our list does not contain a specific category of intersecting inequalities. Nevertheless, its flexible and comprehensive nature allows us to take intersecting inequalities into consideration in the analysis of the budget. When a policy area affects several groups of capabilities at the same time, as is the case for many policy areas, this gives us the opportunity to discuss the reasons and identify the intersecting equalities affected by the policy in question. We understand intersecting inequalities as seemingly independent qualities of an individual which when combined reinforce each other and result in increased marginalisation or oppression, such as sex, gender, race, colour, religion, LGBT status and socioeconomic status (see Crenshaw 1989).

In this methodology, as a second step of analysis, individual policy areas are matched with different capability categories which they can impact in a positive and/or negative way. As a result, policies are flagged in terms of their potential effects on gender equality. This is followed with defining the number of capabilities that each policy is likely to affect (*gender equality spectrum*) and the intensity of the effect of the policy in question as direct or indirect or low, moderate and high (*gender equality impact*).

After identifying a policy's gender equality spectrum and impact, we look at whether the impact and spectrum are acknowledged and reflected on in the policy choices and budgetary decisions. This is followed by a fourth step in which we look into the implementation of the policy in question; and ask specifically, whether the beneficiaries and participants of the policy in question were chosen in a gender-sensitive way reflecting the capabilities that are likely to be affected by the policy. Finally, if we identify a discrepancy between the capabilities that are likely to be affected in the third and fourth stages of analysis, we flag the policy as potentially detrimental to gender equality. As a result, as the final stage of analysis, we call for reflection and policy change in those policy areas in order to reverse those policies' potentially detrimental impacts on gender equality.

## FINDINGS OF A CAPABILITY-BASED ANALYSIS OF THE EU BUDGET

This chapter does not provide enough space to subject the entire EU budget to a capability-based gender budgeting analysis. Nevertheless, the key findings of gender budgeting analysis of six different policy areas will be shared here to illustrate the current status of gender budgeting in the EU (see table 7.1). The six policy areas (namely Employment, Social Affairs and Exclusion, Home Affairs, Justice, Development and Cooperation, Research and Innovation and Education and Culture) are chosen mainly to be provide an illustrative sample of the EU budget within the limited space of this chapter. However, a complete gender budgeting will naturally have to investigate the entirety of the budget, because even policy areas that initially appear remote from gender could affect men and women differently and cause significant implications on gender equality.

A gender budgeting analysis of the six policy areas reveals direct and high impact on all capability areas. Employment, social affairs and inclusion is primarily linked to women's participation in the economic production that is most directly related to capability groups a, b and c. Additionally, some spending programmes within this policy area, such as the Fund for European Aid of the Most Deprived or the European Globalisation Adjustment Fund aim to contribute towards fighting poverty which also affects highly and directly capability groups d and e.

In the context of Home Affairs, gender equality related issues are arising particularly acutely in the context of migration and asylum. Migration and refugee status and their underlying reasons (e.g. war, violence, lack of access to basic resources) affect men and women differently. They are likely to have a direct and high impact on all capability groups: displaced women are likely to experience significant difficulties in terms of access to work, a regular family life, shelter, safety and other basic living conditions that are necessary for a dignified life and mental and physical health. Displaced women's vulnerabilities have been acknowledged at the international and EU levels (Edwars 2010). Among others, the United Nations High Commission for Refugees produced two sets of guidelines[4] to promote a gender-sensitive approach to the interpretation of the 1951 Refugee Convention, which arguably also forms a part of the EU's legal framework, as Article 18 of the EU Charter of Fundamental Rights and Freedoms makes a direct reference to the 1951 Convention.

Justice appears to be the most straightforward area in terms of implications on gender equality. This policy area is expected to be fundamentally impactful on gender equality in capability groups, since protection of rights and freedoms enshrined in the EU legal framework, including gender equality, constitutes an objective of this policy area.

**Table 7.1 Gender Budgeting Analysis of Six Policy Areas Based on the Annual Budgets of 2014 and 2015 and the 2014–2020 Multiannual Financial Framework**

| Policy Area | Employment, Social Affairs and Inclusion | Home Affairs | Justice | Development and Cooperation | Research and Innovation | Education and Culture |
|---|---|---|---|---|---|---|
| **Stated policy objective (as recognized in the budget and the key legislations in the area)** | To support Europe 2020 objectives of smart, sustainable and inclusive growth | Creating an area of free movement where security is provided, and human rights are respected | Effective exercise of EU citizens' rights and promotion of non-discrimination and equality | Crisis prevention, peace-building, promotion of democracy and human rights | To create job opportunities, drive growth and competitiveness, and address pressing societal challenges | Europe 2020 education targets, excellence in science, support to the creative sector |
| **Gender equality spectrum** | a, b, c, d, e | a, b, c, d, e | a, b, c, d, e | a, b, c, d, e | a, b, c, d, e | a, b, c, d, e |
| **Gender equality impact** | Direct, high | Direct, high | Direct, high | Direct, high | Direct, high in a and b. Indirect, medium in c, d, e. | Direct, high in a, b, d. Indirect, medium in c, e. |
| **Whether gender equality impact/ spectrum are reflected in policy objectives** | Gender equality is recognised as an overall policy objective with varying implementation in different budget items | Gender equality spectrum and impact are not recognised. | Gender equality is recognised as an overall policy objective with varying implementation in different budget items | Gender equality spectrum and impact are not recognised. | Gender equality is recognised as an overall policy objective with varying implementation in different budget items | Gender equality is recognised as an overall policy objective with varying implementation in different budget items |
| **Data on the gender of participants/ beneficiaries** | Limited | Not available | Not available | Not available | Not available | Limited |

Financial assistance in Development and Cooperation enables the EU to spread its own norms and values, including gender equality, to its periphery using the soft power of conditionality. Development policies impact gender equality substantially in several interconnected dimensions, including the fight against poverty, the fight against diseases primarily affecting women, international trade policies affecting women's access to production, sustainable development and agriculture and its gender effects (Momsen 2010). This also goes for security and peace building, not only because women are particularly adversely affected by conflict as targets of sexual and otherwise violence but also because they have a significant role to play in conflict resolution.[5] As a result, this policy area is likely to result in a direct and high impact on all capability groups.

In the field of EU Research and Innovation policy gender equality has been an issue of long-standing concern, since the Helsinki Group recognised science in 2002 as a primary area for gender mainstreaming (Rees 2002). The ongoing Horizon 2020 Programme aims to foster gender balance in research teams and leadership and to integrate a gender dimension to science and innovation.[6] Research and Innovation Policy is likely to make a significant and direct impact on capability group a as a result of the mandate to ensure gender balance in research employment and on capability group b as a result of the mandate to ensure gender balance in research leadership. This policy area is also likely to make an impact on other capability areas, as a result of the integration of a gender perspective into science, although this impact is likely to be less direct and substantial (Cengiz and Beveridge 2015, 71).

Education and Culture is also likely to have a significant impact on gender equality, although this impact is less immediate than it is in the area of Research and Innovation. Over time, the focus in education shifted from girls' lower representation in early education to boys' underperformance and higher drop-out rates.[7] Rather than gender on its own, complex intersecting inequalities including immigration status, disability, economic and geographical location of the family and LGBT status seems to affect the performance in education.[8] Education and Culture is likely to make a significant and direct impact on capability groups a, b and d. This is because this policy includes programmes (such as Creative Europe) which if subjected to gender mainstreaming could increase women's access to employment and leadership in the creative sector and would give them the opportunity to express their views and opinions creatively and artistically. An impact on capability groups c and e through improved access to education, employment and leadership is also expected, although these would most likely be less direct and substantial.

Despite the direct and high impact of all policies on the majority of capability groups, there are significant inconsistencies between them in terms of whether or not they recognise gender equality as a policy objective; and in terms of to what extent they show commitment to gender mainstreaming in policy implementation and spending. The majority of EU policies while recognising gender equality as an overarching policy objective, show varying commitment to it when it comes to implementation and spending decisions. More worryingly, the significant impact on

gender equality is not recognised in Home Affairs and Development and Cooperation. For instance, in the context of Development and Cooperation gender equality
is recognised only as an indicator of good governance rather than a policy objective
on its own (Cengiz and Beveridge 2015, 64).

This inconsistent commitment to gender equality contradicts with the EU's overall high-level legal and political commitment to gender equality as a principle and to
gender mainstreaming as an implementation instrument (see for example Beveridge
2007). This means that even those EU policies that show a strong commitment
to gender equality are likely to make limited positive impact on gender equality,
because gender equality issues, such as poverty, immigration and asylum seeking-
status, have complex societal dimensions, which fall under the scope of various policies and which can only be addressed through collective and consistent action. Thus,
if gender equality is not consistently recognised as a fundamental policy objective,
issues with a significant impact on gender equality cannot be addressed effectively.

Equally importantly, several policies are not sufficiently transparent regarding
the allocation of resources to different policy objectives. Programmes and actions
with different policy objectives are grouped together under umbrella policies, which
makes it difficult to observe how the EU spending is distributed among different
policy objectives. This gives the discretion to the European Commission and other
authorities involved in EU spending to strategically prioritise certain objectives over
others in spending; and it potentially raises the risk of gender equality being overshadowed by other objectives. This is also a general problem of budgetary accountability as it makes it difficult for institutions involved in budgetary accountability,
such as the EP, and citizens to observe how resources are used.

This problem is particularly acute in the context of the 'Rights, Equality and Citizenship' programme of Justice policy.[9] This programme brings together the policy
objectives of previously separate Fundamental Rights and Citizenship, Daphne III
and Progress programmes. Daphne III was a highly successful flagship EU programme tackling gender-based violence.[10] Daphne's policy objectives are now mixed
with diverse and distinct other policy objectives, including the protection of personal
data, the protection of the rights of the child and the empowering of consumers.
In other words, the fight against gender-based violence will now have to compete
against other policy objectives to attract sufficient funding and if other policy objectives are prioritised, the fight against gender-based violence will suffer substantially.

Finally, almost none of the EU policies analysed here incorporate a systematic
and consistent data-collection phase to monitor whether the policy has achieved
its objectives and if not, what should be changed to make implementation more
effective. Particularly, the lack of collection of gender-aggregated data with regard to
beneficiaries and participants of EU programmes makes it very difficult to observe
the impact on gender equality and other intersecting inequalities. This is particularly
significant for policies that rely on national authorities and actors in implementation. Programmes that involve a complex multilevel enforcement regime, such as the
European Social Fund, might suffer from varying degrees of commitment to gender

equality across different Member States. As a result, data collection with regard to the implementation of such programmes becomes particularly important to prevent a potential multilevel governance fatigue from jeopardising gender equality objectives.

As a result, at present the EU budget scores very low from the perspective of gender equality and there is substantial room for improvement for the EU budget to satisfy the conditions of gender budgeting. Most notably, gender equality as an overarching objective as well as the gender equality impact and spectrum of individual policies need to be recognised and reflected on in budgetary decisions. Similarly, implications on gender equality need to be taken into account and gender-aggregated data needs to be collected once the policy has been implemented. These are also necessary action points to improve budgetary accountability and democracy and to respect EU's general commitment to gender mainstreaming in the budgetary context.

The primary duty to follow gender budgeting falls to the European Commission and other EU institutions that plan and implement the EU budget. Nevertheless, as the EU institution representing citizen interests and entrusted with the task of budget-making and budgetary accountability, the EP enjoys a unique position as a potential gender budgeting advocate. The following section briefly discusses the EU budgetary process and politics before the chapter turns to the questions of whether and how the Parliament could play the gender budgeting advocate role in the face of some serious exogenous and endogenous challenges.

## EU BUDGETARY PROCESS AND POLITICS

EU budgetary process is technocratic and expertise-driven, as it is in many other polities. Arguably, the EU budgetary process is relatively more complex and potentially less transparent also due to the structure of the EU as a multilevel organisation, which puts Member States in the position of main budget contributors, and the idiosyncratic EU budgetary politics, which involves three institutions in budget-making.

Seventy-six per cent of EU spending comes from Member-State contributions (as a rule, 1.23 per cent of each Member State's Gross National Income).[11] Budget negotiations are a zero-sum political bargaining game, as a decrease in one Member State's contribution must be balanced by an increase in another's (Hageman 2012, 26). Similarly, an increase in spending in one policy area must be balanced out by a decrease in spending in another. As it was reflected on the discourse of the Brexit referendum, national governments' individual contributions are subject to significant checks and balances and at times populist political limitations at the national level.

Since the 2008 economic and financial crisis and the imposition of austerity politics both at the EU and national levels, Member-State contributions have been subject to even more intense political scrutiny at the national level. As a result, national veto players with power over the national budgetary process, most notably national parliaments, political coalitions and at times local and regional governments, significantly limit national governments' budgetary negotiation mandate (Hageman

2012, 25). Since Council negotiations take place behind closed doors and centre on EU expenditure, spending and national contributions as a package deal, individual national contributions rather than the substance of the budget and its strategic priorities dominate budgetary negotiations (Hageman 2012, 28).

In 2008–2009, a budgetary review and reform process took place primarily due to the Member States' dissatisfaction with the inefficiency of the budgetary process.[12] In terms of strategic priorities, the reform process centred on the economic policy objectives of competitiveness and efficiency, and did not pay any attention to social objectives and equality. Additionally, the Lisbon Treaty changed significantly the budgetary procedure in terms of institutional politics between the Commission, EP and the Council. The Treaty brought forward a similar procedure to the ordinary legislative procedure (previously the 'co-decision procedure').

In the light of this procedure, firstly, the Council of Ministers adopts the Multiannual Financial Framework (hereinafter MFF) after receiving the consent of the EP, which defines budgetary priorities and sets spending ceilings for the following five years (Article 312 of the Treaty on the Functioning of the EU, hereinafter TFEU). Before Lisbon Treaty, MFF was a non-binding inter-institutional agreement, which was agreed between the Commission and the Council subject to unanimous common accord of the Member States. The Parliament was able to exercise a take it or leave it veto power on it only. After Lisbon, MFF enjoys elevated status as a binding budgetary agreement setting the spending limits for the next five years and the Parliament enjoys more substantial, formal powers within the MFF process.

Article 314 TFEU establishes the EU budgetary process (see textbox 7.2). Rules 86–98 of the Rules of Procedure of the EP further defines the budgetary process within the EP. According to this, before the adoption of the annual budget, all EU institutions submit requested budgets for the following financial year to the European Commission. The Commission prepares the draft budget by bringing these together with its own resource needs. The Commission then submits the draft budget to the Council as well as the EP. First the Council adopts its position on the draft budget. The Parliament could then propose amendments to the budget, adopt the budget as it is or do nothing (the latter of which is very unlikely to happen). If the Parliament proposes amendments, the budget is adopted as a result of a conciliation committee procedure.

In the light of the Parliament's procedural rules, the Budgetary Committee plays the key role in the budgetary process. The Committee is primarily responsible for drawing up a report on the budget, whereas other committees may deliver an opinion (rule 86a). Individual members of the Budgetary Committee, other committees, a political group or one twelfth of the Members of the Parliament (the so-called low threshold) can table amendments on the Council's position subject to a majority vote (rule 88). The amendments and their justifications are then passed on to the Council and the Commission (rule 88).

EP and the Council collectively subject the Commission to budgetary accountability using budgetary discharge powers (Article 319 TFEU). Within the Parliament,

---

**Textbox 7.2**
**The EU Budgetary Process (Article 314 TFEU)**

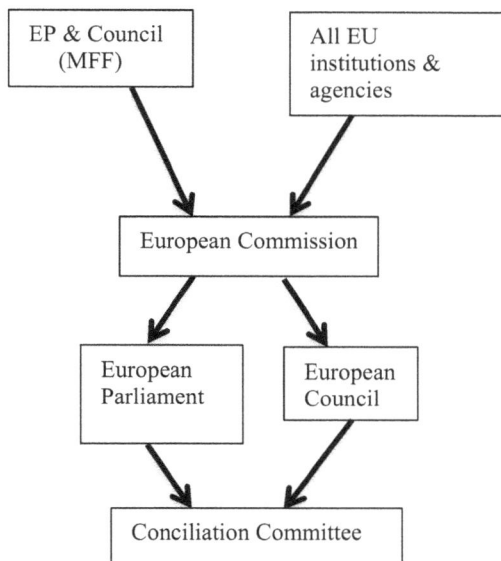

```
┌─────────────┐        ┌──────────────┐
│ EP & Council│        │ All EU       │
│ (MFF)       │        │ institutions &│
│             │        │ agencies     │
└─────────────┘        └──────────────┘
        │                    │
        ▼                    ▼
       ┌──────────────────────────┐
       │  European Commission     │
       └──────────────────────────┘
          │                  │
          ▼                  ▼
  ┌──────────────┐    ┌──────────────┐
  │ European     │    │ European     │
  │ Parliament   │    │ Council      │
  └──────────────┘    └──────────────┘
          │                  │
          ▼                  ▼
       ┌──────────────────────────┐
       │  Conciliation Committee  │
       └──────────────────────────┘
```

---

the Budget Committee and Budgetary Control Committees are primarily responsible for observing the implementation of the budget (rule 92a). The Budgetary Control Committee provides a report on the discharge of the Commission, whereas other committees contribute to the process by delivering an opinion. The Parliament takes the final decision of granting, delaying or not granting the discharge decision with the majority of its members (Annex IV to the rules of procedure of the Parliament).

The budgetary procedure gives seemingly equal power to the Council and the Parliament as co-budget-makers. Nevertheless, in budgetary politics the Parliament enjoys significantly less power than the Council. This is because, particularly in the light of tighter deadlines, the post-Lisbon budgetary procedure makes it easier for the Council and the Parliament to disagree on the entirety of the budget, compared with the pre-Lisbon procedure (see Article 272 of the Treaty Establishing the European Community), which allowed the Parliament to pass amendments subject to the agreement of the Council (Benedetto 2012, 41). Given that the position of the Council on the budget represents a painstakingly negotiated position between twenty-seven governments with different interests and subject to different political limitations, it will be politically extremely costly for the EP to disagree with the budget unless there is a significant reason to do so.

Additionally, it will not be in the best interest of the Parliament to prevent the adoption of the budget. This is because, if the budget fails to be adopted, the previous year's budget continues to stay in force and the Parliament does not enjoy the power to increase EU spending for that year (Article 315 TFEU). Also, the Parliament is not a homogeneous institution, but it consists of several committees and political party groups who might not necessarily represent a unified position with regard to budgetary priorities and objectives. As a result, given the political and institutional repercussions of rejecting the budget, the Parliament has never objected to the budget on substantive policy points, but when the Parliament used its veto power or disagreed with the budget in the past (in 1980, 1985, 2006 and 2011), it was with the aim of increasing the level of EU spending.

## GENDERING THE EU BUDGET: THE ROLE OF THE EUROPEAN PARLIAMENT

Given that the other two institutions involved in the budgetary process primarily look after their own interests as the spender (the Commission) and the provider (the Council) of the budget, the Parliament is the best placed institution to advocate citizen interests in the budgetary process. This position makes the Parliament a potential gender budgeting advocate. Nevertheless, whether or not the Parliament could play this role depends on whether or not the Parliament could use its budgetary powers as a veto power and block the budgetary process if its call for gender budgeting is not recognized by other institutions. So far, the Parliament fell short of playing this role. The FEMM Committee has been calling for gender budgeting with increasing urgency during the budgetary process and the Committee was also pivotal in the passing of a resolution on gender budgeting in the Parliament's plenary.[13] Nevertheless, these efforts have not resulted in any significant change in the EU budgetary process or the procedures and practices of other EU institutions.

As explained in the previous section, budgetary process and politics limits significantly the Parliament's role as a budgetary veto player. Accordingly, in playing the role of gender budgeting advocate, the Parliament faces some crucial endogenous and exogenous challenges. The primary endogenous challenge stems from the fragmented nature of the Parliament as an institution consisting of various committees and political party groups. This is further reinforced by the fact that the FEMM Committee, the key Parliamentary actor representing women's interests, does not enjoy any formal powers within the budgetary process (see also Ahrens 2016; Rolandsen Agustín 2012). As a result, FEMM Committee's mere voicing of its call for gender budgeting during budgetary negotiations is not sufficient to see a policy change but more tangible actions, such as questioning policy choices in terms of their gender effects during budgetary and discharge procedures in the Plenary are necessary.

To achieve this end, FEMM Committee members will have to rely on *internal* coalition building with the Budget and Budgetary Control Committees, who enjoy more tangible powers in the budgetary processes, with the objective of voicing a unified position on gender budgeting. In building this coalition a particularly important role falls on FEMM Committee members who are also members of the Budget and Budgetary Discharge Committees. Similarly, the Parliament's Gender Mainstreaming Network provides a potential strategic platform for coalition building with Members of the Parliament, who are members of other committees but share a strong position on gender equality. Given the strict time limits surrounding the budgetary process, the Parliament's procedural rules at times imposing a straight-jacket on the Plenary debate and the enormity of EU budget as a policy document, gender equality competes against various other political priorities in budgetary debates. As a result, the coalition between MEPs will have to be particularly strong and persistent in order to be able to make a case for gender budgeting during the budgetary process.

The Parliament faces two crucial exogenous challenges in its role as a gender budgeting advocate. Firstly, despite the Lisbon reforms increasing the Parliament's budgetary powers, opaque negotiations between national governments determine the outcome of the budgetary process to a large extent. Secondly, all EU policies and politics with a social dimension seem to have been overshadowed by the neoliberal agenda transfixed on economic policy objectives of growth and competitiveness (Kantola and Verloo 2018). In the specific case of the EU budget, budgetary debates revolve around strategic priorities of border security and migration and growth and competitiveness without a reference to gender, even though both migration and economic growth make a significant impact on gender equality.[14]

In order to take advantage of this general political climate, which is not particularly hospitable to equality, one might be tempted to frame gender equality as a strategic instrument to achieve growth and competitiveness, among others, through women's equal participation to economic production. Nevertheless, this comes with the substantial risk of significantly limiting the ambitions and scope of gender equality as a principle and relegating it to a toothless box-ticking activity. Previous similar experiences in gender mainstreaming illustrate that using the neoliberal frame indeed results in serious caveats and limitations to gender equality (Elomäki 2015).

Instead, in order to overcome both exogenous challenges EP and other advocates of gender equality could rely on alternative political frames and build *external coalitions* with actors, who are influential on the budgetary position of national governments and who share a commitment to gender equality. National parliaments enjoy strong veto powers over the national governments' positions within the EU budgetary process. Thus, national parliaments and in particular parliamentary committees with an interest in equality appear as the natural partners to push the national governments to take gender equality into consideration in the budgetary process.

After the EU's less than perfect management of the 2008 financial and economic crisis and the imposition of austerity policies on the EU Member States, its legitimacy and credibility are under more question than ever. Similarly, the European

Commission and other EU institutions are under intense public and civil society scrutiny with regard to corporate lobbying and revolving doors, particularly after previous Commission President Jose Manuel Barosso's joining to Goldman Sachs upon leaving the office. Arguably the current crisis in the legitimacy of EU institutions compares to the crisis caused by the corruption scandal in the Santer Commission.

This general political climate of distrust towards the EU institutions and calls for increased accountability provides a window of opportunity for coalition building between the EU Parliament, the FEMM Committee, national parliaments and other actors with an interest in gender equality, such as national and EU-level civil-society organisations, with a view to influence the position of national governments in the EU budgetary process. If these actors successfully frame gender budgeting as a mechanism for budgetary accountability, they can push for gender budgeting as part of the general agenda for increased democracy and accountability. Experiences in other countries, where gender budgeting enjoys a constitutional status, such as Austria, show that when accepted as part of a broader agenda for accountability and democracy, gender budgeting is more likely to enjoy a high legal and political status (Steger 2010).

## CONCLUSIONS

This chapter proposed an original capability-based methodology for gender budgeting in the EU. The scrutiny of the EU budget in the light of this methodology reveals that EU's high-level political and legal commitment to gender commitment is not followed through in the budgetary process and spending decisions. In the shadow of the inconsistency between different EU policies regarding whether and to what extent their gender equality spectrum and impact are recognized and reflected on in budgetary decisions, complex gender equality issues with several societal dimensions are unlikely to be addressed effectively. In order to honour the EU's commitment to gender equality and gender mainstreaming, gender equality as a principle needs to be horizontally incorporated into the budget-making and budgetary accountability processes.

EP is the only institution potentially and strategically advocating citizen interests in the budgetary processes and this unique position makes the Parliament a potential gender budgeting advocate. Nevertheless, the Parliament faces significant endogenous and exogenous challenges and limitations in this role, including its fragmented nature as an institution, its limited veto powers within the budgetary process vis-à-vis the national governments and the overarching neoliberal efficiency and competitiveness discourse dominating EU policies and politics. Whether or not the Parliament could make an effective case for gender budgeting very much depends on whether the Parliament could take advantage of the emerging frames of democracy and accountability and build external and internal coalitions to voice gender equality consistently during the budgetary process.

There are other issues significantly connected to gender budgeting this chapter could not address given the limited scope. Most notably, this chapter confined with using the capability approach to screen the EU budget rather than proposing an alternative deliberative participatory budgetary process, which would give citizen's a voice in the budgetary process regarding capabilities essential to their well-being. If the capability approach is to be fully incorporated into gender budgeting, the budgetary process needs to be essentially participatory. Naturally, this depends on the macro-level question of whether or not alternative political frames for democratic citizen-led policy-making could penetrate into the currently significantly technocratic and secretive EU budgetary process. This chapter leaves this essential question of budgetary reform to future research.

## NOTES

1 See European Parliament Resolution of 14 March 2017 on EU funds for gender equality, 2016/2144 (INI). http://www.europarl.europa.eu/sides/getDoc.do?type=TA&reference=P8-TA-2017-0075&language=EN. Also see European Parliament Resolution on Gender Budgeting in the EU Budget – The Way Forward. http://www.europarl.europa.eu/meet-docs/2014_2019/plmrep/COMMITTEES/FEMM/DV/2018/09-03/20180828DraftResolut ionGenderBudgetingintheEUBudget-the way forward_EN.pdf.

2 See Opinion of the Committee on Women's Rights and Gender Equality for the Committee on Budgets on the drafts general budget of the European Union for the financial year 2019 (2018/2046 (BUD)). Opinion of the Committee on Women's Rights and Gender Equality for the Committee on Budgets on the draft general budget of the European Union for the financial year 2018 (2017/2044 (BUD)).

3 Our analysis focused on the EU's 2014 and 2015 annual budgets as well as the 2014–2020 Multiannual Financial Framework. We specifically looked at Budget titles on Employment, Social Affairs and Inclusion (Title 04), Home Affairs (Title 18), Justice (Title 33), Development and Cooperation (Title 21), Research and Innovation (Title 08) and Education and Culture (Title 15). This was for space and scope reasons and also because we expected as an intuition a direct and substantial impact on gender equality in these titles.

4 UNCHR (1991) Guidelines on the Protection of Refugee Women, Geneva: UNCHR and UNCHR (2002) Guidelines on International Protection: Gender-related Persecution within the Context of Article 1A (2) of the 1951 Convention, HCR/GIP/02/01.

5 United Nations Security Council Resolution 1325 (2000) on Women, Peace and Security.

6 See Horizon 2020 Regulation and European Commission Guidance, Gender Equality in Horizon 2020 at http://ec.europa.eu/research/participants/data/ref/h2020/grants_manual/hi/gender/h2020-hi-guide-gender_en.pdf.

7 See European Commission (2014), Education and Training Monitor at http://ec.europa.eu/education/library/publications/monitor14_en.pdf.

8 See Network of Experts on Social Aspects of Education and Training at http://www.nesetweb.eu/policy-priorities/policy-themes-outlines/#dyp.

9 Regulation (EU) No 1381/2013 of the European Parliament and of the Council of 17 December 2013 establishing a Rights, Equality and Citizenship Programme for the 2014 to 2020, 28.12.2013 OJ L354/62.

10  See http://ec.europa.eu/justice/grants1/programmes-2007-2013/daphne/index_en.htm.

11  See Council Decision 7 June 2007 on the system of the European Communities' Own Resources, 2007/436/EC, 23.6.2007 OJ L163/17.

12  See http://europa.eu/rapid/press-release_MEMO-10-503_en.htm.

13  See note 1 above.

14  See the 2019 budgetary debate at http://www.europarl.europa.eu/sides/getDoc.do?pub Ref=-%2f%2fEP%2f%2fTEXT%2bCRE%2b20181022%2bITEM-014%2bDOC%2bXML %2bV0%2f%2fEN&language=EN.

# Part III

## THE ROLE OF MEPs IN STEERING GENDER EQUALITY

# 8

# 'Feminist to Its Fingertips'?

## Gendered Divisions of Labour and the Committee on Women's Rights and Gender Equality

*Mary K. Nugent*

In 2011, Mikael Gustaffson, Member of the European Parliament (MEP) from Sweden's Left Party, took over as chair of the European Parliament (EP) Committee for Women's Rights and Gender Equality (FEMM),[1] becoming the first man to do so since the committee's inception in 1984. The Parliament's press release announcing the change described Gustaffson's appointment as 'a clear signal that championing gender equality is not the sole responsibility of women', and Gustaffson was described as being 'Feminist to His Fingertips' (European Parliament 2011). This personnel change for the FEMM Committee was notable because it is contrary to the expected and usual gendered division of labour, where women take lead when it comes to issues of gender equality in politics (see for example Childs 2001; Childs and Krook 2006; Vega and Firestone 1995; Wängnerud 2009).

This chapter considers the question of gendered divisions of labour in politics, and in particular the gendered responsibility for gender equality. In some respects, the gendered order of the EP has changed dramatically in the past thirty years, with the per cent women MEPs more than doubling in the past thirty years.[2] Yet while 'forces of change' have successfully seen many reforms in terms of women's inclusion into politics in general and the EP in particular, the 'forces of resistance'[3] and the depth of institutional norms and practices mean that in many contexts the gendered division of labour is remarkably enduring.

To explore how competing forces of resistance and change have played out in the case of the EP, I turn to arguably the most explicitly gendered body within the parliament – the FEMM Committee. The chapter first outlines the development and history of FEMM, considering its power, role, and place in the Parliament. The chapter then goes on to evaluate the concept and reality of gendered division of labour in the context of FEMM, ultimately arguing that the relative stability of a gendered division of labour in this case demonstrates how deeply embedded the gendered order of power is within the FEMM Committee, the Parliament, and politics.

## HISTORY OF THE COMMITTEE ON
## WOMEN'S RIGHTS AND GENDER EQUALITY

The first direct elections to the EP in 1979 saw significant progress on the representation of women: with sixty-eight seats women made up 16.6 per cent of all MEPs – more than double the 6 per cent before direct elections. This also stood in stark contrast to most Member States' national parliaments – only Denmark's parliament exceeded the EP in women's representation, and many saw significantly lower proportions of women, with women making up 3 per cent of the UK parliament, and 4 per cent in France and Ireland (Kohn 1981). MEPs keen to see this progress reflected in the committee arrangements called on Parliament President Simone Veil to create an Ad Hoc Committee on Women's Rights (Vainiomäki 2013, 17), and in October 1979 the motion to create an Ad Hoc Committee on Women's Rights was approved. The first set of candidates were elected shortly after, and with twenty-four women and eleven men it was the first committee where women were a majority of members (ibid., 18).

Following the dissolving of the Ad Hoc Committee in 1980, a 'Committee of Inquiry into the Situation of Women in Europe' was set up in 1981, proving to be the immediate predecessor of FEMM. The Committee of Inquiry's purpose was to monitor the situation of women in countries of the European Community. A series of reports later, and the members of the Committee of Inquiry voted on a final resolution to be put to the plenary in December 1983. In addition to its own assessments of the situation of women in Europe, the Committee of Inquiry had legislation referred to it, and itself proposed reports of inquiry and opinions on issues that affect women. It was this engagement with the broader legislative work of the parliament that caused a debate in 1982 on the nature of the Committee of Inquiry, and whether the special temporary committee status was appropriate going forward (Vainiomäki 2013, 29). In its resolution at the close of the 1982–1984 parliamentary session, the Committee of Inquiry expressed its hope that the new parliament will set up a standing committee on women's rights, to ensure that the issues they had raised will be developed further.

The first standing committee was indeed instituted following the second direct elections to the EP in 1984 (Gustafsson 2011a, 6) and named the 'Committee on Women's Rights and Equal Opportunity' (the name was changed to 'Committee on Women's Rights and Gender Equality in 2004). The remit of FEMM has enlarged over time; during 1989–1994 session, for example, responsibility for social and training policy in respect of women was added to FEMM's responsibilities. The current-day FEMM Committee has seven main areas of responsibility,[4] including the definition and promotion of women's rights in the Union, equal opportunities in the labour work, and removal of sex-based violence and discrimination.

## Role and Powers of FEMM

While the remit is broad, and many have argued that it plays a central role in gender policy development in the parliament and in Europe (Jacquot 2015; van der Vleuten 2007), there is a widespread perception, including amongst MEPs, that the FEMM Committee is one of the least powerful in parliament. Hausemer (2006) found FEMM to be the least active committee on a number of measures: it had the lowest mean attendance (36.8 per cent), was the source of the smallest number of parliamentary questions and produced just 45 out of a total of 2,412 reports during the 5th parliamentary term. Renman and Conroy (2014) find similar patterns of activity and status, measuring legislative influence of committees by looking at the production of 'Ordinary Legislative Procedure' (OLP). Though only one of many legislative procedures in the EP, the OLPs are the most commonly used and most important procedures. Of the 433 OLPs produced by committees in the 7th parliamentary term, FEMM produced only 4 (ibid., 4)

The relatively low status of FEMM is perhaps a function of both issue area and limited set of enforcement tools – a finding mirrored in Grace's (2016) work on the Canadian House of Common's Standing Committee on The Status of Women, who concluded that while the presence of a 'feminist voice' was an important contribution to the Canadian Parliament, the committee was limited in its ability to actually compel the government to act and bring about significant gender mainstreaming.

## Neutral Status

A distinct and important feature of FEMM is its 'neutralised' status. One of only two such committees, designation as a 'neutral' committee means that membership of the FEMM Committee falls outside of the usual one committee limit imposed on MEPs. Thus, FEMM members are full members of two committees, and potentially also substitute for a third. FEMM membership therefore involves taking on an additional burden, and the productivity of FEMM is dependent on a degree of voluntary engagement on the part of MEPs. Ahrens (2016) argues that the neutralized status partly explains the limited power of the committee in the parliament, as neutralized status entails 'an additional workload, thematic exclusion and symbolic disregard' (2). The causal direction here is of course difficult to entangle – the neutralised status is not an accident, but rather a procedural feature put in place because of the import and strategic tools given to the issue in the first place. Thus, rarely in charge of legislative and composed of MEPs for whom this is a secondary assignment, FEMM is best understood as a consultative body whose power depends on the desire of its members and the parliament more broadly to enact significant change.

This 'second-order membership' is an important distinction regardless of its causal role in the low status of the committee and is a useful feature for the purposes of studying engagement in gender issues by MEPs. While membership of FEMM is, like all other committees, shaped by party groups (the relative sizes of which determine the group make-up of each committee), the neutral status of FEMM means that MEPs joining and *engaging* in committee activity is much closer to a truly individual act than most examples of legislative behaviour. Thus, membership of and activity within FEMM provides an indicator of a desire and interest in representing women, and thus can be a useful way to understand the place and value of gender equality issues in the Parliament over time.

## GENDERED DIVISION OF LABOUR IN PARLIAMENTS

Both academic research and political discourse would lead one to expect much of the work FEMM to be primarily made up of women MEPs, acting on behalf of women across Europe. Political discourse (and perhaps also common sense) often suggests that democracy should 'look like' the people it represents, with politicians drawing on their own identity and experiences as evidence of their ability to speak with authority on an issue. The scholarly research broadly supports the idea that, both theoretically and empirically, the presence of women matters for both symbolic and substantive reasons (Mansbridge 1999; Phillips 1995).

The theoretical framework for conceptualising facets of representation that many scholars turn to comes from Pitkin (1967), who breaks down the idea of representation in a few interrelated components. Most importantly for this chapter, she distinguishes between 'descriptive representation' – the extent to which the representative resembles the represented – and 'substantive representation', which is the extent to which the actions and views of representatives resemble the interests of those they represent. Significant bodies of work are concerned with how these two concepts interact, asking when, how, and why descriptive representation shapes substantive representation.

The connection between the descriptive and substantive representation has been a particularly interesting and thorny question for scholars interested in understanding changing gender balances of legislative bodies. Though women lawmakers are more similar than they are different to their male counterparts, research in a variety of national contexts suggest that women sometimes deviate from the male norm of political behaviour, and in particular are more likely to favour 'women's issues'. For example, Wängnerud (2000) found that in the case of the Swedish Parliament over twenty years, 75 per cent of women in parliament addressed issues of social and family policy, compared to 44 per cent of men. In the US context, Osborn (2012) and Swers (2002, 2013, 2001) both find a small but significant difference between male and female legislators, with women being more likely to be active on 'women's issues'. These gender differences have been found in a range of national and institutional contexts, and in a range of legislative behaviours including the asking of parliamentary questions, signing of parliamentary petitions, and in the tabling of Private Members Bills (Bird 2005; Childs and Withey 2004; Tremblay 1998).

However, other research finds small and sometimes even non-existent gender differences (e.g. Schwindt-Bayer and Corbetta 2004), especially in contexts where parties are polarised and powerful (Frederick 2009). In a review of the literature, Wängnerud (2009) describes 'mixed' results, and thus limited empirical support for a *clear* connection between the presence of women and increased attention on 'women's issues'; in a similar vein, Dodson (2006) argues that the link between descriptive and substantive representation is at best probabilistic, and not deterministic.

Explanations for this tendency – albeit not homogenously – for women to engage more on issues related to women often incorporate some form of 'mandate' as a driver of representation. Bergqvist, Bjarnegård, and Zetterberg (2016) argue that men are less likely to be drivers of gender equality because of what they term the 'gendered leeway'. In the case of advocating for gender equality, the male gender confers a political advantage: the power to choose not to advocate for gender equality without cost. There is an unequal, and gendered, set of perceived mandates as to who has a responsibility to advocate for gender equality, such that 'Female politicians are blamed if they do not pursue "women's issues" while male politicians get credit if they do' (6).

This gendered leeway to substantively represent women comes from differential 'external mandates' – expectations from others (colleagues, voters) to support issues and groups – as well as from differential 'internal mandates' – those expectations politicians place on themselves to particular issues and groups (which in part result from informal gendered rules, and external mandates imposed on individuals). In the case study that Bergqvist, Bjarnegård, and Zetterberg use to illustrate their theory, the Swedish Social Democratic Party and the issue of parental leave and gender equality, they find that male politicians 'have the privilege of larger manoeuvring room that enables them to speak within the gender equality discourse without being delegitimised when they prioritise other issues'. This concept is also illustrated with examples outside of politics; Bekkengen's (2002) study of Swedish couples and their use of parental leave concludes that while it is possible and even desirable for men to take primary responsible for child care, it is not expected. Thus, when men do take on child care responsibilities, they are met with gratitude and reward where a woman would only be fulfilling that which is expected of her (cited in Bergqvist, Bjarnegård, and Zetterberg 2016, 6).

Ideas of internal and external mandates have been implicitly or explicitly present in many theories of women's substantive representation – Franceschet and Piscopo (2008) also describe a 'mandate effect' felt amongst women in the Argentinian Parliament – with female legislators felt a greater sense of obligation to act on behalf of women constituents. While in part these mandates are a result of a broader societal expectation, and perhaps a self-interest to act, the gendered leeway that Bergqvist et al. describe is a result of gender power structures (within and outside of parliament) that determines the place and value of gender equality issues.

## Gendered Committee Membership

The nature of the gendered distribution of members of parliament on committees is an important question for political scientists because of the aforementioned ways such patterns illustrate legislator preferences, party priorities, and the varied perceptions of power and prestige among the range of legislative issues. In addition, legislative committees and the gender dynamics therein are important because committee activity represents an important aspect of legislative behaviour in the EP (McElroy 2006; Yordanova 2011) and in parliaments more broadly (Beloff and Peele 1985; Brazier and Fox 2011; Jogerst 1993; Russell and Benton 2011). The make-up of committees has the potential to change the shape of policy, and in addition the membership of committees can be an important determinant of legislators' career trajectories.

As in other areas of legislative behaviour discussed above, women and men MPs are generally more alike than they are different with constraints such as party allegiances and constituent interests often determining political behaviour. However, consistent patterns have emerged with gender differences in assignments, with women being more likely to be found on committees concerning issues explicitly addressing women, or other 'softer' policy areas. This finding holds true in a variety of national and political contexts, including on English local authorities (Yule 2000), in parliaments across Western Europe (Bolzendahl 2014; Diaz 2005), Danish local politics (Baekgaard and Kjaer 2012), US State legislatures (Carroll 2008), and Latin American legislatures (Barnes 2014; Heath, Schwindt-Bayer, and Taylor-Robinson 2005; Piscopo 2014).

Because of the important place of legislative committees and consistent observation of gendered patterns of memberships, scholars have had to attempt the difficult task of distinguishing between the possibility of men's and women's different preferences on the one hand, and the discrimination – explicit or implicit – that leads women to be limited to committees on policy areas more traditionally associated with women. O'Brien (2012) tries to disentangle these two potential explanations by looking to select committee membership in the UK Parliament, following the introduction in 2010 of elections for committee chairs and members. O'Brien finds no support for the gender-bias hypothesis, and even finds evidence of an advantage for women seeking a committee position. This points to gendered divisions of labour on committee being a function of legislator's policy priorities – a finding supported in other studies, including work on Danish local councils (Baekgaard and Kjaer 2012) and US House of Representatives (Friedman 1996; Frisch and Kelly 2003; Gertzog 1995).

While this conclusion of limited discrimination towards women in committee assignments emerges as a consistent finding, many studies have indicated that as the institution of parliament, and women's presence and place, changes so too does the gendered division of labour of committees. Gertzog (1995) found in the case of the UK parliament that there was strong gender differentiation in committee assignments prior to 1960s, but no apparent pattern since. In their study of the assignments of women senators, Arnold and King (2003) found that the breadth of women's committee assignments increased with their numbers. Similarly, while Carroll's (2008) study of women in US State legislators found 'remarkably persistent' gender different in the types of committees men and women ended up on, gender differences do appear to be less prevalent over time. And Barnes (2014) finds that, in the case of women in Argentine provinces, it is only once women are a sizable proportion that they become less marginalized and confined to women's specific committees (a finding that cannot be explained by women's seniority alone).

Murray and Sénac (2018) seek to explain the traditional gendered divisions on committees, and to account for women's over-representation on 'soft committees' (such as FEMM) and men's over-representation on 'hard' and traditionally masculine committees. They argue that it is 'multiple hidden forces' steering these gendered divisions, with three core explanations: expertise (prior gender gaps in knowledge and experience), seniority (with more established legislators usually having better access to prestigious committees), and gender stereotyping (men and women associate themselves and others with distinct policy areas). Murray and Sénac also point to the subtleties of gendered patterns and pressures within an institution – while explicit discrimination may be rare in many contexts, multiple small implicit pressures and expectations on women may combine to shape membership outcomes. Diamond (1977) finds this to be true in the case of women in four New England legislatures where women were 'channelled' toward certain committees and faced subtle difficulties when women's interest didn't coincide with expectations.

It is worth noting that the study of gendered divisions of labour has focused on the location of women in committees; a key argument of this chapter is to consider not only how women's place changes – with more areas opening up as possible committees for women to become members of – but also when and how men step into the traditionally 'women's' committees, and how institutional shifts broaden the potential place of men on committees. In part this is important because if a changed gendered division of labour means *only* that more areas are now open for women to engage in, but not also any changes in the place and priorities of men, then women's increased engagement on areas outside of traditional women's areas either means that those issues get neglected, or that women take on mainstream issue areas *in addition* to their work on women's issues. The role of men is key not only because they make up a majority of parliament, but also because men's legislative activity shapes what women are able to do.

The nature of FEMM – it's explicit mandate to represent women and second-order membership – along with evidence from other political contexts we would expect the work of the committee to be done mostly by women. This is largely true – both historically and in present, as will be shown later in the chapter. However, the headline figure that women make up a majority of members and leaders of FEMM obscures a more complex picture. The gendered division of labour in an institution, particularly in an area as explicitly 'gendered' as FEMM, is both an important institutional feature and itself indicative of power dynamics and gender norms at play in the institution, and the trajectory of change can give us a glimpse of the ways in which these gendered power dynamics have (or have not) changed over the time in the past three decades.

In order to investigate these questions, my primary source of data comes from membership records and meeting minutes for the FEMM Committee, obtained from the EP's archives.[5] The gender balance of the committee was taken based on membership immediately following committee elections at the beginning and mid-way through each term. Each MEP in the dataset was coded by sex, their membership status (full vs. substitute), and any leadership position they held. The dataset includes 802 MEPs.[6] The activity measurement comes primarily from the meeting minutes from each meeting since 1984, which noted the appointment of authors for reports and opinions for the committee. A total of 409 reports and opinions were identified.

### Gendered Responsibility for Gender Equality

When Mikael Gustaffson took over as chair of FEMM after incumbent chair Eva-Britt Svensson stepped down,[7] as noted in the introduction, many (including Gus-taffson himself) claimed that this turn events as a 'a clear signal that championing gender equality is not the sole responsibility of women' ('Women's Rights Commit-tee's New Chair "Feminist to His Fingertips"' 2011).[8] The quote suggests a sense of inevitable 'progress', with ever increasing levels of gender equality in political institutions, with men stepping up in the area of gender equality both a contribution towards, and illustration of, a trajectory of progress.

Research on changing cultural values and public opinion also gives us reason to believe that male support for feminism is, and will continue to be, an increasingly widespread phenomenon. Norris and Inglehart's 'Rising Tide' (2003) thesis posits that economic development leads, somewhat inevitably, to increasingly broad accep-tance of gender equality. The shift to industrial and later post-industrial society leads to a change in values – from traditional to secular-rational values, and from survival to self-expression values. Thus, as societies develop economically, the centrality of the traditional family declines, and value placed on gender equality increases. As the title of the book indicates, gender equality values are viewed as 'tide', that inevitably sweeps the modern world as economies develop and people (both men and women) change accordingly. This view of gender equality sees the arc of history of linear: there is more development and greater acceptance of gender equality over time, and the diffusion of 'progressive' views of gender equality is a continual and inevitable process.

While Norris and Inglehart's argument does not offer specific predictions as to who will be responsible for the issue of gender equality advocacy, the logic of their argument suggests that over time gender equality is increasingly embraced as a key political value – by women *and* men. This idea is reflected in other work on public

opinion. Bolzendahl and Myers (2004) looked at trends in men and women's attitudes to gender equality in the United States between 1974 and 1998.[9] Broadly
speaking, they find that over time attitudes towards gender equality 'liberalize and
converge' amongst both men and women – with an increasingly clear consensus in
favour of feminist attitudes over time.[10] In a more recent study on social attitudes,
the analysis of the Finnish Gender Equality Barometer[11] offers another example of
this trajectory in public opinion, with public opinion on gender equality liberalising
and converging over time (Kiianmaa 2013). For example, the proportion of men
who agree 'men also benefit from an increase in gender equality' has increased over
time and has begun to catch up with women's (higher) levels of support for this statement (10). Similarly, the number of men supporting the statement 'women should
play a more active role in politics to diversify the range of political expertise' has
increased each year. In each of the years of the survey, a majority of both men and
women believe that equality will increase over the next ten years (9).

Patterns of increased support for the importance of gender equality, particularly
among men, are also evident in recent high-profile initiatives and platforms on the
part of global elites. The UN launched their 'HeForShe' campaign in 2014, with a
stated goal of engaging men and boys as agents for change in the fight for gender
equality. It received widespread attention and discussion; launched at the UN in
New York by actress Emma Watson in September 2014, it has since attracted attention and endorsement from a range of high-profile men, in politics and outside,
including Barack Obama, UN Secretary General Ban Ki-moon, along with business
leaders, university presidents, and other heads of state. The HeForShe campaign
currently has more than 1.3 million men registered as supporters.[12] Similarly, high-
profile male politicians around the world have begun to talk about men's responsibility for gender equality; Canadian Prime Minister Justin Trudeau has become known
for his outspoken support for issues of gender equality, and often refers to himself as
a feminist,[13] and Barack Obama at the 'United State of Women Summit', organised
by the White House in June 2016, declared, 'This is what a feminist looks like.'[14]

This increased prominence of male supporters of gender equality supports the
idea that we are seeing a move towards broad acceptance and male engagement in
gender equality. Progressive political discourse itself often cites the positive relationship between the passage of time and the mainstreaming of gender equality issues.
Canadian Prime Minister Justin Trudeau illustrated this belief in 2015: when asked
why appointing a gender-balanced cabinet was so important to him, he simply
answered 'Because it's 2015'.[15] His answer suggested not only that he viewed male
commitment to feminism as a norm that he both advocates for and sees as non-
controversial, but his stating the year was also meant to indicate that while this might
not have been an obvious decision in previous times, society has progressed enough
no explanation should be required.

There appears then, to be some shifts in normative arguments surrounding the
responsibility for gender equality, as well as organisational changes by groups seeking women's rights. Combined, these offer support for a hypothesis predicting the

gendered division of labour in an institution such as the FEMM Committee in the EP would equalize over time.

However, the 'rising tide' thesis (in the various guises outlined here) has been criticised for its singular and ethnocentric understanding of progress and modernity, and some critics suggest that gender equality is an incidental byproduct of modernisation in the context of existing advanced industrial democracies rather than an inevitable and universal shift in values that will come with the passage of time (Rowley 2006). As the next section goes on to demonstrate, the shift of power is rarely a straightforward of linear process, particularly when it is a question of the less powerful gaining power – at the cost of those currently yielding power.

## Institutional Stability and Women's Roles

By contrast, institutionalist literature emphasises the persistence of institutional norms and practices, and thus would hypothesise a slower and more resistant path to institutional change. Institutionalism is premised on the idea that rules and designs of institutions are powerful in shaping political actors and outcomes, and institutional dynamics have far-reaching effects on political outcomes and activities. New institutionalism (or neo-institutionalism) seeks to incorporate not only formal rules but also informal rules and practices to the study of politics and institutions (see Thelen and Steinmo 1992). Institutional analysis is important not only because it seeks to explain key features of political life, but also because of the persistence of institutions once created – as Mahoney and Thelen (2010) note, 'The idea of persistence of some kind is virtually built in to the very definition of an institution' (4).

Building on these traditions, feminist institutionalism seeks to use gender to understand not only individual actions but also institutions themselves as gendered entities and practices. Acker (1992) was an early articulation of such a fusion, when she argued in 'From Sex Roles to Gendered Institutions' that gender roles and identity are too narrow a unit, and instead an individual's gender only exists in and because of the formal and informal institutions they are situated in. Acker posits that there is a gendered 'understructure' of society's institutions shaping the creation and function of every institution. Feminist institutionalism has continued to develop theoretical and empirically, and in the case of the study of legislatures has explored how in how the 'maleness' of these institutions persist. The embeddedness of male norms in political institutions can sometimes be seen in an institution's literal physical form – Ross (2002) describes multiple ways in which parliamentary buildings[16] are explicitly designed with male and masculine legislators in mind, including a lack of female toilet provision, unwillingness to install crèche provisions in favour of maintaining many bars, and in the case of South Africa a gym that was accessible only through the men's urinals. There are clearly practical barriers created when an institution's facilities are gendered in these ways – but perhaps more importantly these physical expressions of an institution's gendered nature are both symptomatic of, and contributing to, the symbolic meaning created around an institution, that perpetuates the idea that it is a male space. Similarly, Puwar (2004) describes the British Parliament as a 'Palace of Mirrors' – where white men can walk the halls and feel like they belong, seeing a reflection of themselves when they look at the walls adorned with pictures of the previous occupants. As Ross puts it, political institutions were mostly designed with men in mind as the somatic norm, and modern political institutions are filled with signifiers that women's presence is 'tolerated' (194).

Work in contexts outside of the EP points to the 'stickiness' of maleness in political institutions, even where some aspects of the institutions 'progress'. Coffe and Schnellecke (2013) do not find a decrease in the long-standing over-representation of women on committees handling women's issues over time, even as the number of women in the German Parliament increases. Crawford and Pini (2011), in their analysis of the Australian Parliament, conclude that it is hegemonic masculinity in parliament marginalising women into less prestigious politics and keeping men in positions of more comparative power, even (or perhaps especially) when women's presence is increasing.

Applied to the case of the EP in general, and the FEMM Committee in particular, feminist institutionalism offers a number of insights. Ahrens offers a feminist institutionalism analysis of the FEMM Committee as an actor within the parliament and discusses the ways that the actors in the committee have worked with a set of (gendered) rules and norms in order to maximize their power (2016). Ahrens' argument offers support for the idea of 'institutional stickiness'; she argues that institutional norms and practices (such as the formal status of the committee, and issue area responsibility) are have proved persistent in their form, and thus it is only via adaptation to these conditions that the committee has been able to have any effective role in the Parliament.

Feminist institutionalism, and institutionalist approaches more broadly then, would be more pessimistic about the likelihood of a significant change in the place, status, and male interest in the FEMM Committee. Institutionalist approaches do not preclude the possibility of change – change is a key theme of institutionalist work – but draws attention to the power and existence of institutional forms and practices. Through concepts such as path dependency, institutionalism predicts argues that actions that follow the development path established happen more easily than changes to the path that has been undertaken. 'Incentive structures' aid this path dependency; once a set of institutions is in place, actors adapt their strategies of action in ways that reflect and thus reinforce the 'logic' of the system and are generally rewarded when doing so. And 'distributional effects' remind us that institutional are not neutral coordinating mechanisms, but reflect, reproduce, and thus magnify power distributions in politics – those in power become further entrenched as they are increasingly able to garner benefits from the current order. These mechanisms along with the insights from gender politics scholars on the power of patriarchy would predict 'institutional stickiness' and limited change within the FEMM Committee over time.

These two possible expectations – of cultural and political progress towards greater gender equality on the one hand, and institutional persistence on the other – while in some senses are opposites, in reality, forces of change and resistance are present simultaneously, as Hughes and Paxton's important framework notes (2008). To assess the relative strength of these competing forces, I turn to the archival data of FEMM's membership and activity.

## GENDERED DIVISIONS OF LABOUR ON FEMM

### Committee Members

The archival data on committee membership suggest that there has not been a significant shift in the proportion of men on the FEMM Committee, either in absolute terms or relative to their proportion of parliament. As shown in figure 8.1, apart from a relatively high proportion of substitute members in the mid-1980s, the proportion of men on FEMM has remained consistent over time, hovering somewhere around 10 per cent of the committee membership.

As the top line of figure 8.1 shows, the per cent men MEPs in the EP as a whole has declined over time. To test whether any changes over time are simply a reflection of the broader Parliament; in figure 8.2, I compare the proportion of FEMM membership that is male with the proportion of the EP that is male, creating of a ratio of the proportion of men on FEMM: proportion men in the EP. A score of '1' would indicate that the gender balance of FEMM and the EP was the same; a score of 0.5 indicates that the per cent of men on FEMM is half that of the per cent of men in the EP.

A woman MEP is, on average, approximately ten times more likely to be on FEMM than a male MEP, and this has remained fairly consistent for the past thirty years. The ratio ranges from a low of 0.04 to and a high 0.22 – in other words, at

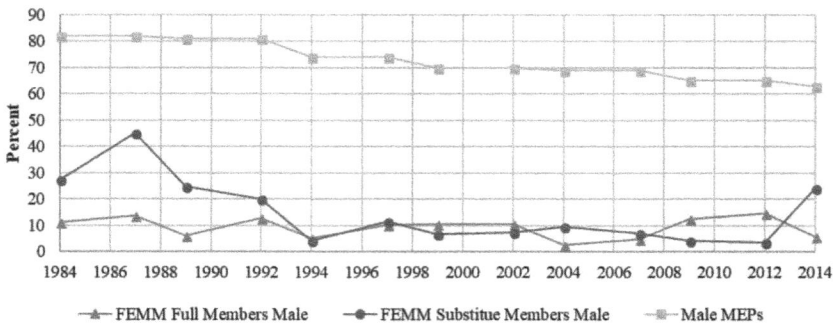

**Figure 8.1   Proportion of Men in European Parliament and on FEMM Committee**

Source: Compiled by author using data from the European Parliament Historical Archives Unit in Luxembourg, with thanks to Alexandra Devantier for her assistance.

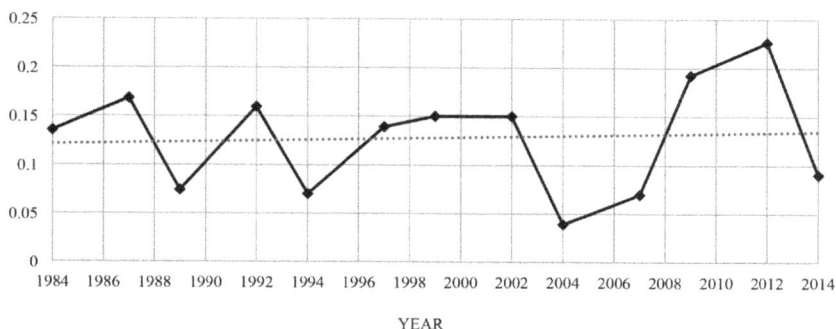

YEAR

**Figure 8.2    Ratio of Per cent Men on FEMM versus Per cent Men in EP**

Source: Compiled by author using data from the European Parliament Historical Archives Unit in Luxembourg, with thanks to Alexandra Devantier for her assistance.

its most gender balanced, the proportion of men on FEMM is less than a quarter of the proportion of men in the EP. As the dashed trend line indicates, there is slight positive increase of this relationship over time, (meaning men become somewhat less under-represented on the committee as time goes on), but the change over time is not statistically significant. There are, at best, only tentative indications that there might be a move towards male MEPs joining FEMM.

This data of course offers limited insight into why male membership is so consistently low. Some tentative hypotheses come from public comments by former committee members. Former committee chair Eva-Britt Svensson said in an interview with a journalist in 2011: 'We have a very conservative majority in Parliament, where gender equality issues have very low status, therefore men are not interested in participating in the work, that's what I believe is the main reason' (Reporting the EU 2011). Svensson echoes the findings of research in other legislative contexts, finding that women's issues have low status and are often left to women.

This sentiment in an exploratory conversation with a former MEP who was a member of the committee in the early 2000s; she said of the committee, 'This particular committee suffered . . . from a slight feeling of guilt that it was not carrying out "proper" EP work'. Of men in particular, she notes, 'The men joined unwillingly and seemed to feel out of place. It was not a popular committee for men to join'. By contrast, another female interviewee I spoke with, who was a substitute member of the committee in the late 1980s and MEP in the socialist political group, was more optimistic about the opinion of the committee held by the broader parliament:

> The need for such a committee became more and more obvious. So, at the beginning [of the discussions about forming a committee] some people, particularly some speeches in the parliament saying that this committee wasn't necessary and so on. . . . That was when we were trying to set up the ad hoc committee. But, as the time went on, those kinds of views were very much in the minority, as it made total sense for a committee

of the parliament to monitor what was happening to all the EEC equality directives and look at the situation of women in the different countries of the European Community.

A more favourable reading of the consistent lack of men on the committee comes from Marc Tarabella, MEP and former FEMM Committee member in a media interview (Reporting the EU 2011): 'I regret that there are so few men on the committee, but I think it might have to do with the fact that a lot of women unfortunately have experienced being treated differently because they are women. And if you can relate, it's easier to engage'.

Such explanations – that women better represent women and are best placed for women in Europe – is not only logical but in line with women and politics scholarship on the substantive representation of women. However, the consistency over time of the degree of men's engagement on FEMM remains puzzling. Many of these public comments and conversations expressed a desire to see more men engaged in the mission and activities of FEMM. One former MEP I spoke with said, 'Both genders are essential when discussing discrimination against one or other one'. Given this seeming desire to change the place of gender equality in the parliament, and the gendered division of labour of this issue, the lack of movement on the place of men on the committee should cause one to question the degree of 'progress' in terms of gender in the institution of the EP.

## Leadership

The leadership of the FEMM Committee consists of a chair, and either three or four vice-chairs. There have been fifty-six appointments to the leadership team of FEMM during the period of study, and of these two have been men (just over 3 per cent). Spanish MEP Raül Romeva served as vice-chair 2007–2009, and Mikael Gustaffson chair 2012–2014. Despite the headlines, there is no clear indication that Mikael Gustaffson's chairship was a part of a broader pattern of men taking on leadership roles with FEMM. Interrogation into the circumstances of these two cases suggests that these men were outliers, rather than a sign of a changing institutions. Mikael Gustaffson was a Swedish MEP representing the Left Party, which describes itself as a socialist feminist political party, while Raül Romeva was an MEP representing the green Catalonia independence party, Iniciativa per Catalunya Verds, which also boasts a distinctly feminist manifesto. This doesn't preclude the possibility that institutional change and feminisation of politics made it possible for these ideological positions to be viably held by men, but in purely descriptive terms, there does not appear to be a systematic shift in leadership team balance.

## Activity and Engagement

Finally, we turn to the activity of men once on the committee, in particular the authoring of reports and opinions. In total, there was record of 409 reports and

**Table 8.1 Reports and Opinions by Men**

| Term | Male-Authored Reports and Opinions | All Reports and Opinions (%) | Male FEMM Members (%) |
|---|---|---|---|
| 1984–1989 | 3 | 7 | 11 |
| 1989–1994 | 2 | 4 | 6 |
| 1994–1999 | 3 | 7 | 5 |
| 1999–2004 | 3 | 4 | 11 |
| 2004–2009 | 3 | 2 | 3 |
| 2009–2014 | 4 | 8 | 13 |

opinions from 1984 to 2014 produced by FEMM, and of these 18 were authored by men. The distribution of this was fairly even over time, as shown in table 8.1.

Male members on the committee are, on average, less likely to author a report or opinion than female FEMM members. Further examination of the reports and opinions written by men suggest two patterns. First, most of these authors were reported by a handful of men who each wrote multiple report; Raül Romeva is an acute example of this, being the source of at least a third of all reports authored by men. Women and politics scholarship terms such people 'critical actors'; as per Childs and Krook's definition (2009), critical actors can be either men or women 'who act individually or collectively to bring about women-friendly policy change' (127).

The second broad pattern is a move away over time from men only authoring reports or opinions on 'masculine' topics, and towards men being seemingly willing to author similar topics to that of women members. For example, one of the first male-authored reports from FEMM was by British Conservative MEP Andrew Pearce, and was about spouses in agriculture and family business.[17] Not only is agriculture a traditionally masculine sphere, but the assumption behind the report (and the interest of the women's rights committee) is that women had a distinct and different role in agriculture – as spouses and supporters of husbands. Less traditional conceptions of gender roles appeared to be present in the more recently authored reports; Raül Romeva's reports varied in topic area, from femicides in Central America and Mexico, to the role of women in the Common Fisheries Policy. The extremely small sample sizes make it hard to claim systematic or institutional change, but the few men who have engaged in the work of FEMM seem to be doing so without limiting themselves to traditionally masculine fields of inquiry.

## FUTURE OF FEMM AND CONCLUSIONS

Though he might have been an outlier, Gustaffson hoped that his leadership position would have lasting impact. In the FEMM newsletter in 2011, he wrote:

Finally, I would like to add that gender equality is not the sole responsibility of women. We can only achieve gender equality with the full cooperation and participation of men

and boys. As chair of this Committee, I hope that my position can contribute to send-
ing this clear and strong message to all those concerned both within and outside the
Parliament. (Gustafsson 2011a)

This message was repeated in a 2011 FEMM report Gustafsson authored, entitled
'Report on Gender Mainstreaming in the Work of the European Parliament', where
it reads

> Awareness of the need for a gender balance in decision-making processes, to be achieved
> by increasing the representation of women on Parliament's governing bodies, on the
> bureaus of political groups, on the bureaux of committees and delegations, in the
> composition of delegations and in other missions, such as election observation, and by
> increasing the representation of men in areas where they are under-represented. (Gus-
> tafsson 2011b)

There is evidence of dynamics of both resistance (or 'stickiness') and change; the
data suggest that men are significantly less likely to be on the FEMM Committee
than women, and once on the committee are less likely to take an active role in the
work of the committee. While this is perhaps unsurprising – women are, after all,
probably more likely to effectively advocate for women's rights – the lack of change
over time is less predictable. Both the academic literature and 'real world' politics
engage in a narrative that suggests there is a degree of inevitable progress towards a
more gender-equal society. While of course this trajectory and 'progress' is seen very
clearly in many areas – especially in gender balance of cabinets and in parliaments
improving – we must also attend to the areas of stability and resistance, and despite
its long history of impressive relatively gender balance, the EP is one such area. In the
case of the FEMM Committee, the resistance and stickiness of the gendered order
that sees women as primarily engaged in the issue of gender equality is a result of both
individual decisions about the relative merits and importance of the issue, but also
of the continued low status of the committee. FEMM likely has fewer men because
it is low status and relatively unimportant to the work of the parliament – but since
the power remains primarily with men and male-dominated structures, that the lack
of men on FEMM likely also perpetuates the low status nature of the committee.

This stability, however, has been taking place within the context of drastic change
in some respects for the EP. In 1984 the EP consisted of MEPs from ten member
countries (of which 18 per cent were women), and by 2014 there were twenty-eight
countries represented (37 per cent of MEPs were women). The powers of the EP
have also changed significantly over this period, from essentially a consultative body,
to one able to legislate and oversee executive functions of the European Union. These
changes are broad ranging; David Farrell said of the parliament, in a quote that is
a favourite of the EP, 'For much of its life, the EP could have been justly labelled a
"multi-lingual talking shop". But this is no longer the case: the EP is now one of the
most powerful legislatures in the world both in terms of its legislative and executive
oversight powers'.[18] Such large-scale changes make it hard to easily track one aspect

of institutional change – in this case the place of gender equality. While this, in some ways, a limitation of this analysis, in other ways the consistency in the levels of male participation FEMM is all the more puzzling.

## NOTES

1 FEMM is the EP abbreviation given to the committee. I here use FEMM to refer to the committee from its 1984 conception to present day rather than the full name, because it has held two different names during this time.

2 From 16 per cent in the first election in 1979, to 37 per cent in the 2014 election (see http://www.europarl.europa.eu/elections2014-results/en/gender-balance.html).

3 'Forces of resistance' and 'forces of change' as concepts in understanding changes over time in the gendered ordered here come from Hughes and Paxton (2008).

4 Rules of Procedure of the European Parliament, Annex VI: 'Committee responsible for: 1. the definition, promotion and protection of women's rights in the Union and related Union measures; 2. the promotion of women's rights in third countries; 3. equal opportunities policy, including the promotion of equality between men and women with regard to labour market opportunities and treatment at work; 4. the removal of all forms of violence and discrimination based on sex; 5. the implementation and further development of gender mainstreaming in all policy sectors; 6. the follow-up and implementation of international agreements and conventions involving the rights of women; 7. encouraging awareness of women's rights'. See also http://www.europarl.europa.eu/sides/getLastRules.do?language=en&reference=RESP-FEMM.

5 With thanks to Alexandra Devantier at the EP's Historical Archives Unit in Luxembourg, for generously facilitating my study visit.

6 But does not represent 802 unique individuals, as many MEPs are reappointed and thus appear in the dataset more than once.

7 Svensson stepped down due to ill health, and Gustaffson was Svensson's alternate.

8 The circumstances of his ascension – that of an incumbent chair unexpectedly stepping down due to ill health – perhaps make the fact of Gustaffson's leadership less indicative of wider attitudes and conditions regarding men's role (compared to, for example, an instance of a man actively seeking out and winning the chair of the FEMM committee). However, the fact remains that a man voluntarily, and with the support of his committee and political leaders, became the chair of a body that for the entirety of its history was led and dominated by women.

9 Using data from the General Social Survey.

10 On most issues, the key exception being abortion.

11 The Gender Equality Barometer surveyed approximately 1,500 Finnish adults in each of 1998, 2001, 2004, 2008 and 2012.

12 See http://www.heforshe.org/en.

13 See http://fortune.com/2016/03/10/justin-trudeau-feminist/.

14 See http://www.huffingtonpost.com/entry/president-obama-this-is-what-a-feminist-looks-like_us_57605770e4b053d433068d9e.

15 See http://www.huffingtonpost.ca/2015/11/05/justin-trudeau-s-because-it-s-2015-comment-gets-international-media-attention_n_8480104.html.

16  She focuses on Parliaments in the UK, Australia and South Africa.

17  Pearce wrote in his memoir of his time on the committee, 1984–1989: 'I was posted to the Committee on Women's Rights. This was a stomping ground for feminists. While I never had any doubts about the rights of women to equality under the law and within the economy, I found some of the affirmative action proposed in the committee to be beyond all sense. My main role on the committee on behalf of our Group was to combat the more nonsensical suggestions brought forward' (Pearce 2013, 78).

18  See  http://www.europarl.europa.eu/sides/getDoc.do?language=EN&type=IM-PRESS &reference=20070615IPR07837.

# 9

# Politicisation of Gender Equality in the European Parliament

## Cohesion and Inter-Group Coalitions in Plenary and Committees

*Markus Warasin, Johanna Kantola[1],*
*Lise Rolandsen Agustín and Ciara Coughlan[2]*

After every crisis, whether constitutional, migration or financial, the image of the EU has been damaged, and the EU has presented itself as a cumbersome and convoluted political system. Growing Euroscepticism is producing significant political upheaval, as seen in the British people voting to leave the EU in 2016 – the ultimate rejection of European integration. Across the continent, both left and right populism is mobilising against the EU as an elite actor and populist parties have gained in popularity and power in the aftermath of the 2008 financial crisis. Populism has transformed national party systems and posed challenges to EU integration.

Gender equality is at the heart of these developments. The consequences of the economic crisis have been highly gendered as austerity policies have erased women's jobs in the public sector and reduced the public services on which women are more dependent than men (Kantola and Lombardo 2017; Karamessini and Rubery 2014). Minority women – who have lived in a permanent state of crisis as a result of structural inequalities and racisms – have been worst effected (Bassel and Emejulu 2017). At the same time, (radical) right populism has challenged gender equality as a key European value, portraying it as either part of the 'elite' EU project to be opposed or best left to the national level (Kuhar and Patternotte 2017). Opposition to gender equality now comes from many directions in Europe (Verloo 2018), including from within the European Parliament (EP) (Kantola and Rolandsen Agustín 2016).

It is within this context that this chapter will explore our key objectives. Firstly, the increasingly politicised nature of gender equality as a policy area within the EP will be investigated. We suggest that the stakes are high in this area, as it relates to conflicts over fundamental values – equality and non-discrimination – which are at the heart of the European integration project. More practically, this politicisation is reflected in intra-group cohesion rates in the parliament when voting on issues of gender equality at plenary and committee level. This is the key empirical issue on which we focus in our analysis. Our second aim relates to the way in which this politicisation affects dynamics at committee level. Here we are interested in the key gender equality actor of the EP, namely the Committee on Women's Right and Gender Equality of the European Parliament (FEMM). We explore its political dynamics and how the FEMM Committee shifts from a consensus orientation (based partially on feminist alliances) to conflictual inter-group relations. The FEMM Committee is not only the most prominent and important EP arena for the promotion of equality between women and men, but also the main arena for politicisation of gender equality policy at the EU level. Political groups are the main agents in this arena and most conflicts are fought along the lines of the parliamentary groups. Intra-group cohesion and inter-group coalition remain key tactical considerations in this politically competitive environment.

More specifically, we argue that inter-group coalitions and intra-group cohesion differ between plenary and committee levels (i.e. FEMM) and that they are particularly relevant in terms of revealing the gendered dynamic of the policy-making processes in the context of the EP as a complex and changing political environment. Thus, we argue that higher levels of intra-group cohesion in addition to inter-group coalition between the political groups of the European People's Party (EPP), Socialists & Democrats (S&D), and Alliance of Liberals and Democrats for Europe (ALDE) are significant in explaining plenary-level patterns. In contrast, at committee level in the FEMM Committee, the coalition between S&D, ALDE, Greens/European Free Alliance (Greens/EFA) and European United Left/Nordic Green Left (GUE/NGL) give the groups a disproportionate influence on the agenda-setting, especially when combined with lower levels of intra-group cohesion in some groups such as the EPP. In this chapter, we explore specific policy processes in order to investigate such intra-group cohesion and inter-group coalitions in the EP and the ways in which they impact decision-making and political dynamics in the increasingly fraught field of gender equality policy-making.

We seek to shed light on these complex processes by combining quantitative and qualitative data. Empirically, the chapter builds on document analysis, voting patterns and MEP interviews. The voting patterns are analysed through data from Vote-Watch Europe,[3] which is an independent organisation producing data on the voting behaviour of MEPs. This data provides a relevant overview of policy processes, but it tells little about the quality of the single vote; caution is therefore needed to avoid overestimating these data (Cicchi 2017). Semi-structured interviews (eighteen in total, conducted in 2014–2016) were carried out with current and former female MEPs from the ALDE (5), S&D (4), Greens/EFA (4), EPP (3), GUE/NGL (1) and EFDD (1). These interviews covered the issues of gender-specific alliances within and across political groups; content and contestations on key policy issues in the field of gender equality; the EP policy-making process; and the role, function and dynamics of the FEMM Committee. Document analyses of key EU policies are used to illustrate controversial and particularly complicated processes where key dynamics of EP party politics in relation to cohesion and coalitions come to the fore.

# THEORETICAL FRAMEWORK:
## COHESION AND COALITIONS IN THE EP AND CONSTRUCTIONS OF GENDER EQUALITY

Previous literature has generated knowledge about the practices, policy-making functions and ideological divisions within the political groups. Firstly, the literature provides key insights into the formal-institutional role and practices of the political groups. The political groups select committee members, decide on leadership positions, appoint the political group coordinators of committees and influence the choice of rapporteurs for committee reports. EP committees are the key sites of political group politics. Unlike many Member-State parliaments, the committee work is consensus-oriented, meaning that political groups seek to cultivate majorities in committee votes. The roles of the committee chair, the rapporteur and potential shadow rapporteur, and the coordinators appointed by the political groups, are central in this consensus building (Collins, Burns and Warleigh 1998; McElroy 2006; Settembri and Neuhold 2009).

Secondly, the central role played by political groups in EU policy-making ensures that policy positions form the blueprint for their legislative activity in the EP, and new group members usually agree to follow existing group policy (McElroy and Benoit 2010). Empirical research shows that over time, political groups have become increasingly cohesive, showing a heightened emphasis placed on maintaining voting cohesion; with the two largest political groups operating a whipping system (Hix 2008; McElroy and Benoit 2010; Raunio and Wagner 2017). The EPP and the S&D have a long history of cooperation to increase the powers of the Parliament vis-à-vis the Commission and the Council and they continue to vote together around two-thirds or 70 per cent of the time (Raunio and Wagner 2017, 8; see also Abels this volume). Political groups, which are less institutionalised or ideologically more divided, for instance, on the radical left, do not necessarily attempt to have unitary group positions (Raunio and Wagner 2017, 7). Political group discipline and cohesion is promoted by allocating rapporteurship of legislative reports to MEPs as a reward for loyalty (Yordanova 2013). Previous research has established that MEPs vote along political group lines over 90 per cent of the time. Nevertheless, building and maintaining cohesion is a constant struggle and political groups and MEPs negotiate between European and national party positions (McElroy and Benoit 2010).

Thirdly, the literature focuses on the role of political ideas in the functioning of political groups. On the ideological and normative level, the composition of the European political groups has fluctuated; new groups have become established and others have dissolved. Historically, policy-making in the EP was dominated by grand coalitions between the two largest political groups, the EPP and the S&D. However, coalition formation has become increasingly ideology-driven and formed around the left/right divide, resulting in centre-left or centre-right coalitions (Yordanova 2013). Scholarship on the political dynamics of the EP has generated insights about when, and how, inter- and intra-political-group divisions emerge. Similarly, research on political contestation shows that there is strategic competition among political parties at the domestic level between mainstream and radical, populist parties (Hooghe and Marks 2009).

Feminist scholarship on the EU has studied extensively the ways in which gender equality has been framed, understood and put forward in the EP. Such approaches represent discursive approaches (see Kantola and Lombardo 2018), where it is stressed that the issue of gender inequality can be represented in many different ways, that a particular problem conceptualisation or solution to the problem is at the same time silencing other representations of a problem and alternative solutions to it, limiting possibilities of change (Bacchi 1999, 2009; Ferree 2012; Kantola 2006 and 2010; Verloo 2007). EU gender equality policies are an arena of construction and contestation of gender and intersectional norms, meanings, and power relations (Kantola and Lombardo 2018).

The EP is often represented as a champion for gender equality among the EU institutions (see van der Vleuten this volume). It has not only voted in favour of many legislative proposals – first debated and voted for in the FEMM Committee – that have later been stalled in the Council (such as the maternity directive in the 2010s), it has also adopted a strong human-rights perspective to women's rights, by, for example, framing violence against women as a violation of women's human rights, and constantly supporting European-wide action to combat gender-based violence (Kantola 2006; Kantola and Lombardo 2018; Rolandsen Agustín 2013). More recently, gender scholars have stressed the need to differentiate the EP as an actor in gender policy in contrast to constructing it 'as the most gender equal actor of the Union'. This necessitates studies of the discursive battles and controversies, for instance, between and within the different EP political groups that are fundamental in framing EP gender policy (Kantola and Rolandsen Agustín 2016).

In this chapter, we focus on the ways in which gender equality is politicised within the EP and how this is reflected in intra-group cohesion as well as inter-group coalitions, at plenary and committee levels. Politicisation is defined as contestation and increased political power struggles (in this case among the political groups of the EP) over a specific policy issue (here, gender equality). Whereas politicisation is often used to characterise the process whereby an issue is introduced into the political debate, from closed elite circles into the public arena or from apolitical to political terms (Nitoiu 2015; Statham and Trenz 2012), we consider the politicisation of gender equality issues here more as a process of increased attention and struggles. The issue is not new on the EP agenda and our analysis is confined to the parliamentary sphere (rather than the broader public debate in mass media) but we do find traits of politicisation processes in the sense of contestation around gender equality policy issues; an increased number of actors engaged in political debate on the issues as well as divergence and polarisation of opinions; as well as strengthened interest from various actors in power positions in the policy area (such as committee chairmanship, for instance). In other words, the stakes have become higher and this is translated into shifts in cohesion and coalition dynamics, which at times make consensus impossible and compromises difficult. Hence, politicisation addresses the 'increasing contentiousness' and 'controversiality' (Hooghe and Marks 2012) of gender equality policies as a specific part of regional integration in Europe. Thus, we refer to one part of the process of politicisation, namely the one related to the 'increase in the polarisation of opinions, interests or values' (De Wilde 2011, 560) within the realm of the EP, more so than the public saliency of gender equality as a policy issue on the European level (see also Rauh 2018, for a classification of the main elements of politicisation). The latter is also relevant, and we observe a parallel politicisation process in this regard; it is nevertheless not the aim of this chapter to shed light on those aspects of politicisation of gender equality in Europe.

## REPRESENTATION OF WOMEN AND GENDER EQUALITY INFRASTRUCTURE OF THE EUROPEAN PARLIAMENT

The overall representation of women in the EP rose slightly from 35 per cent female MEPs in the 7th legislature (2009–2014) to 37 per cent in the 8th legislature (2014–2019). Significant differences in female representation can be observed across the eight political groups of the Parliament. In the 8th legislature the share of female MEPs is highest in the groups of GUE/NGL (50 per cent), S&D (46 per cent), Greens/EFA (42 per cent), ALDE (40 per cent) and EFDD (38 per cent), whereas EPP (31 per cent) and European Conservatives and Reformists (ECR) (21 per cent) present the lowest levels of female representation among the political groups.[4] Combining the overview of the representation of women in the political groups, as well as the representation of women in leadership positions, with their positions on gender equality policies and programmes, we find that GUE/NGL and Greens/EFA have strong gender equality profiles, S&D and ALDE relatively strong, EFDD and EPP moderate, while ECR has the weakest gender equality profile among the political groups (Kantola and Rolandsen Agustín forthcoming).

Within the policy-making processes of the EP, parliamentary committees, like the FEMM Committee, draw up, amend and adopt legislative proposals and own-initiative reports. They consider Commission and Council proposals and, where necessary, draw up reports to be presented to the plenary assembly. During the 8th legislative term, the EP has twenty standing committees, covering policy fields like Foreign Affairs (AFET) and Economic and Monetary Affairs (ECON), over Employment and Social Affairs (EMPL) and Internal Market and Consumer Protection (IMCO), to Culture and Education (CULT) and Civil Liberties, Justice and Home Affairs (LIBE). Each committee is headed by a chairperson and three or four vice-chairs who are elected according to the agreements reached at the Committees constituent meetings, so that the positions allocated to each political group reflects its size. The committees differ in size as well as workload and work

performance. The vast majority of EU legislation is endorsed through early agreements – that is, at first or early second reading, when parliamentary committees de
facto sit in the driving seat. This trend towards early agreements is as strong as ever,
representing 97 per cent of files concluded in the first half of the 8th legislature
(July 2014–December 2016) (European Parliament 2017b; see also Mushaben,
this volume).

The FEMM Committee was established as an ad-hoc committee following the
first direct elections 1979, and in 1984 – after the second European elections – a
standing committee was created (Brunn 2012). According to Annex V of the EP
Rules of Procedures, the FEMM Committee is responsible for the definition,
promotion and protection of women's rights as well as initiatives in the areas of
equal opportunities in relation to the labour market, combatting gender-based
violence, and development of gender mainstreaming. Since its creation and from
one legislative term to the next, the committee has been the most prominent
and important EP arena for the promotion of equality between women and men
(European Parliament 2017c). Occasionally, the FEMM Committee is branded as
a non-legislative committee or as an opinion-giving committee, implying that it
does not work on legislation or on files, which are genuinely its competence, but
rather provides opinions to other committees, which are in charge of the files.
However, data show that other committees issue more opinions than the FEMM
Committee (see figure 9.1).

The Committee Statistical Report for the 7th Legislature (2009–2014) (European Parliament 2014d) also revealed that, compared to the other committees,
the FEMM Committee is a low performer when it comes to legislative procedures; a high performer when it comes to non-legislative resolutions, which have
the character of political declarations rather than of legal acts; and an average
performer when it comes to public hearings with civil society and experts (see
figure 9.2).

The FEMM Committee has traditionally thrived on strong, feminist alliance-
building within the Committee, but in recent years these dynamics have been
challenged leading way to more internal disagreements and a questioning of the
Committee's overall feminist nature (see also Kantola and Rolandsen Agustín 2016).

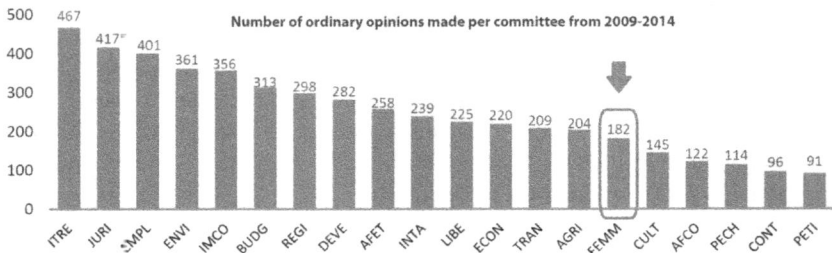

**Figure 9.1   Committee Statistics, 7th Term, 2009–2014 (opinions)**

Source: Data from the European Parliament.

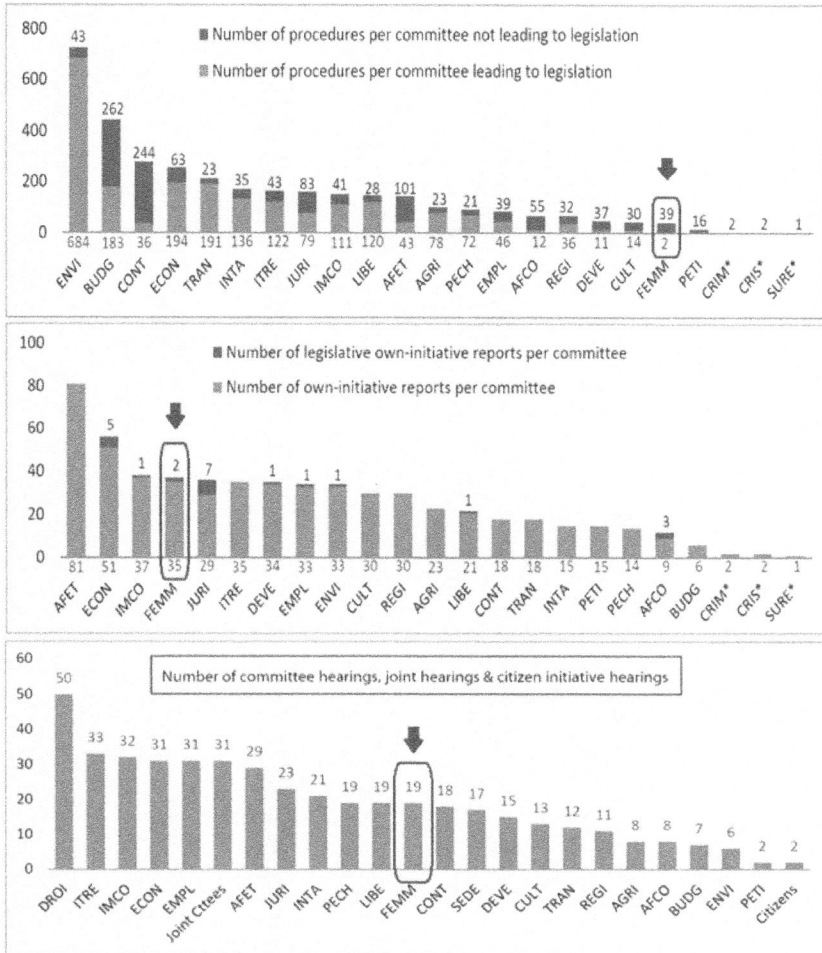

**Figure 9.2   Committee Statistics, 7th Term, 2009–2014 (procedures, reports, and hearings)**

Source: Data from the European Parliament.

Thus, in the following we pursue two hypotheses. The first relates to the increasingly politicised nature of gender equality as a policy area. The stakes are high in this area, as it relates to conflicts over fundamental values. This, among other things, is reflected in intra-group cohesion rates when voting on gender equality matters at plenary and committee level. The second hypothesis relates to the way in which this politicisation affects dynamics at committee level, where the FEMM Committee develops from consensus orientation (based partially on feminist alliances) to conflictual inter-group relations.

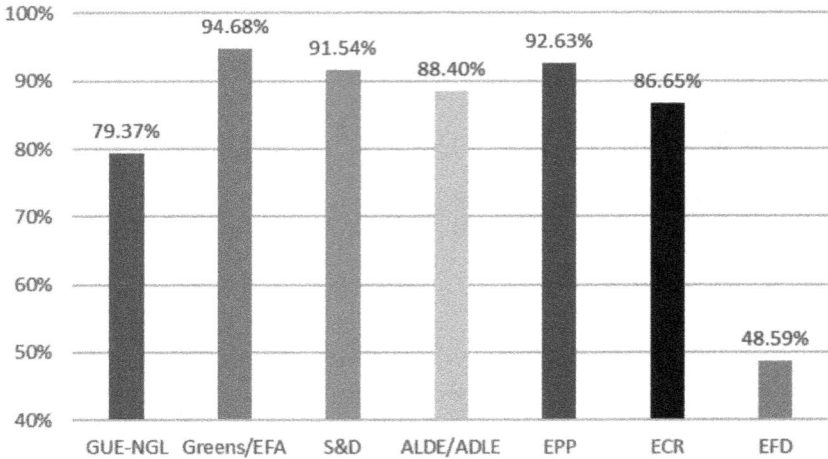

**Figure 9.3   Cohesion Rates Political Groups EP 7 – All Policy Areas**

Source: Data from Vote Watch Europe.

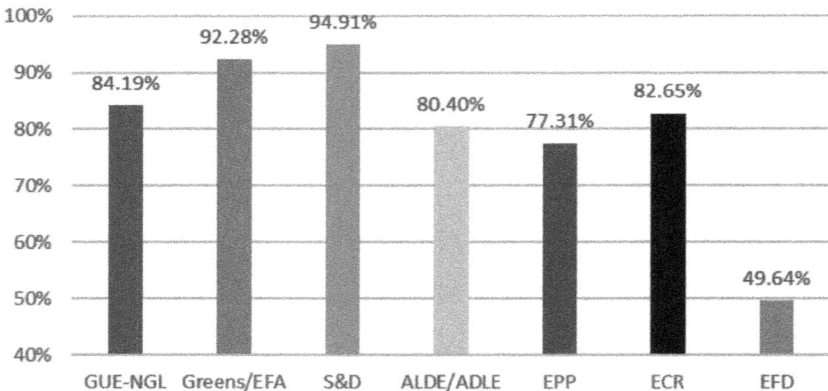

**Figure 9.4   Cohesion Rates Political Groups EP 7 – EU Gender Equality Policy**

Source: Data from Vote Watch Europe.

## INTRA-GROUP COHESION IN GENDER EQUALITY POLICY AREAS AND OVERALL

At plenary level, the voting behaviour of MEPs in the 7th legislative term shows rather high cohesion rates in the different political groups. Thus, considering the cohesion rates for the different political groups overall, that is, across all policy areas,

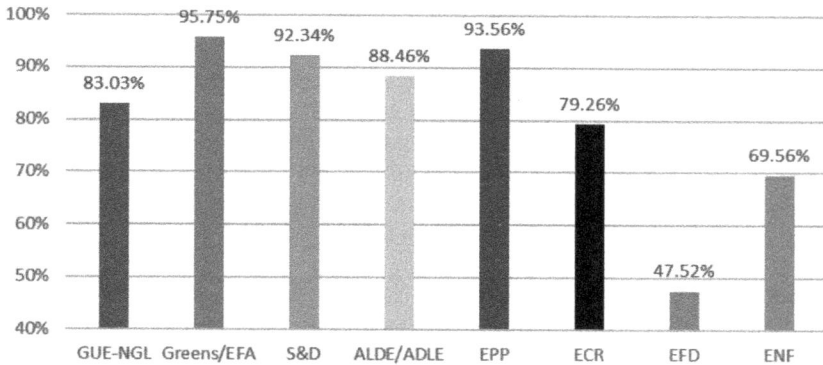

**Figure 9.5  Cohesion Rates Political Groups EP 8 – All Policy Areas**
Source: Data from Vote Watch Europe.

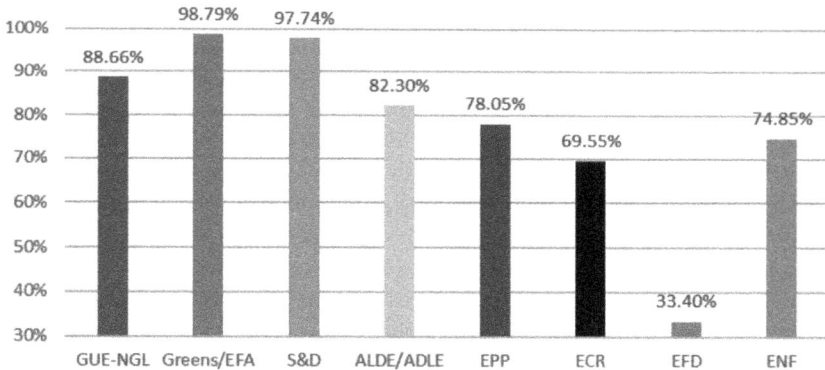

**Figure 9.6  Cohesion Rates Political Groups EP 8 – EU Gender Equality Policy**
Source: Data from Vote Watch Europe.

we find that intra-group cohesion is high, not least in the large EPP and S&D groups as well as Greens/EFA. Only EFD shows low figures at 49 per cent (see figure 9.3).

When comparing the cohesion rates in all policy areas with the rates and voting behaviour in gender equality policies, the differences are notable, especially for the EPP group, where rates drop from 93 per cent across policy areas to 77 per cent on gender equality policies, and ALDE dropping from 88 per cent to 80 per cent. Greens/EFA (95–92 per cent) and ECR (87–83 per cent) also experience reductions in cohesion rates, albeit to a lesser degree. Notably, S&D (92–94 per cent), GUE-NGL (79–84 per cent), and EFD (49–50 per cent) experience higher cohesion rates when voting on gender equality issues (see figures 9.3 and 9.4).

Similar conclusions can be drawn when comparing the cohesion rates for the 8th legislature. The rates drop most prominently for the EPP group, from a cohesion rate of 94 per cent across all policy areas to 78 per cent in the area of gender equality policies. The cohesion rates increase for the groups on the left of the political spectrum (GUE/NGL, Greens/EFA and S&D), as well as ENF, whereas they drop for the ALDE group as well as the right-wing groups ECR and EFDD (see figures 9.5 and 9.6).

There is, as shown, lower cohesion in gender equality policy areas for some political groups, most significantly EPP and EFDD, as well as ECR and ALDE. However, in politically important votes, the fragmentation of political groups may be much higher than the overall cohesion rates suggest.

> What is generally overlooked is that the high levels of party cohesion in the EP may be a 'statistical artefact', in the sense that a substantial number of divisive votes are drowned out by a large majority of votes where political groups are highly or almost completely cohesive. (Cicchi 2017, 1)

Furthermore, when comparing the inter-group coalitions in the five committees dealing with transport policy, internal market, agriculture, fisheries, and regional affairs, patterns are comparable to plenary, with EPP, S&D and ALDE in the driving seat. The FEMM Committee is different. In no other committee, do GUE/NGL and Greens experience a greater footprint when compared to EPP. In no other committee, do they win more votes than the EPP. This is an expression of the committee's high degree of polarisation. Every committee occasionally experiences polarising debates. However, in the FEMM Committee left/right polarisation is the norm. One reason for this counter-trend in the FEMM Committee is the low cohesion rate (77 per cent) of the EPP on issues of gender equality policy. Contrary to other policy areas, EPP MEPs are not conditioned to follow a line to take, thus leading to a heterogeneous voting result.

The lower cohesion rates on gender equality policy in comparison with the rates averaged across all policy areas provide support for the assumption that gender equality policies are particularly characterised by polarisation in the context of the EP. This resonates with previous qualitative findings in the area which point to significant internal splits on gender equality policies within the political groups, with minority fractions voting against the party line in areas such as sexual and reproductive health and rights (EPP and ALDE) as well as gendered consequences of the economic crisis (EPP and Greens/EFA) (Kantola and Rolandsen Agustín 2016; see also Chiva this volume).

One of the most prominent examples of such a legislative dossier deadlock was the recast of the maternity leave directive (Council Directive 92/85/EEC). The EP concluded its first reading on the recast of the maternity leave directive in 2010 under Edite Estrela (S&D). However, the file did not find enough support in the Council of the European Union to progress further. Because of the obvious lack of progress, the Commission decided to withdraw its proposal in 2015 (European Commission 2015). In the same year, Maria Arena (S&D) and Iratxe García Pérez (S&D) launched a rescue attempt on behalf of the FEMM Committee and submitted a resolution on maternity leave calling on all institutions to conclude the file in a cooperative spirit. As during the vote on the Estrela resolution in 2010, more than 60 per cent of MEPs voted in favour. However, the changing pattern in voting behaviour of the EPP group is notable. The Estrela resolution was adopted in plenary with 390 votes in favour, 192 against and 59 abstentions, according to the roll call votes on October 20 2010. Of 641 voting members, 255 were members of the EPP group. More than half of them (146) had voted in support of the resolution submitted by the S&D members. Only twenty-five – less than 10 per cent – had abstained. The motion for resolution submitted in 2015 was adopted with 419 votes in favour, 97 against, and 161 abstentions, according to the roll call votes on May 20 2015. Of the 193 EPP members, only 30 voted in favour, 35 against and more than half of them (128) abstained. While in 2010 more than half of the EPP members voted in favour of the legislative resolution on maternity leave, in 2015 more than half of them abstained from the vote on a non-legislative resolution. This was mirrored in the FEMM Committee vote, with the 2010 vote seeing nineteen votes in favour, thirteen votes against and one abstention in comparison to the 2015 committee-level vote which was approved by nineteen votes, with three votes against and eleven abstentions. Chiva (see this volume) finds that, overall, female MEPs from the new Member States were more likely to vote against control over reproductive rights than female MEPs from the old Member States.

Although there are internal splits in the groups, or perhaps precisely due to this fact, we find networks within political groups which focus explicitly on women's rights and representation. For example, the unofficial women's network of the EPP group, 'the W' (W stands for 'women'), was originally initiated to gather support for a specific FEMM report within the EPP group. This informal network was established as 'we seem to have similar interests in these questions, and we know the pains of our own group and the ways in which these things need to be taken care of' (interview with MEP from the EPP group, January 2014). The women in the W have exchanged information before votes and have sought to advance gender equality questions within the EPP party programme and election manifestos (interview with MEP from the EPP group, January 2014).

In conclusion, divisions within some political groups, the EPP in particular, are pronounced with respect to gender equality policies. These divisions, represented by cohesion rates, are greater with respect to the issues dealt with by the FEMM Committee than on average across all policy areas, indicating that the debates around gender equality in the EP are particularly polarising.

## INTER-GROUP COALITIONS
## AT PLENARY AND COMMITTEE LEVEL

The analysis of all the votes which took place during the 7th legislative term shows that three potential coalitions were possible in order to reach the absolute majority in the EP. In 70 per cent of votes, a grand coalition was established by the EPP and the S&D group, and sometimes included ALDE. Fifteen per cent of the votes were characterised by a centre-right coalition of EPP, ALDE and ECR; and another 15 per cent of the votes by a centre-left coalition of S&D, ALDE, Greens/EFA and GUE/NGL.

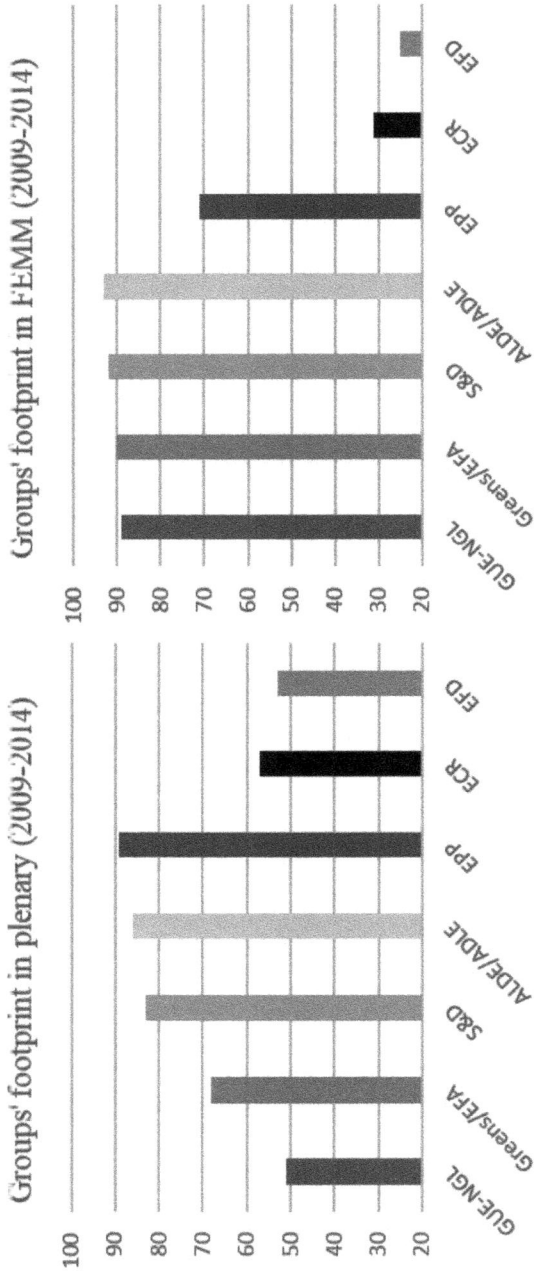

Groups' footprint in plenary (2009–2014)

Groups' footprint in FEMM (2009–2014)

**Figure 9.7   Relative Influence of the Political Group in Plenary versus in FEMM (2009–2014)**

Source: Data from Vote Watch Europe.

These findings confirm the fact that from an overall point of view with all policy areas included, the 7th term was largely dominated by a grand coalition with a minor percentage of the votes determined by the two-alternative coalition-building options. However, votes in the FEMM Committee in the same legislative term exhibit a clear left–right division with 90 per cent of the votes won by a coalition comprising S&D, ALDE, Greens-EFA and GUE/NGL. Thus, at plenary level, a smaller political group – ALDE – enjoys a greater footprint than other smaller parties outside of the grand coalition. However, in the FEMM Committee, it is GUE/NGL and Greens/EFA, in addition to ALDE, that experience a greater footprint when compared to similar smaller groups on the right, and even, remarkably, the much larger EPP group (see figure 9.7).

The different coalitions in the plenary and in the FEMM Committee, respectively, have resulted in policy processes where a report, which initially had been adopted at the committee stage, was voted down at plenary stage. This occurred in the case of the Estrela Report on Sexual and Reproductive Health and Rights (Committee on Women's Right and Gender Equality 2013b) and the Zuber Report on Equality between Women and Men in the European Union (Committee on Women's Right and Gender Equality 2014; Pimminger 2015). During the 8th term a similar trend can be observed, but with one significant difference – the only possible configuration which could achieve a majority vote was the coalition between the EPP and the S&D groups, with the regular support of ALDE.

The composition of the FEMM Committee allowed, however, for an alternative coalition building. S&D, ALDE, Greens/EFA and GUE/NGL together commanded a majority of one vote over the other groups until shortly before the end of the first half of the term, and this has marked the coalition building of the 8th legislative term in the committee.[5] This allowed the political groups, as the main agents of politicisation in the FEMM Committee, to cultivate a considerably higher level of polarisation and conflict, than was the case for the plenary (see figure 9.8).

The Estrela report (Committee on Women's Right and Gender Equality 2013b) on sexual and reproductive health and rights is a good example of the controversies that are rife in the EP with respect to gender equality policies. The report itself, approved by the FEMM Committee after extended amendments, emphasised the human rights and bodily integrity perspective of sexual and reproductive health and rights. In the plenary debate however, the more traditionalist and conservative views of the right conservative political groups, the EPP in particular, won out and the Estrela report was turned down. As a result, sexual and reproductive health and rights as an issue was framed as outside EU's sphere of influence and the parliament adopted a very minor statement stressing subsidiarity and Member-State responsibility (Kantola and Rolandsen Agustín 2016). Similarly, the politicisation of gender equality within the EP had an impact on the way in which the economic crisis was eventually framed (Kantola and Rolandsen Agustín 2016). The gendered aspect of the economic crisis changed from a consensual political issue and a shared concern among the majority of the EP's political groups to a highly politicised one where

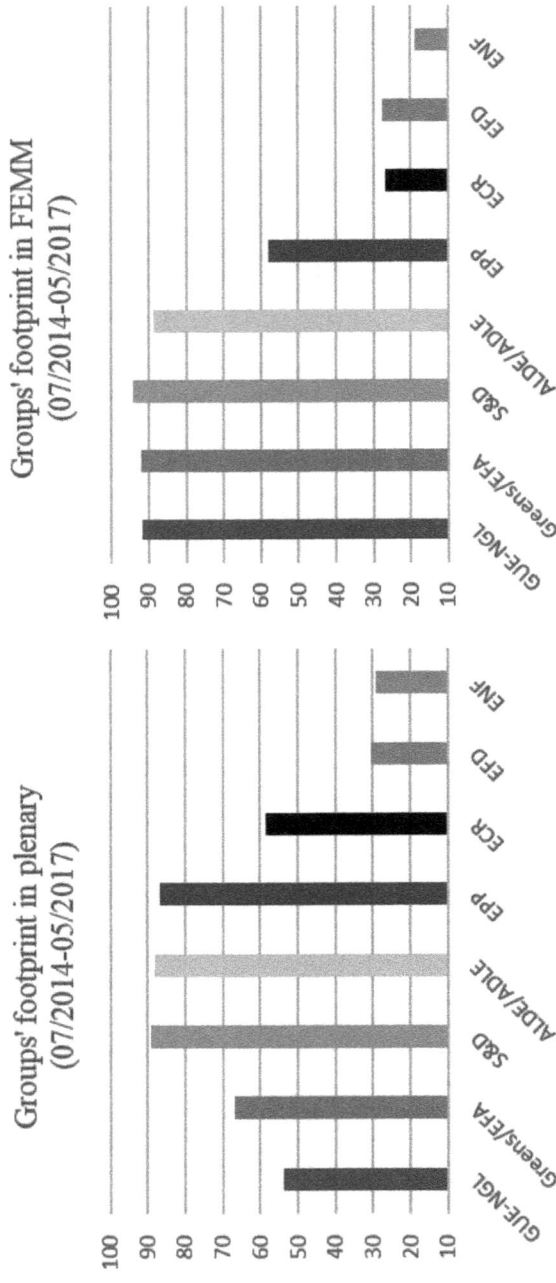

**Figure 9.8  Relative Influence of the Political Group in Plenary versus in FEMM (2014–2017)**

Source: Data from Vote Watch Europe.

the differences between the political groups were exacerbated. This trajectory can be traced from the parliamentary debates that took place arising from three FEMM-initiated reports (Committee on Women's Right and Gender Equality 2010, 2013a, 2014) on gender and the economic crisis (Kantola and Rolandsen Agustín 2016). The reports framed the crisis as gendered, highlighted the ways in which it was disproportionately damaging to the position of women in the labour market and curbing their social rights, reducing their pensions, all of which was resulting in increased gender discrimination and gender-based violence, and leading to the downgrading and dismantlement of gender equality policies and institutions. However, over time party-political differences in the framing of these issues came to the fore. In the case of the 2014 report, right-wing, conservative groups strongly rejected its gendered framing of the crisis by the FEMM report (Committee on Women's Right and Gender Equality 2014), and the report was eventually rejected (Kantola and Rolandsen Agustín 2016). In these two examples, the EP appears as a more contested and far less unified and progressive actor for gender equality than it is sometimes portrayed (Kantola and Rolandsen Agustín 2016).

An example that shows the complexities of both intra-group cohesion and alternative inter-group coalition building with respect to gender equality policies is the 2015 FEMM non-legislative report on the occasion of the twentieth anniversary of the Beijing Platform for Action and the Millennium Development Goals. The report was drafted by Maria Noichl (S&D) in 2015, the same year in which the European Commission (EC) Strategy on Gender Equality ended. The draftsperson therefore aimed to use the report to encourage the EC to draft a new, ambitious strategy. However, it soon became evident that it would be difficult to build a sufficiently broad coalition on the issue for it to be successfully adopted. Nonetheless, in June 2015 the resolution was adopted in plenary with 341 votes in favour, 281 against and 81 abstentions. Contrary to common practice, the draftsperson invited representatives of all political groups that had supported the resolution to attend the subsequent press conference. Hence, Maria Noichl (S&D) held the press conference, together with Angelika Mlinar (ALDE), Malin Björk (GUE/NGL) and Terry Reintke (Greens-EFA), during which, the voting behaviour of the EPP group was criticised. One hundred thirty-five EPP MEPs had voted against the resolution, while 53 had abstained, contrary to the dominant trend of a grand coalition between EPP and S&D. The text could be adopted regardless however, as a simple majority (and not an absolute majority of at least 376 votes) was necessary for a non-legislative resolution. Furthermore, the vote in favour of some, as well as the abstentions of many, EPP members helped to pass the resolution. The common press conference of the left-leaning 'winners' and the expressed criticisms against the centre-right 'losers' conveyed an atmosphere of a highly polarised vote between FEMM MEPs as agents of politicisation.

However, the FEMM Committee still shows some traits of being a consensus-seeking committee. When interviewed, MEPs reported that they found it relatively easy to reach agreements within the FEMM Committee as members, across the major political groups, generally shared a concern about gender inequalities (interview with MEP from the ALDE group, April 2015; and MEP from the EPP group, April 2015):

> I think we have a lot of consensus in the gender equality committee. This I have to say. We are hardcore feminists all of us. And we know what this is about, and we know what we are up against. (Interview with MEP from the S&D group, December 2014)

A Gender Mainstreaming Network has been established across the parliamentary committees in order to enhance the focus on, and coordination of, women's rights and gender equality issues (see chapter by Ahrens in this volume). Similarly, cross-group alliances have been made on the issue of equal representation of women and men and the need to have both women and men represented at leadership level of the EU institutions (interview with MEP from the Greens/EFA group, April 2014). This has also been observed in a different manner in relation to the nomination of Beatrix von Storch (ECR) as the 4th Vice-President of the FEMM Committee. A feminist cross-group alliance was formed to prevent the nomination and contrary to the agreement between political groups in the EP based on the d'Hondt method, the candidate of the ECR did not receive the necessary support at the constitutive meeting of the FEMM Committee on 7 July 2014, when the committee was expected to elect its chair and four vice-chairs. In the following meeting on 22 July, the ECR presented an alternative candidate, who eventually received the necessary support.

Previous research shows that cross-group alliances on gender equality policies are issue-specific and change over time (Kantola and Rolandsen Agustín 2016). Thus, sharing views on issues of gender equality seems to be a greater uniting factor than political group or party membership, or country of origin. Alliances are largely individual- or issue-based; thus, cooperation specific to gender equality policy across political groups and in the formation of networks at FEMM Committee–level stand out (interview with MEP from the EPP group, January 2014; and MEP from the Greens/EFA group, January 2014). Personal contacts and shared convictions on gender equality are more important than political group affiliation for alliance-building (see also European Parliament 2014a).

Cross-party networks are considered to play a greater role in the context of the EP compared to the national level as national parliaments are marked by government-opposition dynamics. These dynamics are less significant in the EP, even though the left/right divide has become increasingly important at the transnational level also. In particular, issues of sexual and reproductive health and rights such as abortion, prostitution, and LGBTQ rights stand out as issues considered by our interviewees to be particularly controversial and where agreements are not easily reached. An increase in MEPs with conservative views on women's rights was raised as one reason for the increased polarisation on issues like sexual and reproductive health and rights:

> You have really these two [. . .] strands on the two sides of the spectrum: on the one hand, those who want to get rid of this whole gender equality discourse, and who even dare to argue against parts of women's rights, for example if you look at the discussions in Poland about the ratification of the Istanbul Convention, where conservative and Catholic circles really say that this convention is against the Polish values of the family, and of course you have representatives of this stream, of these arguments in the Parliament, and on the other hand, you have not only representatives from the Nordic countries, but also for example from France and from Spain, who know these discussions from the national level, and who are quite well armed rhetorically to respond to this, and who have very much advanced ideas of gender equality. (Interview with EP Administrator, March 2015)

The dividing lines on controversial issues are most often attributed to ideology, national belonging and, with regard to abortion, East/West differences (interviews with MEP from the EPP group, April 2015; and MEP from the S&D group, December 2014). Additional factors also play a part. For example, Cullen (see this volume) concludes that national party loyalty also matters regarding conflicts over the issue of abortion, and Chiva (see this volume) finds that national salience of the issue of abortion predicts voting patterns among female MEPs, more so than the difference between old and new Member States.

It is clear that the grand coalition of centre-right and centre-left political groups at plenary level does not appear to hold strong when it comes to the field of women's rights. The debates raging around gender equality issues disrupt existing inter-party coalitions in the EP both through polarising MEPs along left–right divide and through unique feminist network and coalition building in the FEMM Committee and beyond on issues of gender equality.

# CONCLUSION

Research literature in the field of political group dynamics in the EP point towards the existence of largely consensus-seeking committees; increasing coherence in the political groups; and a development away from grand coalitions (EPP and S&D) determining votes to growing divisions between centre-left and centre-right coalitions, respectively.

In this chapter, we have combined quantitative data on voting behaviour with qualitative data on specific policy processes in order to shed light on intra-group cohesion and inter-group coalitions and the ways in which they affect decision-making and political dynamics in the field of gender equality. Our findings show that gender equality policies are increasingly politicised. This is reflected in the fact that levels of intra-group cohesion are lower in the gender equality field than on average for all EP policy-making processes. Some groups are more challenged than others in this regard; the EPP group and, to some extent, the ALDE group are faced with internal splits and minority groups of MEPs going against the party discipline when voting. Polarisation is, in other words, visible not only at the general level, that is, between the different political groups in plenary, but also within some of the political groups themselves. Similarly, we see a move away from consensus towards an increase in conflictual inter-group relations. This is expressed not least at committee level where we find greater polarisation and alternatives to the traditional grand coalition emerging and gaining strength. Cross-group alliances do still exist, but they are highly issue-specific, especially within the FEMM Committee.

The findings confirm that political groups are indeed the main arena for politicisation within the EP. They also reinforce the argument that it is not enough to just carry out detailed analyses of the individual institutions within the EU in order to capture the EU in all its complexity, rather than seeing it as a coherent actor with one voice. We also need to investigate the differences within the EP and differentiate between dynamics at plenary and committee level as well as between political groups and specific policy-making processes in our empirical analyses.

## NOTES

1 Johanna Kantolas work received funding from the European Research Council (ERC) under grant agreement No 771676 of the European Union's Horizon 2020 research and innovation programme.

2 Ciara Coughlan contributed to this work in a personal capacity.

3 VoteWatch.eu is an independent international NGO, based in London, which monitors the decision-making activities of the EP and the Council.

4 Among the Non-Inscrits (NI), the female representation was 29 per cent.

5 Although the EP Rules of Procedure (article 199) stipulate that the composition of the committees shall, as far as possible, reflect the composition of Parliament, this is not the case in relation to the FEMM committee.

# 10

# The European Parliament and Irish Female MEPs

## Female Political Agency for Gender Equality

*Pauline Cullen*

This research explores the relevance of the European Parliament (EP) for Irish female members of the European Parliament (MEPs) to advance gender equality. A specific focus is placed on the dynamics between the national context and the EP in shaping Irish female MEPs political agency on gender issues. Ireland has been understood as net beneficiary of EU membership exemplified in the role of EU policy as a catalyst for advancing gender equality and equal treatment initiatives within a historically conservative gender regime. However, while the EP has expanded its remit and power, its executive role has been circumvented by a decline in legislative proposals alongside a rise in populist and anti-European opposition, some of which is directed at gender equality issues (Mushaben this volume; Verloo et al. 2018). When combined with the impact of permanent austerity on gender equality in Europe (Kantola and Lombardo 2017) and the overall decline in EU gender equality level initiatives (Guerrina 2017; Jacquot 2017) questions arise as to the relevance of the EP as a forum to advance gender justice. In this chapter, I seek to understand how Irish national politics and society and the opportunity structures of the EP operate as a multilevel context that shape how Irish female MEPs construct their role and understand their function regarding gender equality.

The eighth EP (2014–2019) marked the first time since Irish accession to the EU in 1973 that Irish female MEPs achieved a majority status in their national representation. Irish women MEPs held six of eleven seats as compared to the national level where Irish female MPs constitute 22.2 per cent of the Irish parliament. While historic in terms of descriptive representation of Irish female politicians what this means for how female politicians understand and advance initiatives on gender equality in the EP is less clear. Irish female MEPs can be characterised as holding a variety of positions, from traditional to explicitly feminist on what constitutes women's interests and gender equality. As such, this work connects to debates on how women with different levels or none of feminist identification, maybe viewed as 'gender conscious' actors (Celis and Childs 2018) in a transnational parliamentary context. Drawing from feminist institutionalist assessments of the EP and theorisation of representation as a process this chapter is interested in how female MEPs experience, understand and act on issues of gender equality. A focus on the gender political identity of female MEPs also reveals how MEPs perspectives on gender equality can evolve over time. Profiling individual MEPs allows for a consideration of the complexity in attitudes that female politicians hold about gender and social change, and the role of context and political culture, including constructions of high and low politics, as factors shaping attitudinal commitment to gender equality.[1] Questions that guide this analysis include: How do Irish female MEPs understand their role in the EP? What focus if any do, they place on using their office to promote gender equality? How does party-political affiliation and national political culture influence female MEP's political agency?

I begin with an overview of the methodology used and debates on gender and representation. I continue with a brief overview of the influence of EU membership on Ireland, Irish political culture, the gendered nature of Irish political institutions and structures as conditions under which Irish MEPs operate. Next, I profile Irish female MEPs, their assessments of the EP as a context for female politicians and for addressing gender inequality. I place particular emphasis on the case of reproductive rights to illustrate the tensions and contradictions that shape the actions of female MEPs on gender equality at national and European level.

Previous studies have employed large-scale survey and quantitative analyses of roll-call voting behaviour and or gender gaps in political attitudes to explore patterns of female representation in the EP (McEvoy 2016; Rittenberger and Rittenberger 2015). This study differs in exploring in small case qualitative terms the experiences and attitudes of a national delegation of female politicians to drill down into the micro-level practice of doing politics and pursuing women's interests at the transnational level. Adopting a sociological and qualitative approach this work draws on in-depth semi-structured interview data with six sitting and past female MEPs to access their understandings of the EP as a workplace for women, and their roles as a female politician vis-à-vis gender equality. Document analysis of parliamentary portfolios, work records and media communications are also analysed to explore how Irish female MEPs define and act on gender equality. Social media or Web 2.0 profiles of MEPs are also analysed as a form of political communication. Analysis suggests that MEP's use Twitter as a representational tool, with Irish MEPs amongst the nationalities with the most prolific median use of this medium (Scherpereel et al. 2017, 123). A focus on a specific national delegation of female politicians also affords analysis of the role of national and transnational political contexts in configuring female MEP political agency in terms of motivation and opportunity to pursue gender equality. This method carries with it the contingencies of a small sample single case approach in terms of limits on the explanatory range (Yin 2014). The relatively small number of Irish MEPs limits the sample size and has implications for the confidentiality of the participants. Where necessary, the identity of the participants has been concealed.

Case selection of Ireland is an opportunity to examine transnational gender politics in a context absent strident forms of right-wing populism evident in other European contexts yet featuring the legacies of social conservatism that despite a 2014 candidate gender quota, maintains significant over-representation of men in national politics. Ireland at the same time reflects broader trends in what the EU means for gender equality in Member States, in exemplifying a gender regime liberalised as a function of EU membership, that more recently embraced EU sanctioned austerity with deleterious gendered effects (Murphy and Cullen 2018).

The peculiarities of Irish national political culture as a mediating factor for female MEP action are also instructive. Localism is a key form of political capital and works alongside low levels of public interest and knowledge of European integration to marginalise MEPs while allowing national politicians to use the EU to selectively amplify domestic policy agendas (Murphy and O' Brennan 2013). These dynamics construct MEPs as EU ambassadors at the national level as well as 'distant' elected representatives (Blomgren 2003) beholden to local constituents and party discipline on EU matters with implications for their potential to pursue gendered interests. A focus on reproductive rights allows us to consider an issue of increasing divisiveness in the EP (Agustín 2012) and a gendered conflict that reflects populist claims for national sovereignty. The Irish ban on abortion, often critiqued at EU level, yet supported by national political interests, sat uneasily with Ireland's credentials as a modern EU Member State and has acted to shape Irish MEP's voting patterns on gender equality. This case also allows for future theorisation of how national and or European venues can work to secure gender equality. A 2018 referendum that repealed the constitutional ban on abortion, frames Ireland as a poster child of successful feminist collective action at the national level, in contrast to increasing opposition to gender equality across Europe, while Brexit locates Ireland and its EU political actors at the centre of the future of EU integration.

## THEORISING FEMALE POLITICAL AGENCY IN THE EP

For this case study the actions and perceptions of a specific group of female MEPs is conceptualised in terms of level of interest, motivation, will to act and power to effect change on women's interests (Childs and Krook 2009, 127). How women's interests are defined is also a key issue. Scholars have argued for a shift from predefined definitions to an approach that captures how women's interests become constituted through the act of deliberation and representation by women and men across the ideological spectrum and in a variety of contexts (Celis and Childs 2018), Given the centrist orientation of many of the Irish female MEPs, a focus beyond feminist substantive representation (ibid.), to include gender conscious actions (ibid.), affords a more nuanced assessment of whom and what constitutes acting for women in Parliamentary contexts. While this chapter does not aim to evaluate what is 'good' representation for women (ibid., 1–3), and is attuned to the critiques aimed at an elastic notion of substantive representation of women (Dovi 2015) it does argue for a process oriented and dynamic approach to understanding female politicians' actions on behalf of women.

Research has also detailed factors that raise the likelihood of women politicians acting for women, these include legislators' feminist awareness, gender consciousness, contacts with women's organisations, membership of an equality committee, and the incentives they receive from the party-political context (Erzeel 2015, 457–8). While this complex web of variables can indicate broad patterns of agenda-setting behaviour on women's interests assessing the testimony of female politicians, and the context and resources within which they operate can help us to highlight the factors that may influence their perceptions and actions in this transnational political assembly. Added here to Erzeel's (2015) analysis, is a focus on the influence of national political culture including electoral rules. Party loyalty has worked in particular to trump gender equality in debates on abortion in Ireland, where female politicians declared they are pro-choice privately but conform to a pro-life party line. In the context of reproductive rights this has undermined efforts at the national level to construct party-political support to create pressure for change (Thompson 2017, 9–10). The following section outlines the influence of Irish political culture and the implications of EU accession for Irish women understood here as key aspects shaping Irish female MEPs political agency and capacity to act on women' s interests.

## IRELAND AND EU MEMBERSHIP: POLITICAL CULTURE AND GENDER EQUALITY

Irish accession to the European Economic Community (EEC) in 1973 was motivated by economic concerns relating to the United Kingdom's membership in 1972. Irish public support for European Integration is highly contingent. Ireland's initial rejection of both the Nice (2001) and Lisbon (2008) revisions to the EU Treaties is understood as a testament to the power of the Catholic Church and Eurosceptics use of a version of morality politics to link national sovereignty and abortion with further European integration (Nelsen and Guth 2015). Analysis of the 2014 European elections in Ireland suggested these were 'second-order' elections with voter choice mainly influenced by a backlash against austerity. EU issues gained little traction in the campaign and opinions on the EU had minimal impact on party choice suggesting that domestic politics remain key to understanding EP elections in Ireland (Quinlan and Okolikj 2016).[2]

Local political capital in particular is a key asset for political office in the Republic of Ireland and is a highly gendered resource (Culhane 2017). A system of multi-constituent proportional representation means that political candidates and incumbents must engage in permanent campaigns based on establishing and maintaining a reputation for service delivery at the local level including holding local clinics in their constituencies (ibid.). Irish MEPs are accordingly strongly influenced by pressures of what they can bring back to their local constituents. This reinforces certain elements of localism, populism[3] and clientelism at both national and EU level and shapes decisions of female MEPs as to what portfolios and committee work to pursue. Nevertheless, the EU has been an important modernising influence on gender equality legislation in Ireland. Irish social policy is less patriarchal and less familial because of EU social policy. In 2018, over thirty pieces of legislation with a bearing on gender equality in Ireland had origins in EU membership. However, feminist mobilisation on EU equality legislation has met with resistance from the state and Irish political elites. In reality the state foot dragged on implementing EU equality law illustrating a reluctance to deviate from a familialist gender frame of Irish law and social policy and a model of low public expenditure (Devitt 2015). Women's increased labour-market participation was one of the most important outcomes of EU funds that were used to support education, and some minimal support for working mothers in disadvantaged contexts. However, changes in gender roles are slow, with caring responsibilities particularly invisible (Murphy and Cullen 2018). While the European Court of Human Rights (ECHR) has been important to loosen the restrictive abortion regime, until the 2018 constitutional referendum a near-total ban existed on abortion. Overall high-cost childcare, care work unrecognised and male-gendered institutional norms in legislatures and political parties in Ireland maintain gender inequality (Galligan and Buckley 2013).

## IRISH WOMEN, POLITICAL AGENCY AND REPRESENTATION

Despite the introduction in 2012 of candidate gender quota legislation for national elections in Ireland (enacted in the 2016 general elections), the Irish Parliament ranks eighty-first in the world for women's representation.[4] Until the enactment of the gender quota, Irish political parties had made meagre progress on gender representation, as illustrated by a rise in female MPs from 4.1 per cent in 1977 and to 15.5 per cent in 2015 (Buckley 2013). Analysis confirms little support among Irish political parties for a woman-oriented policy platform (Buckley, Galligan and McGing 2016). Resources in the form of gender expertise and connections to women's organisations are also considered important factors in supporting a politician's capacity and attitudinal commitment to pursue women's interests. Equality infrastructure and women's organisations have fared poorly in the context of austerity, with a dismantling or mainstreaming of gender equality supports and services and funding cuts for women's community organisations. The overall effect is a weakening of feminist mobilisation as the state offloaded service provision to women's organisations and tied funding to conditionalities that suppressed advocacy (Cullen and Murphy 2016). Such significant deficits in gender representation and female political agency in the Irish party-political environment suggest a lack of incentives and opportunities for female politicians to actively pursue gender equality.[5] A resource-poor women's movement and the absence of a dedicated women's policy agency also undermines political representatives' access to gender expertise. Irish female MEPs operate in this multilevel context. If domestic opportunities and incentives for mobilisation on women's interests are weak, does the EU, and more specifically the EP, provide a favourable context for Irish female MEPs to act for women's interests?

## THE EUROPEAN PARLIAMENT, WOMEN AND REPRESENTATION

While EU legislative commitments to gender equality have declined, the EP remains an important context for the representation of women (see Rolandsen Agustín and Ahrens this volume). However, intergovernmentalism in EU policy-making and the rise of conservative political parties has left gender equality advocates in the EP with stalled initiatives including on quotas for corporate leadership posts and the expansion of maternity leave protections (Mushaben and Abels 2015). An increase in MEPs with conservative views on gender relations is mentioned as one of the reasons for the strengthened division on issues like sexual and reproductive health and rights (SRHR). A consequence of this is that opposition to gender equality initiatives were often framed by right-wing MEPs as an issue of over-reach of the EU into the private sphere of family life and the domestic sovereign competencies of the nation state (Kantola and Agustín 2016). These trends lend support to the significance of party-group identification and have specific relevance for the case discussed below. Next a profile and assessment of individual Irish female MEPs power, perceptions and reported actions on women's issues and gender equality reveals information on levels of attitudinal commitment supportive of gender equality (see table 10.1).

## IRISH FEMALE MEPS

Irish female MEPs reflected the major political party cleavages at the national level, where there is no large political party representing either a hard left or hard right constituency.[6] Female MEPs party-political affiliations included two representatives from the opposition centre-left nationalist party, Sinn Fein (traditionally a Eurosceptical force),[7] two members including a vice-president of the EP from the incumbent centre-right party Fine Gael and two independent representatives, one originating from a centre-left and one from a centre-right political affiliation. Irish female MEPs could be categorised as a combination of younger women acquiring experience at the beginning of their political careers and older women who have committed to the EP as a career serving periods of ten years or more.

Assessment of the background of the six female MEPs reveals four of the six women had served previously as elected officials, in Parliament, or at local or mayoral level. Irish female MEPs have qualifications in journalism, media and

**Table 10.1 Irish Female MEPs: Party-Political Affiliation, EP Portfolio and Terms Served**

| | National Political Party/ EP grouping | Term | EP Committee 2014–2019 |
|---|---|---|---|
| Lynn Boylan | Sinn Fein (centre-left – nationalist) GUE/NGL | First term 2014–19 | ENVI: (Full Member) EMPL: Employment and Social Affairs (Substitute Member) |
| Liadh O Riada | Sinn Féin (centre-left – nationalist) GUE/NGL | First term 2014–2019 | BUDG: Budgets (Full Member) PECH: Fisheries (Full Member) CULT: Culture and Education (Substitute Member) |
| Nessa Childers | Independent S and D Group | Second term 2009–2019 | ENVI: (Full) ECON: (Substitute) **FEMM: Women's Rights and Gender Equality (Substitute)** |
| Mairead McGuinness | Fine Gael (centre-right) EPP VP of the EP | Third term 2004–2019 | AGRI: (Full Member) ENVI: (Substitute Member) |
| Deirdre Clune | Fine Gael (centre-right) EPP | First term 2004–2009 | TRAN: Transport and Tourism (Full Member) EMPL: Emp and Social Affairs (Substitute Member) |
| Marian Harkin | Independent Group Alliance of Liberals and Democrats | Third term 2004–2019 | EMPL: Employment and Social Affairs (Full) ECON: (Substitute PETI: Petitions (PETI) (Substitute Member) |

cultural management. One MEP is a former civil engineer, and another is an agricultural economist. Two centre-right MEPs belonged to the EPP (Group of the European People's Party – Christian Democrats) centre-right grouping, one centre-right independent was a member of the ALDE (The Alliance of Liberals and Democrats for Europe) grouping, the other centre-left MEP belonged to the S&D (Group of the Progressive Alliance of Socialists & Democrats). The remaining two centre-left MEPs were affiliated with the GUE/NGL (see table 10.1).

Executive incorporation is an additional aspect in assessing the capacity of female representatives to exercise political agency. Abels's (2015, 8) analysis of the gender representation of the EP emphasises its quality as a 'working parliament' in the central role played by committees, which are understood as central to the legislative process and where holding a formal leadership position or office affords influence. Committee membership is also highly competitive, and membership on the most important committees is politicised (McElroy and Benoit 2012). One of the two longest serving MEPs, Harkin, was a coordinator for the ALDE group for the Employment and Social Affairs Committee. The other MEP with a long tenure, McGuinness, is a Vice-President of the EP, serving on the EP's Agriculture and Rural Development Committee and the Committee on the Environment, Public Health and Food Safety. Notably the two longest serving female MEPs have occupied the most powerful positions. A position on the Agriculture Committee, one of the most prominent areas of EU policy, is particularly important for Irish national interests, and McGuinness is noted as having significant influence in this committee. McGuinness has also taken a prominent role in negotiating the Brexit agreement that has specific implications for the border between Northern Ireland and the Republic in the South in terms of security, migration, trade and agriculture.

The other MEPs were full members of environment, budget, fisheries, agriculture and transport committees. Interview data suggest that Irish female MEPs' expertise at the national level, local issues (especially for rural-constituency MEPs), and guidance from their political parties oriented their interest in seeking a specific committee membership. Only one Irish MEP, the independent centre-left Childers, sat on the Women's Rights and Gender Equality or FEMM Committee of the EP as a substitute member. Childers has been the most explicitly feminist MEP and as an independent is unrestricted in ways that other female MEPs are by the party whip system which is strongly articulated in the Irish context. This said, as an independent she lacked the power and leverage associated with national party-political patronage.

Attitudinal commitment and access to resources are also key factors influencing representatives' political agency. As such next I examine female MEPs assessment of the EP as a context for female parliamentarians, their perceived role in pursuit of women's interests, relationship to the EP FEMM Committee and their actions on SRHR. In this assessment, I emphasised the gender ideologies and constructions employed.

## IRISH FEMALE MEPS
## REPRESENTATION AND GENDER EQUALITY

The gender composition of Irish MEPs in the eighth EP was five male and six female representatives, an increase of 29.5 per cent on the previous term where ten male and five female MEPs were elected. As shown in table 10.2, this marked the first time since entry into the EEC in 1973 that female MEPs have outnumbered male MEPs.[8] The success that female politicians have had in the EP, compared to the national context, can be understood as an indication in part of the historically low status that this position holds in Irish political culture (McElroy and Benoit 2012). Echoing similar findings to Chiva (this volume) a first time Irish female MEP contrasted her experiences at the national level with the EP noting, 'There is such a difference going into meetings and not being the only woman in the room, also it is not as adversarial, it is more about consensus and you also realise there are a lot of women in very important positions'. Another female Irish MEP suggested, 'The EP is so different from national politics in that you don't need to actively seek out other women to create an alliance, sometimes depending on the issue women may be the majority in a room'. Irish female MEPs, while asserting that the EP offered a contrast to the national political scene, in that 'there are certainly more females' were in turn careful to underplay gender deficits at national level. Instead, many of the women interviewed detailed their own leadership achievements, suggesting they had not personally been held back by gender bias, while at the same time aware that it did exist. Asked to assess if the greater presence of women in the EP created a space for raising gender equality issues, most female MEPs agreed in principle. However, differed in whether they understood this was a part of their own role. A centre-right female MEP suggested, 'The EP is a place where we legislate for citizens for men and women not for women explicitly'. Assessing the relative merit of the national compared to the EP context to secure progress on gender equality a first term centre-left MEP asserted, 'Of course the EP has been beneficial for gender equality in Ireland, but I think the way the EP works with co-decision you need change to come from

**Table 10.2  Descriptive Representation of Irish Female MEPs, 1979–2014**

| EP Legislature | Irish MEP Delegation | Men | Women |
|---|---|---|---|
| 1979–1984 | 22 | 20 | 2 |
| 1984–1989 | 17 | 15 | 2 |
| 1989–1994 | 17 | 15 | 2 |
| 1994–1999 | 15 | 12 | 3 |
| 1999–2004 | 15 | 10 | 5 |
| 2004–2009 | 13 | 8 | 3 |
| 2009–2014 | 12 | 9 | 3 |
| 2014–2019 | 11 | 5 | 6 |

Source: http://www.europarl.europa.eu/portal/en.

National Parliaments'. Noting the lack of legislation within the EP, this MEP added, 'In reality there is so little legislation related to equality issues at all moving through the Parliament at this time, it doesn't seem the place to look for change'.

Female MEP's also discussed the EP as a working context for career advancement of female politicians, a centre-right MEP suggested, 'I am not conscious of gender bias at all, it is just about the work'. Overall female MEPs were reluctant to critique their party groups, a function perhaps of the relatively positive scenario compared to the national context and in line with other research (Kantola and Agustín 2016). This said, Irish female MEP members of the EPP grouping stated that the presence of 'ultra conservative' women was creating problems for those interested in supporting gender equality initiatives. When asked directly if they held a feminist identification, a typical response from the centre-right MEPs, included, 'No I don't use that label, I avoid blaming men, I am more interested in pushing for a balance and quality of life for men and women'. Another stated, 'Not a label I take on or reject it is just that I think it is better to normalize the issue of gender equality'.

Aside from an explicit rejection of feminist identification, another measure of gender consciousness amongst female MEPs is their perspective on what female MEPs could do to advance their careers. In line with Kantola and Agustín (2015) the majority of female MEPs emphasised the responsibility that individual women had to seek opportunities to make themselves visible, and gain credibility, absent any acknowledgement of a gendered institutional context. The most experienced MEPs argued that women needed to make themselves 'specifically visible and associated with a particular expertise or they would not progress'. Advice to new female MEPs included 'engage in committee work with a concrete piece of high-profile legislation and maintain your focus, communicate clearly and negotiate'. This focus on pursuing high visibility or 'high' politics issues to gain credibility suggests a strategy that reflects ideas about what is important for national interests that may work to inhibit a focus on women's issues often considered as 'low' politics. Overall, most Irish female MEPs did not indicate a high level of attitudinal commitment as MEPs to address gender equality; however, further assessment of levels of gender consciousness and actions reveals a more complex picture of their engagement with gendered interests in this multileveled context.

## IRISH FEMALE MEPS ACTING ON GENDERED INTERESTS

The majority of Irish female MEPs supported an extension of EU legislation on maternity leave, a directive that has been blocked in the Council of the EU, and all have called for EU legislation to guarantee paid paternity leave in Member States. However, consistent with a resistance to feminist frameworks and in alignment with party ideology centre-right female MEPs evoked familial, human capital, the business case for gender equality, as well as demographic concerns stating that

Employees being absent is a cost to business; I recognise that, especially for small businesses. But I think we are going to have to accept that it is a cost to business just like rent, rates, holiday pay, electricity costs and other benefits. Overall it is the cost to businesses of not retaining their female staff in the long run which is also at stake.

Centre-left MEPs are more likely to evoke the issue of fairness and justice, broadening the issue to paternity leave and pushing back at more conservative frameworks on family life evident in this statement,

Fathers too have a right to experience and contribute to the earliest stages of development of their children across the Union. Paid paternity leave legislation is long overdue too. It's interesting to see how conservative forces harp on about family values when they see fit, and yet show such little enthusiasm for a modest improvement in the conditions of working people's family lives.

It is evident how ideological cleavages shape the gender constructs that MEPs draw on in the EP even if they broadly agree on similar issues (Pristed Nielsen and Agustín 2013). Analysis of speeches, voting records and hosting of civil society delegations indicate that Irish female MEPs have mobilised on women's interests in a diverse range of areas including women in masculinised occupations, including fishing and farming and on challenges faced by carers of older people and people with disabilities.

As a VP of the EP, the longest serving Irish female MEP Mairead McGuinness, has a record of support for the deinstitutionalisation of orphans and children with disabilities in central and eastern Europe. Other Irish female MEPs supported the rights of Palestinian women and development aid more generally. Many of the gendered issues championed by Irish female MEPs can be understood as 'safe claims'. This term has been used to assess the ways that centrist and conservative women advance women's interests on issues including sex trafficking, women's development aid and women in decision-making (Celis et al. 2009, 221). Safe claims often involve gender constructs of women as victims from outside a respective national context, rather than a focus on domestic women's issues which might require a disruption of the gender regime and or substantial state intervention or cost (Erzeel and Celis 2016).

Female MEPs also pursue policy agendas without highlighting any gendered aspects. In negotiations on the proposed trade deal Transatlantic Trade and Investment Partnership (TTIP) centre-right and centre-left female MEPs focused on protections sought for Irish industry and agriculture rather than any gendered assessment. One of the centre-left MEPs working on TTIP, when asked if gender was part of her approach, answered that her focus was on workers' rights, belatedly mentioning her efforts to secure social clauses including those that address gender equality in public procurement processes. In this way, an issue where national imperatives shape female MEP engagement became gendered in part at the transnational level as a function of EP gender mainstreaming processes. However, the two longest serving and most powerful Irish female MEPs, Harkin and McGuinness, both highly engaged with Brexit negotiations, have not raised gender as an issue: unsurprising perhaps in the overall degendered perspective taken in official negotiations on Brexit (Guerrina and Masselot 2018).

Erzeel (2015) argues that exposure to feminist attitudes and gender-related information from women's organisations are key resources in feminist awareness and by extension support for women's interests. Centre-right MEPs with no specific connection to feminist organisations recounted their misgivings about the use of gender quotas. In contrast, one of the centre-left MEPs admitted to being against gender quotas until she attended several events at national level held by the state feminist organisation the National Women's Council of Ireland (NWCI). Understandings and definitions of women's interests are not fixed but evolve over time and become constituted in political action (Squires 2008). As such this first time MEP, sensitised initially at the national level to feminist frameworks had spent the past 4 years interacting with networks of left-wing feminist MEPs and engaging with EP gender mainstreaming processes When interviewed in 2014 she did not commit to any strong feminist identification, however, by 2018 she listed feminist in her social media profile and stated that in part due to what she viewed as 'her socialisation in the EP', gender issues had taken an increased role in her portfolio, including work on EP reports on gender diversity in the media and austerity and gender. This evolution was evident in her recounting of working on food security at the national level, that her time in the EP and the requirement for gender proofing each policy area revealed to her this issue had specific implications for women. This 'revelation' in turn pushed her to think about her work on food poverty in the ENVIRN committee in gendered terms.

## IRISH FEMALE MEPS AND THE FEMM COMMITTEE

Research suggests that a strong indicator that women representatives may act on women's interests is their membership of a parliamentary equality committee (Erzeel 2015). Equality committees are key contexts where gender expertise is accessed. In the EP, the FEMM Committee is an important site for political struggles over how women's interests are constructed and politicised at EU level (Agustín 2012). Although its recommendations are non-binding its members, who are predominantly female, nonetheless bring substantial gender expertise to bear in other committees where they serve (Mushaben and Abels 2015). FEMM membership is also voluntary and can be carried out in addition to other committee memberships, which means that MEPs can hold membership alongside other portfolios. However, Irish female MEPs have almost unilaterally declined membership of this committee. Over the history of Irish EU membership only three women have either occupied full or substitute membership of the women's rights committee. The most significant presence was a centre-right politician and a long serving MEP (1984–2004) Mary Bannotti who held either full or substitute membership between 1987 and 2002. Irish female MEPs have also played a retrograde role on gender equality issues in the past. For example, conservative MEP Dana Scallon agitated to refuse the EU women's rights NGO the European Women's Lobby funding and in effect abolish the FEMM Committee in 2000 (Agustín 2012). In the past ten years, only one Irish female MEP has held membership but as a substitute.

An experienced female MEP when asked about the FEMM Committee responded, 'The FEMM committee is not relevant as I am an engineer by training the transport committee is a better fit'. Another remarked:

> The FEMM Committee does some good work but is has no legislative power, it is not in a position to push. There are other ways to secure gender equality, such as gender mainstreaming, gender proofing, or funding through the European Social Fund and European Regional Development Fund and so forth. Gender equality is integral to my work as a normal part of my work not an extra or an add on.

Centre-right Irish female MEPs also referenced gender mainstreaming as an initiative that displaced the need for specific committee membership on women's rights. 'Gender mainstreaming means that in all my work there is a gender element'.

Here Irish Female MEPs evoke constructions that suggest that either gender mainstreaming principles negate the need for a specific focus on gender equality or that gender is irrelevant or outside of their own interests and expertise. Either construction supports the idea that female MEPs need not feel responsible for pursuing a specific gender equality portfolio.

In the view of another centre-right female MEP, the FEMM Committee has made some important mistakes particularly on the long stalled proposed revision of EU law on maternity leave. She commented, 'Sometimes the Committee makes gender an issue in a way that inhibits legislation, they are not willing to compromise enough. Their position was inflexible the result was that everybody's time was wasted'. In the end, this female politician commented, 'I came to the EP to legislate to be where the influence is and that is not in the FEMM committee'.

The centre-right Irish MEP who is also a VP stated that 'I have never attended a FEMM committee meeting, it is too left leaning, there are too many divisive voices and it is too adversarial'. She continued, 'When we look at the EU, what are the major legislative priorities? not on the FEMM committee, where are Ireland's national interests? not there'. In her view, committees that are 'womanised' are marginal; instead there needs to be more women who are visible in other contexts such as agriculture. For these female MEPs the FEMM Committee does not serve their core objectives to pursue national interests in spaces powerful enough to effect policy change. Irish female MEPs have little experience of gender equality policy machinery reflected in the absence of national state feminism and despite the establishment of a women's political party caucus in 2017 there is no national Parliamentary committee for women's equality. Aside from these characterisations of the FEMM Committee, it is the issue of SRHR that has created difficulty yet also a near consensus amongst the Irish female MEP contingent.

## IRISH FEMALE MEPS AND SRHR

National party ideology and loyalty have long inhibited Irish female MEPs actions on reproductive rights. Eager to maintain the party line and the support of their local and for some MEPs, rural constituents, voting on abortion in the EP was out of bounds.

When queried about why only Irish MEP holds membership of the FEMM Committee a centre-left MEP confirmed this in her response: 'Abortion, all the political parties instruct their MEPs not to become members of the FEMM committee for this reason'. Asked to expand further, she explained that until the issue of abortion had been *dealt with at home* no MEPs were encouraged to sit on the FEMM Committee. She elaborated on this with reference to her rejection of the 2014 FEMM Tarabella report on gender equality that included the clause 'women must have control over their sexual and reproductive health and rights, not least by having ready access to contraception and abortion' (paragraph 45). She explained, 'It is very frustrating when you cannot vote in favour of something like that, it is a pity that abortion was in there, as it would have gotten much broader support because there are so many other really important things in that report'. When probed further she admitted that she was personally pro-choice but that she had to comply with her party's diktat. The EP record shows that only one MEP the Independent Nessa Childers voted for the Tarabella report prompting the Irish civil society group, the Abortion Rights Campaign (ARC) to publicise those who did not support the amendment with the statement, 'Most of our representatives in Europe think it is acceptable to cherry-pick when it comes to human rights and gender equality'.[9]

Another centre-right MEP commented, 'I am prolife that is on the record but also in this context subsidiarity is the reality. This insistence on trying to federalise the issue of abortion is futile'. The issue of subsidiarity does play a significant role for most political parties. Sinn Fein in particular, the nationalist centre-left party, rejects a federalist position and has in the past constructed the issue of reproductive rights as directly tied to this. Positioning on issues of gender equality in instrumental ways aimed at reducing EU influence has increased in EP, a strategy employed particularly by Eurosceptical right-wing political interests (Kantola and Agustín 2016, 9).

The centre-right MEP Deirdre Clune, who belongs to the Fine Gael party, offered a clear articulation of this position in her speech in plenary:

> 'I welcome the elements of this report that deal with equality for women. However, it is my view that the formulation and implementation of policies on abortion are a matter for each individual Member State and not the European Parliament. Parliament must not overstep its competence and must recognise the principle of subsidiarity, which is a founding principle of the EU'.[10]

As one centre-right female MEP remarked, 'high profile issues such as reproductive rights maybe feminist issues but are they are really what concerns women in the everyday life, such as caring for older parents, disabled children or working for low pay?' These lines of argumentation indicate how feminist spaces such as the FEMM committee are constructed as too radical, extreme or irrelevant to the pursuit of 'real' gender equality. Combined with discourses of national interest and sovereignty, gender equality is used here in way that block EP level initiatives, relieve Irish female MEPs of any specific responsibility for pursuing gender justice and confirm the national context as the appropriate venue for gender equality policy change.

Interestingly in a significant break with the past, in 2018 all Irish major political parties endorsed a repeal of the ban on abortion. For the centre-left Sinn Fein, in a spectacular volte face party discipline was applied with members required to support the repeal. While overall, most centrist parties played at best a low-key role in campaigning, notably Lynn Boylan, Sinn Fein female MEP, took a strong and central role orchestrating events in Brussels and canvassing in a highly visible way at the national level and in her urban constituency. Boylan's party colleague MEP Liadh ni Riada, who represents a predominantly rural constituency also campaigned at the national level and at events held in Brussels, albeit less frequently and with less visibility. Deirdre Clune, the centre-right Fianna Gael MEP, who refutes any feminist identification, campaigned for repeal, adhering to her national party-political mandate. Her position was enabled by campaign messaging that avoided feminist frameworks and highlighted women's health concerns.[11] Crucially this messaging was consistent with that adopted by the leader of her ruling political party. Marian Harkin, MEP, on the record as prolife did not support repeal yet there is no evidence she campaigned against the change. Analysis of her social media and Twitter profile during the campaign indicates no reference at all to the issue. The other most senior MEP also a ruling party member McGuinness, avoided declaring her position, and was the subject of national media coverage with headlines 'McGuinness refuses to say which way she will vote'.[12] Analysis of her social media profile during the campaign, indicates no reference to the one of most high-profile referendum campaigns on gender equality in modern Irish history. However, at the last moment, two days before the vote, McGuinness announced a reticent decision to support repeal absent any support of abortion.[13] Analysis of Twitter timelines of all Irish female MEPs during the period between the announcement of the referendum in March 2018 to May 2018 indicates that the most senior and powerful MEPs had no mention of the issue or related events, focusing predominantly on a mix of local constituent issues and or their role in Brexit related processes. Twitter profiles of the senior MEPs also indicate strong messaging of attendance at Catholic rituals and conservative stakeholders in the local constituencies, key tactics to maintain resonance with their base in advance of the upcoming 2019 EP elections. In sum, party loyalty, an inhibiting factor in supporting SRHR in the EP, became an enabling factor in the domestic context. How this will affect how female MEPs vote on FEMM Committee reports in the future is open to question.

## CONCLUSION

Irish gender equality policy owes much to EU membership. More recently while a decline in EU gender equality initiatives may offer MEPs less opportunities to pursue women's issues, forces within the national political context including localism and party-political discipline limit female MEPs political agency in gendered ways. However, Irish female MEPs do act as gender conscious actors yet in doing so advance women's issues largely in tangential ways, mainstreamed into committee work and portfolios that have other priorities. Success in this gendered institution is understood by female MEPs as best achieved through entrepreneurial, instrumental and human capital approaches to career advancement. This said, the EP provides female politicians opportunities absent at the national level and has worked as a context to deepen some left-wing female MEPs gender awareness and feminist identification. While extreme right-wing populism is not evident in national party-political terms, centrist Irish female MEPs exemplify dynamics across Europe in invoking gender ideology and constructions of gender equality in ways that constrain support for EU-level initiatives for gender justice. They refused membership of the FEMM Committee indicating no incentives from their parties to pursue women's issues in the EP and until recently disincentives on reproductive rights. Change on this issue was to come at the national level from a rupture in the party-political consensus and an effective grass roots woman led campaign that lowered the threshold for Irish female MEPs to act. That said, the most powerful centre-right MEPs chose to sidestep or minimise their role, actions consistent with their morality politics and or the marginal status of gender equality in their professional projects. Analysis of MEPs inaction in the EP and action on the national level on abortion reveals the constraints and opportunities shaping female political agency on different levels. It also illustrates how female MEPs deliver on substantive representation of women when party loyalty coincides with gender equality goals. In sum national political culture, party ideology, the lack of political capital associated with gender issues in the EP and an absence of strong feminist agency diminish opportunities for female MEPs to deliver on gender equality.

## NOTES

1 Given the historical minority status of Irish female MEPs and the lack of feminist analysis of Ireland's relationship to the EU, the focus here is on the experience and perspectives of female MEPs and their relationship to gender equality. Future research should examine Irish male MEPs as a constituency from a gendered and or feminist perspective.

2 The 2019 election suggests a changing dynamic away from a second-order model with a more EU-conscious electorate and Brexit increasing the 'value' of the MEP role. Notably at the date of publication, five female MEPs were elected to the ninth EP, reversing the female majority.

3 Populism in Ireland exists in right- and left-wing forms; however, it is not expressed in the same extreme xenophobic ways evident in other European countries.

4 Electoral (Amendment) (Political Funding) Act 2012 specifies that payments to political parties 'shall be reduced by 50 per cent, unless at least 30 per cent of the candidates at general national elections are of either gender,. The threshold is due to rise to 40 per cent from 2023 onwards.

5 This said, in late 2017 a Women's Parliamentary Caucus was established.

6 There are smaller hard-left parties in Ireland, but they did not have representation in the EP in 2014–2019 period.

7 Sinn Fein's position on EU membership has evolved, shifting from a strong form of Fein's to a 'critically engaged' position.

8 See http://www.europarl.ie/en/your_meps/irish_meps_since_1973.html.

9 See http://www.abortionrightscampaign.ie/2015/03/11/thank-you-procedure-non-legislative- resolution-20142217ini-was-passed/.

10 See http://www.europarl.europa.eu/sides/getDoc.do?pubRef=//EP//TEXT+CRE+20 150310+ ITEM -012-10+DOC+XML+V0//EN&language=en&query=INTERV&detail=2-298-369.

11 Campaigning under the slogan *Together for Yes* women's organisations from across the ideological spectrum eschewed feminist frameworks.

12 See https://www.independent.ie/irish-news/abortion-referendum/mcguinness-refuses-to-say-which-way-she-will-vote-36937035.html.

13 See http://maireadmcguinness.ie/2018/05/23/statement-8th-amendment/.

# 11

## Overcoming Male Dominance?

### The Representation of Women in the European Parliament Delegations of the Postcommunist EU Member States

*Cristina Chiva*

Feminist scholars have long been intrigued by the higher levels of descriptive representation for women in the European Parliament (EP) by comparison to the national legislatures of the European Union (EU) Member States. Vallance and Davies (1986) were the first to argue that, across Europe, party selectors were more inclined to recruit women candidates in European elections than in national parliamentary elections. These findings have withstood the test of time well: ever since the first European elections in 1979, the proportion of women elected to EP delegations has continued to exceed the proportion of women elected to national legislatures in the overwhelming majority of the EU's Member States (Fortin-Rittberger and Rittberger 20142015; Lühiste and Kenny 2016).

Women's descriptive representation thus constitutes a foundational puzzle for feminist scholars working on the European legislature, with numerous studies mapping and explaining the different outcomes of the European and national parliamentary elections for women's representation (Chiva 2014; Kantola 2009, 2010; Fortin-Rittberger and Rittberger 2014, 2015; Lühiste and Kenny 2016; Norris 1997). In contrast, women's substantive representation has received much less scholarly attention. This is a curious omission, not in the least because of the large and growing literature on the topic during the past decade (Celis and Childs 2012; Celis et al. 2008, 2014; Childs and Krook 2009; Erzeel and Celis 2016; Franceschet and Piscopo 2008; Wängnerud 2009;).

This chapter argues that integrating the descriptive and the substantive dimensions of representation into the analysis of the European legislature can help to shed new light onto the ways in which the relationship between gender and representation plays out within Europe's transnational political arena.

Throughout the analysis presented here, two types of representation are defined as in Hanna Pitkin's influential formulation: while descriptive representation consists in 'standing for' others 'by virtue of a correspondence or connection between them, a resemblance or a reflection' (Pitkin 1972, 61), the concept of substantive representation refers to 'acting in the interests of the represented, in a manner responsive to them' (Pitkin 1972, 209).

This chapter therefore examines the descriptive and substantive representation of women in the EP by focusing on the women MEPs from the postcommunist Member States of the European Union. These countries constitute a distinctive group within the EU in that they all embarked on transitions to democracy and market economies in the late 1980s and early 1990s, and all were deemed to have successfully completed the process of democratic consolidation by the time of their accession to the EU in 2004, 2007 and 2013, respectively. Overall, the eleven postcommunist Member States belong to three distinct regional clusters: the former Soviet 'satellite' states (Bulgaria, the Czech Republic, Hungary, Poland, Romania and Slovakia); the Baltic republics that were once part of the Soviet Union (Estonia, Latvia and Lithuania); and the former Yugoslav republics (Slovenia and Croatia). These differences notwithstanding, as far as women's representation is concerned, the different historical legacies and trajectories of Europe's new democracies coalesce around one shared regional pattern characterised by the following features: the descriptive under-representation of women in national legislatures, the marginalisation of women's voices in political debate and policy-making, and perpetuation of gender stereotypes concerning women's roles within the traditional family unit in political debate (Chiva 2017; Einhorn 1993, 2006; Ilonszki 2004; Matland and Montgomery 2003; Roth 2008, 2009; Rueschemeyer 1998; Rueschemeyer and Wolchik 2009). Thus, patterns of unequal representation for women in the national legislatures of postcommunist Europe are present not only within the arena of descriptive representation, but also within the arena of substantive representation. In sum, it is not simply that women are numerically a minority in national legislatures; it is also the case that critical actors' ability to 'act for' women is also constrained by a heavily male-dominated environment. The implications of this situation for studying women's representation in the EP delegations of the postcommunist Member States are set out in greater detail below in the section on male dominance.

The overarching argument presented in this chapter is that the representation of women in the postcommunist Member States plays out differently in the European political arena by comparison to the national political arena not only in terms of descriptive representation, but also in terms of substantive representation. In sum, I argue that European elections mark a shift away from the established rules of the game of the national political arena and towards the set of rules characteristic of European politics, and this applies to *both* descriptive and substantive representation. As far as descriptive representation is concerned, mainstream parties of postcommunist Europe belonging to the three main European political groups (the European People's Party (EPP), the Party of European Socialists (PES) and the Alliance of Liberals and Democrats for Europe (ALDE)) tend to elect more women MEPs than their proportion of women MPs in national legislatures would suggest. As far as substantive representation is concerned, women MEPs from the postcommunist Member States enter a European legislature where gender equality forms an established part of policy-making and legislative activity, rather than, as in the domestic arena, a hotly contested issue across the political divide. In turn, this means that women MEPs may well find themselves in a position where they are better able to act for women than do women parliamentarians in the national arena.

The chapter seeks to answer two questions, both of which relate to the overall trends in political representation over the three EP legislatures elected since the accession of the first postcommunist Member States to the EU in 2004. The first question regards descriptive representation in postcommunist Europe: what are the main trends in the representation of women in the EP by comparison to national parliaments over the three European legislatures elected since 2004? The second question concerns substantive representation: do women MEPs from postcommunist Europe engage in the substantive representation of women in the EP and, if so, how? Throughout, I also seek to address variation among the postcommunist Member States along the descriptive and the substantive dimensions of representation, respectively.

This chapter proceeds as follows. First, I provide a broad outline of the core characteristics of the national political arenas of the postcommunist Member States in terms of women's representation. These characteristics form the benchmark for comparing the descriptive and substantive representation of women in European elections in the next two sections of the chapter. The core question is: just how different are the national political arenas of the postcommunist Member States from the European arena and what does this mean for women's descriptive and substantive representation? Secondly, I examine trends in women's descriptive representation in postcommunist Europe, paying particular attention to the differences between national legislatures and the EP, as well as to the ways in which the new Member States compare with the EU-15. Thirdly, I look at substantive representation by examining how women MEPs voted on four different items on the agenda of the EP: reproductive rights, gender quotas, maternity leave and political representation. These policy areas were chosen due to their salience in domestic debates not only in the postcommunist Member States, but also in the EU-15. In particular, I examine the extent to which postcommunist Member States differ from the EU-15 when it comes to women MEPs' willingness to 'act for' women in the European legislatures.

## WOMEN'S REPRESENTATION IN POSTCOMMUNIST EUROPE: THE NATIONAL ARENA

How does the representation of women in the EP delegations of postcommunist Europe differ from women's representation national legislatures? This chapter contends that the key to understanding the difference between the European and the national political arenas as far as the postcommunist Member States are concerned lies with the concept of male dominance. Here, I draw on recent literature on the causes and consequences of male dominance in politics (Bjarnegård 2013; Bjarnegård and Murray 2015; Chiva 2017; Dahlerup and Leyenaar 2013a, 2013b). As conceptualised here, male dominance is defined in relation to both descriptive and substantive representation. In descriptive terms, male dominance refers to a situation where men are numerically over-represented, and women are correspondingly under-represented, in politics. Dahlerup and Leyenaar (2013b) distinguish between different degrees of male over-representation: male monopolies (a situation where men comprise more than 90 per cent of elected MPs), a small minority of women (between 10 and 25 per cent), a large minority of women (between 25 and 40 per cent) and gender balance (over 40 per cent women MPs). In substantive terms, male dominance refers to a situation where women's voices are consistently silenced, to the degree where women MPs' ability to act for women is severely constrained. In male-dominated legislatures, the likelihood of the emergence of critical actors seeking to engage in the substantive representation of women is low, especially in combination with low levels of descriptive representation. This is because the few women who *are* present may well feel vulnerable to de-selection if they act in ways that run counter to male leaderships' agendas or expectations. Furthermore, when critical actors do seek to act for women, their chances of success are low because they find it difficult to mobilise sufficient support for their proposals from like-minded MPs.

As the literature on Central and Eastern Europe has amply demonstrated, the national legislatures of the region have been characterised by male dominance on both dimensions of political representation (Chiva 2017; Ilonszki 2004; Matland and Montgomery 2003; Saxonberg 2000; Wolchik and Rueschemeyer 2009). Let us begin with descriptive representation, defined in this context as male over-representation in politics. Figure 11.1 presents the data on women's descriptive representation in the national legislatures of the EU-28 in the elections immediately preceding the EP elections of 2014. The postcommunist countries are well under the EU-28 average, while the overwhelming majority of the EU-15 Member States are well above the EU-28 average. Regional averages make for a bleak picture indeed: while the fifteen established democracies elected, on average, 30.9 per cent women MPs, the eleven new Member States formerly under communist rule elected, on average, 19.8 per cent women MPs to their national legislatures. In other words, on average there is a gap of 10 per cent between the EU-15 and the postcommunist Member States. In some cases, most notably in Hungary, the proportion of male MPs fits Dahlerup and Leyenaar's (2013b) description of the most egregious cases of male over-representation as male monopolies (fewer than 10 per cent women MEPs). In other cases, such as in Poland in 2011, the introduction of legislated gender quotas failed to yield the anticipated rise in the proportion of women MPs across the political spectrum, although it did encourage the main liberal party

% women

0                                                                                        100

| Country | % |
|---|---|
| Hungary (2014) | 9.5 |
| Cyprus (2011) | 10.7 |
| Romania (2012) | 13.3 |
| Malta (2013) | 14.3 |
| Ireland (2011) | 15.4 |
| Slovakia (2012) | 16 |
| Estonia (2011) | 18.8 |
| Czech Republic (2013) | 19.5 |
| NMS-11 average | 19.8 |
| Greece (June 2012) | 21 |
| Latvia (2011) | 21 |
| United Kingdom (2010) | 22 |
| Luxembourg (2013) | 23.3 |
| Croatia (2011) | 23.8 |
| Poland (2011) | 23.9 |
| Lithuania (2012) | 24.1 |
| Bulgaria (2013) | 24.6 |
| Portugal (2011) | 26.5 |
| France (2012) | 26.9 |
| EU-28 average | 27.1 |
| Italy (2013) | 28.4 |
| EU-15 average | 30.9 |
| Slovenia (2011) | 32.2 |
| Austria (2013) | 33.3 |
| Spain (2011) | 36 |
| Germany (2013) | 36.4 |
| Netherlands (2012) | 38.7 |
| Denmark (2011) | 39.1 |
| Belgium (2010) | 39.3 |
| Finland (2011) | 42.5 |
| Sweden (2010) | 45 |

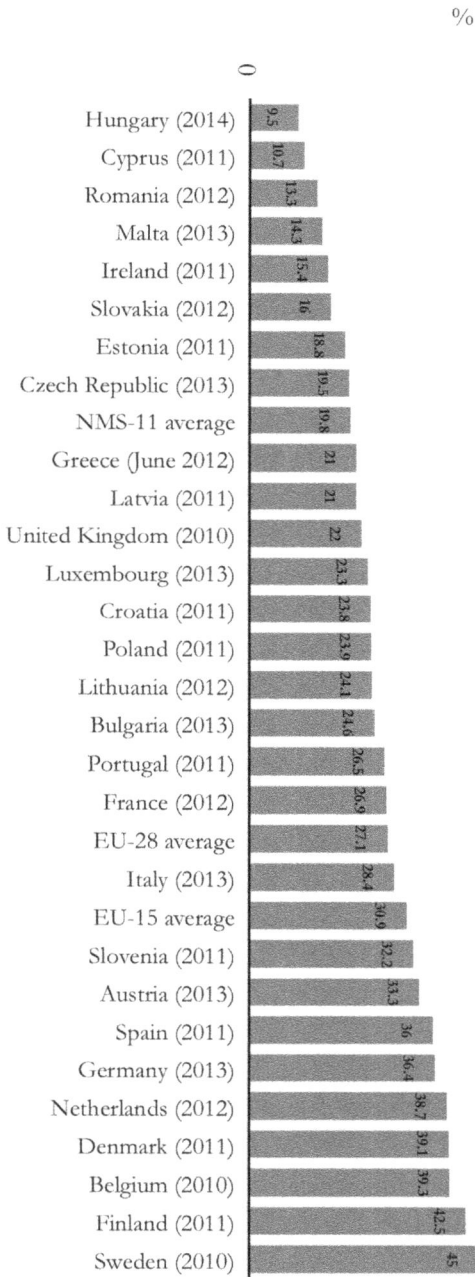

**Figure 11.1   The Proportion of Women Elected to the National Legislatures of the EU Member States**

(Civic Platform (PO)) to increase the proportion of women among its candidates and elected MPs (Chiva 2017; Millard 2014).

How do postcommunist countries perform by comparison to the EU-15 when it comes to European elections? The discussion above suggests that we can formulate two opposing hypotheses with respect to descriptive representation.

*Hypothesis 1.* The postcommunist Member States are as reluctant to recruit women candidates in European elections as they are in national parliamentary elections, while the EU-15 countries are comparatively more committed to recruiting women candidates in European elections than in national parliamentary elections. In the case of postcommunist Europe, this amounts to stating that patterns of male over-representation in politics are equally present at the European and the national levels.

*Hypothesis 2.* Postcommunist countries select women candidates for European elections in a much greater proportion than for national parliamentary elections. In this case, some of the new Member States may approximate the high levels of women's descriptive representation found in the delegations of the EU-15 Member States. Overall, both groups of countries, East and West, are equally likely to be characterised by the pattern of higher descriptive representation for women characteristic of European elections since 1979 by comparison to national elections. These hypotheses are tested in the second section of this chapter.

The relationship between male dominance and substantive representation has seldom been discussed in the literature (for an exception, see Chiva 2017). This is somewhat surprising, not in the least because the question of whether (and how) women MPs' behaviour is constrained by the institutions of male dominance can shed new light on to the strategies employed by critical actors to achieve policy change in situations where the overarching environment is far from friendly to their initiatives. Recent work by Krizsan and Popa (2015) and Krizsan (2015) has begun to cast new light onto the precise reasons why, in postcommunist Europe, successful policy change initiated by critical actors has been relatively rare. Thus, Krizsan and Popa examine three sets of factors: 'women's movement resources and capacity, movement strategies including forming alliances, and finding voice' (2015, 15). These factors coalesce into 'critically institutionalized patterns of action' which, in turn, explain women's movements' influence on policies and account for variation among policy outcomes on gender-based violence across the countries of the region. This framework is equally applicable to other policy areas, where it is clear that critical institutionalisation has occurred, enabling women to press for women-friendly policies, such as the adoption of candidate gender quotas in Poland in 2011 (see Millard 2014).

These achievements are, however, relatively recent. As I argue elsewhere (Chiva 2017), for most of the postcommunist period, the distinctive combination of weak states and weak civil societies have severely hampered the opportunities for the substantive representation of women in the public sphere. This is in line with previous research on this topic, which has shown compellingly that, whether at the beginning of the postcommunist period (Einhorn 1993) or a decade and a half afterwards (Galligan and Clavero 2008), a large proportion of women MPs were not particularly keen to take on the cause of gender equality. Thus, the effects of male dominance on women's substantive representation include silencing or co-opting critical actors to male-dominated agendas. For instance, one of the ways in which this occurs is via party discipline, so that women parliamentarians are induced to vote along party lines on pieces of legislation on gender equality because they feel more vulnerable than men to deselection at the next election. Yet, we should also bear in mind that critical actors were not altogether absent within the parliaments of postcommunist Europe. For example, in Romania, one of the very first bills on incentivising political parties to recruit more candidates was introduced in 1997 by social democratic MP Paula Ivanescu. The bill was summarily rejected, and Ivanescu roundly ridiculed for her lack of understanding of the gender-neutral norms of modern democracies. This brief example suggests that, in male-dominated legislatures, what can only be described as truly heroic acts of substantive representation do occur, but the likelihood of success is minimal.

When women MEPs from the postcommunist Member States enter the EP for the first time, they encounter an environment that is very different from the national legislatures and the national political arena. For instance, the EP is a co-legislator with the Council in the field of gender equality, which, in turn, forms a well-established area within the EU's *acquis* (see the chapters by Abels and van der Vleuten in this volume). The question, then, is how women MEPs from postcommunist Europe behave in very different context at the European level. Two main hypotheses are available in this respect. As above, they are opposites of each other.

*Hypothesis 3.* It is possible that postcommunist women are precisely as conservative as the literature on the region has suggested (Einhorn 1993; Galligan and Clavero 2008; Matland and Montgomery 2003; Rueschemeyer and Wolchik 2009). This means that we should find evidence of a clear gap between the voting record of women MEPs from the postcommunist Member States, on the one hand, and the voting record of women MEPs from the EU-15.

*Hypothesis 4.* Once away from the constraints of the national political arena, MEPs (whether male or female) respond to the new environment by adapting to the specific norms and demands that it contains. For instance, if equality between men and women is a well-established area of policy-making and legislative activity, MEPs will become gradually socialised into new patterns of behaviour, as evidenced by their voting activity.

The testing of these hypotheses are discussed in the third section of this chapter. Having thus outlined our main hypotheses, let us turn to each of them in turn. I begin with descriptive representation, and then move on to discuss substantive representation.

## WOMEN'S DESCRIPTIVE REPRESENTATION:
## THE EU-15 AND THE EU-10 COMPARED

Do party selectorates in the postcommunist Member States behave differently from their counterparts in the EU-15 when it comes to recruiting women candidates in European elections? The answer to this question is a qualified 'no'. As shown in table 11.1, the descriptive representation of EU-10/EU-11 women is, in most cases, higher in the EP delegations than in the national legislatures. In this respect, the postcommunist Member States behave very similarly indeed to their EU-15 counterparts, with the 'European effect' of high levels of representation for women apparent for most EU Member States, whether they are established or new democracies. However, there are also significant differences between the two groups of countries. As shown in table 11.1, over the last three sets of elections to the EP, the overall proportion of women MEPs from the EU-15 Member States has increased, while the overall proportion of women MEPs from postcommunist Europe has decreased slightly. In this respect, the EU-10/EU-11 do behave differently than the EU-15. Thus, the data suggest that, while postcommunist countries may well have paid particular attention to recruiting women candidates in the first elections to the EP, established patterns of male-overrepresentation in politics are beginning to push back against this outcome. In order to make this case, it is necessary to examine the data on descriptive representation in the EP over the period 2004–2014.

Table 11.1 summarises the data on women's descriptive representation in the EP for each EU Member State after the 2004, 2009 and 2014 elections (with the 2007 elections for Romania and Bulgaria included with the 2004 results, and the 2013 elections for Croatia included with the 2009 results). Given the fact that, on the whole, EP delegations from postcommunist Europe are quite small, one should be careful not to over-emphasise the importance of country-specific trends over time: even a small change in the absolute number of women MEPs can have a disproportionate impact of the overall percentage of women in a country's EP delegation. The small delegations notwithstanding, it is clear that we have three groups of countries: those where the proportion of women MEPs has decreased (such as Bulgaria and Lithuania), those where the proportion of women has been stagnating (e.g. the Czech Republic and Romania), and those where it has been increasing, if slightly, over time (e.g. Estonia and Poland). Overall, these trends are more erratic over time than those in most EU-15 Member States, especially in larger Member States, such as Germany or Spain. Furthermore, the gap between the EU-11 and the EU-15 has been increasing over time: from 4.2 per cent in 2004, it went up slightly to 6.5 per cent in 2009, and then almost doubled to 12.5 per cent in 2014. Currently, the proportion of women within the EU-15 delegations in the EP stands at 40.2 per cent, while the proportion of women within the EU-11 delegations stands at 27.6 per cent (the latter is also a drop from the 30.5 per cent elected in 2009). There are significant variations within both groups of countries. For example, Cyprus and Malta display somewhat erratic patterns of recruitment for women MEPs (and have

**Table 11.1 The Proportion of Women Elected to the European Parliament by Member State (2004–2014)**

| | 2004 | | | 2009 | | | 2014 | | |
|---|---|---|---|---|---|---|---|---|---|
| | No. of Women | No. of Seats | % Women | No. of Women | No. of Seats | % Women | No. of Women | No. of Seats | % Women |
| **Austria** | 6 | 18 | 33.3 | 7 | 17 | 41.2 | 8 | 18 | 44.4 |
| **Belgium** | 8 | 24 | 33.3 | 8 | 22 | 36.4 | 6 | 21 | 28.6 |
| **Bulgaria**[a] | 8 | 18 | 44.4 | 7 | 17 | 41.2 | 5 | 17 | 29.4 |
| **Croatia**[b] | – | – | – | 6 | 12 | 50.0 | 5 | 11 | 45.5 |
| **Cyprus** | 0 | 6 | 0.0 | 2 | 6 | 33.3 | 1 | 6 | 16.7 |
| **Czech Republic** | 5 | 24 | 20.8 | 4 | 22 | 18.2 | 5 | 21 | 23.8 |
| **Denmark** | 5 | 14 | 35.7 | 6 | 13 | 46.2 | 5 | 13 | 38.5 |
| **Estonia** | 2 | 6 | 33.3 | 3 | 6 | 50.0 | 3 | 6 | 50.0 |
| **Finland** | 5 | 14 | 35.7 | 8 | 13 | 61.5 | 7 | 13 | 53.8 |
| **France** | 34 | 78 | 43.6 | 33 | 72 | 45.8 | 32 | 74 | 43.2 |
| **Germany** | 31 | 99 | 31.3 | 37 | 99 | 37.4 | 35 | 96 | 36.5 |
| **Greece** | 7 | 24 | 29.2 | 7 | 22 | 31.8 | 5 | 21 | 23.8 |
| **Hungary** | 8 | 24 | 33.3 | 8 | 22 | 36.4 | 4 | 21 | 19.0 |
| **Ireland** | 5 | 13 | 38.5 | 3 | 12 | 25.0 | 6 | 11 | 54.5 |
| **Italy** | 15 | 78 | 19.2 | 16 | 72 | 22.2 | 29 | 73 | 39.7 |
| **Latvia** | 2 | 9 | 22.2 | 3 | 8 | 37.5 | 3 | 8 | 37.5 |
| **Lithuania** | 5 | 13 | 38.5 | 3 | 12 | 25.0 | 1 | 11 | 9.1 |
| **Luxembourg** | 1 | 6 | 16.7 | 1 | 6 | 16.7 | 2 | 6 | 33.3 |
| **Malta** | 0 | 5 | 0.0 | 0 | 5 | 0.0 | 4 | 6 | 66.7 |
| **Netherlands** | 12 | 27 | 44.4 | 12 | 25 | 48.0 | 11 | 26 | 42.3 |
| **Poland** | 7 | 54 | 13.0 | 11 | 50 | 22.0 | 12 | 51 | 23.5 |
| **Portugal** | 6 | 24 | 25.0 | 8 | 22 | 36.4 | 8 | 21 | 38.1 |
| **Romania**[a] | 12 | 35 | 34.3 | 12 | 33 | 36.4 | 10 | 32 | 31.3 |
| **Slovakia** | 5 | 14 | 35.7 | 5 | 13 | 38.5 | 4 | 13 | 30.8 |

(continued)

Table 11.1  (continued)

| | 2004 | | | 2009 | | | 2014 | | |
|---|---|---|---|---|---|---|---|---|---|
| | No. of Women | No. of Seats | % Women | No. of Women | No. of Seats | % Women | No. of Women | No. of Seats | % Women |
| **Slovenia** | 3 | 7 | 42.9 | 2 | 7 | 28.6 | 3 | 8 | 37.5 |
| **Spain** | 18 | 54 | 33.3 | 18 | 50 | 36.0 | 22 | 54 | 40.7 |
| **Sweden** | 11 | 19 | 57.9 | 10 | 18 | 55.6 | 11 | 20 | 55.0 |
| **UK** | 19 | 78 | 24.4 | 24 | 72 | 33.3 | 30 | 73 | 41.1 |
| **EU-27/EU-28** | 240 | 785 | 30.6 | 264 | 748 | 35.2 | 277 | 751 | 36.9 |
| **EU-15** | 183 | 570 | 32.1 | 198 | 535 | 37.0 | 217 | 540 | 40.2 |
| **NMS-10/11** | 57 | 204 | 27.9 | 64 | 202 | 31.7 | 55 | 199 | 27.6 |
| **Difference** | – | – | 4.2 | – | – | 5.3 | – | – | 12.5 |

Notes: [a] The data for the first EP elections in Bulgaria and Romania are for 2007, when the first elections after accession to the EU were held. [b] The data for Croatia for 2009 are for the first elections after the country's accession to the EU, which were held in 2013.

Source: Own datasets, compiled on the basis of the European Parliament Elections Results 2004, http://www.europarl.europa.eu/elections2004/elections.html (last accessed 12 September 2011); *Durzhaven Vestnik* (Official Gazette of Bulgaria) No. 42, 29 May 2007; *Monitorul Oficial* (the Official Gazette of Romania) No. 818/30 November 2007; European Parliament Elections Results 2009 at http://www.europarl.europa.eu/elections2014-results/en/country-results-at-2009.html (last accessed 15 September 2011); The State Electoral Commission of Croatia – 2013 elections results at https://www.izbori.hr/site/UserDocsImages/Izbori_izvjesca/Eu_parlament/2013_izvjesce_final.pdf (last accessed 8 July 2018), and the European Parliament elections results 2014 at http://www.europarl.europa.eu/elections2014-results/en/election-results-2014.html (last accessed 8 July 2018).

a very small delegation size), until 2014 Italy and the UK had a smaller proportion of women MEPs than the majority of the other Member States, while Sweden and Finland have reached gender parity in their EP delegations.

How can we explain the increasing gap between the EU-15 and the EU-11 in terms of women's descriptive representation? Some of this outcome is clearly accounted for by the steeper increase in the proportion of women MEPs across the EU-15 Member States, from an average of 32.1 in 2004 to an average of 40.2 per cent in 2014 (table 11.1). However, the drop in the proportion of women MEPs in the EU-11 delegations between 2009 and 2014 also needs to be accounted for. One possible explanation is that enthusiasm for recruiting women candidates has been cooling in Central and Eastern Europe. In order to gauge whether this is the case, I collected the data on the proportion of women candidates in each of the EU-10/ EU-11 Member States from official bodies and publications, such as the official gazettes and Electoral Commissions of the countries concerned. These data are presented in detail in table 11.2.

As shown in table 11.2, the decrease in the proportion of women MEPs from the postcommunist Member States over the period 2004–2014 cannot be attributed to political parties' increasing reluctance to recruit women candidates. There has been no substantial decrease in the proportion of women candidates in the European elections held in postcommunist Member States; furthermore, countries such as Poland have witnessed a significant increase in the recruitment of female candidates due to the introduction of a 35 per cent candidate quota in 2011, coming into force in the European elections of 2014. The explanation for the lower proportion of women MEPs from the EU-10/EU-11 must therefore lie elsewhere.

This chapter highlights the tentative hypothesis that high levels of party system fragmentation across the region, combined with the requirement for proportional representation in EP elections, holds the key to accounting for the decrease in the proportion of women MEPs within the delegations of the EU-11 Member States. A brief survey of the party systems of postcommunist countries provides some evidence in this respect. In the Czech Republic, no fewer than seven political parties were elected to the twenty-one-strong EP delegation in 2014, by comparison to four in 2009; in Hungary, six parties won the country's twenty-one seats in 2014, against a number of four parties for twenty-one seats in 2009; in Slovakia, no fewer than eight parties won seats to the thirteen-strong delegation, by comparison to five in 2009. In all of these cases, increasing party system fragmentation has led to a rise in the number of parties passing the electoral threshold. This means that the relatively small number of seats of the postcommunist Member States was split between an increasingly high number of parties, resulting in much smaller party delegations in 2014 than in 2004. Given the well-documented tendency of postcommunist party selectorates to place male candidates at the top of the lists (Chiva 2017; Matland and Montgomery 2003; Rueschemeyer and Wolchik 2009), this resulted in a situation where fewer women MEPs were elected from postcommunist Europe than from the

**Table 11.2  The Proportion of Women Candidates and MEPs in the Postcommunist Member States (2004–2014)[a]**

| | 2004/7 | | | | 2009 | | | | 2014 | | | |
|---|---|---|---|---|---|---|---|---|---|---|---|---|
| | Candidates | | MEPs | | Candidates | | MEPs | | Candidates | | MEPs | |
| | No. of Women | % Women | No. of Women | % Women | No. of Women | % Women | No. of Women | % Women | No. of Women | % Women | No. of Women | % Women |
| **Bulgaria** | 41 | 45.6 | 8 | 44.44 | 37 | 36.27 | 7 | 41.18 | 32 | 37.6 | 5 | 29.4 |
| **Croatia** | – | – | – | – | 19 | 52.8 | 6 | 50.0 | 16 | 48.5 | 5 | 45.5 |
| **Czech Republic** | 33 | 20.6 | 4 | 18.18 | 31 | 27.93 | 4 | 18.18 | 50 | 25.8 | 5 | 23.8 |
| **Estonia** | 12 | 25.0 | 2 | 33.33 | 20 | 41.67 | 3 | 60.00 | 18 | 37.5 | 3 | 50.0 |
| **Hungary** | 53 | 22.6 | 8 | 33.33 | 42 | 18.92 | 8 | 36.36 | 47 | 22.3 | 4 | 19.0 |
| **Latvia** | 26 | 36.1 | 2 | 22.22 | 32 | 35.56 | 3 | 37.50 | 26 | 33.3 | 3 | 37.5 |
| **Lithuania** | 35 | 25.9 | 6 | 46.15 | 41 | 29.08 | 3 | 25.00 | 45 | 29.6 | 1 | 9.1 |
| **Poland** | 252 | 25.1 | 7 | 12.96 | 95 | 18.27 | 11 | 22.00 | 277 | 42.6 | 12 | 23.5 |
| **Romania** | 57 | 25.3 | 12 | 35.29 | 54 | 25.12 | 11 | 34.38 | 69 | 31.7 | 10 | 31.3 |
| **Slovakia** | 102 | 29.1 | 18 | 36.73 | 18 | 23.38 | 5 | 38.46 | 26 | 25.0 | 4 | 30.8 |
| **Slovenia** | 41 | 45.1 | 3 | 42.9 | 39 | 48.1 | 2 | 28.6 | 20 | 50.0 | 3 | 37.5 |

Notes: [a] The candidate data was collected only for those parties winning seats in the EP, rather than for all the parties running in the elections.

Source: Own datasets on the proportion of women candidates, compiled on the basis of the candidate lists published in/by: Durzhaven Vestnik (Official Gazette of Bulgaria) No. 42/29 May 2007, 33–37, No. 44/12 June 2009, 113–18, and No. 45/30 May 2014, 19–26; The Elections Server of the Czech Statistical Office; the Hungarian National Elections Office; National Electoral Commission of Poland; Central Electoral Bureau of Romania; Central Electoral Commission of Slovakia; Estonian National Electoral Commission; Central Election Commission of Latvia; the Central Electoral Commission of Lithuania; The State Electoral Commission of Croatia and the State Election Commission of Slovenia. For the elections results: as for table 11.1.

other EU Member States. Conversely, the proportion of women MEPs was relatively stable in countries where party system fragmentation remained relatively low, and the size of the country's EP delegation was relatively large, such as Romania (where five parties won representation in the EP I 2007 and 2009, and six in 2014). In sum, party system fragmentation has clear gendered effects that are detrimental to women candidates' chances of success. This situation is compounded by a region-wide pattern of male dominance, which is frequently expressed in the form of allocating the most desirable places on the lists to male candidates.

As this section has shown, a region-wide pattern can be clearly identified with respect to the descriptive representation of women in the EP delegations of postcommunist Europe. On the one hand, the 'European effect' of relatively high level of representation by comparison to the national legislatures holds true for the EU-11 as well for the EU-15. On the other hand, since old habits die hard, male candidates continue to stand a better chance of success, especially under conditions of high party system fragmentation.

## WOMEN'S SUBSTANTIVE REPRESENTATION: THE EU-15 AND EU-10 COMPARED

How do women MEPs from postcommunist Europe vote on gender equality issues by comparison to women MEPs from the EU-15? As outlined in greater detail above, the literature on Central and Eastern Europe suggests two different hypotheses in this respect. The first hypothesis ($H_3$) states that women MEPs from the new Member States are more conservative, and therefore more likely to vote against policies designed to redress inequalities between men and women. The second hypothesis ($H_4$) states the opposite: when entering the EP, women from the postcommunist Member States are no longer constrained by the institutions of male dominance present in national legislatures, while also finding themselves in a new environment where the major European party groups are considerably more inclined to endorse norms of gender equality than national political parties. This hypothesis therefore suggests that, overall, women MEPs from Central and Eastern Europe behave in the same way as women MEPs from the EU-15, and no significant differences exist between the two groups of countries.

I test these hypotheses by looking at four different votes taken in the EP between 2010 and 2015 on a range of issues in the policy area of gender equality: legislating for the extension of the minimum entitlement to maternity leave from fourteen to twenty weeks across the European Union (procedure file 2008/0193 (COD)); a resolution seeking to introduce a 40 per cent quota for women on corporate boards in the EU Member States (procedure file 2010/2215 (INI)); a resolution on measures to improve the representation of women in politics in the Member States (procedure file 2011/2295 (INI)); and a highly controversial vote on the issue of reproductive rights (procedure file 2014/2217 (INI)). In all four cases, the FEMM Committee was the committee responsible (for a discussion of the committee's role in the EP, see Ahrens 2016; Pristed and Rolandsen Agustín 2013). The rapporteurships were held by the two main political groups: the S&D for the maternity leave proposal and for the amendment on reproductive rights (the rapporteurs were MEPs Edite Estrela and Marc Tarabella, respectively), and the EPP for the two resolutions on women's representations (the rapporteurs were MEPs Rodi Tsagaropulou-Kratsa and Sirpa Pietikäinen, respectively). It is important to note that, while the first vote was on a legislative proposal, the remaining votes were held on resolutions that the EP adopted under its own initiative.

Overall, this section of the chapter finds support for hypothesis H4: there are no discernible differences between women MEPs from the postcommunist Member States and women MEPs from the EU-15 in three of these cases. In the fourth case – reproductive rights – women MEPs from some of the postcommunist Member States are less likely to endorse full access to abortion and contraception, but so do women MEPs from some of the EU-15 Member States. In this respect, the salience of reproductive rights at the national level is the best predictor of how women MEPs will vote at the European level.

The first EP vote analysed here concerns extending the minimum duration of maternity leave from fourteen weeks to twenty weeks across the EU Member States. In 2008, the European Commission published a legislative proposal seeking to revamp Directive 92/85/EEC on the safety and health at work of pregnant workers or workers who have recently given birth or are breastfeeding. The proposal was voted on in the EP on 20 October 2010 (Procedure 2008/0193(COD)). The most contentious amendment was Amendment 12 to the bill, which sought to extend the duration of maternity leave. In the event, it passed very narrowly, with 327 votes for, 320 against and 30 abstentions.

Table 11.3 summarises how male and female MEPs from the EU-15 and the EU-10 Member States voted on Amendment 1 on extending maternity leave. Interestingly, the votes for and against were evenly spread among women MEPs from the EU-15 Member States (47.6 per cent for and 46.5 per cent against), while women MEPs from postcommunist Europe were much more likely to vote in favour (67.3 per cent) than against (30.9 per cent). The precise reason why women MEPs from postcommunist Europe were much more likely to vote in favour is unclear. One potential explanation may be that maternity leave is an issue that conservative women find relatively easy to support, given that the issue resonates with traditional gender norms of women as mothers. However, this idea is only partially supported by the evidence. On the one hand, it is clear that the narrow vote was only carried because of a significant rebellion within the EPP group: thirty-one women MEPs and fifty-one male MEPs voted for Amendment 12, even though the EPP position was to vote against the amendment. The EPP vote in favour was relatively evenly distributed between EU-15 and the postcommunist Member States' MEPs; for example, sixteen women from the new Member States and fourteen women from the EU-15 voted for the amendment. Thus, there is no indication that women MEPs from the new Member States behaved significantly differently than women MEPs from the EU-15 (although male MEPs' vote was evenly split in the case of the new Member States, while men from the EU 15 Member States were slightly more likely to vote against – see table 11.3).

The second and the third EP votes analysed here concern measures to increase women's participation in economic and political life. Within this context, the issue of quotas figures somewhat prominently. As far as Central and Eastern Europe is concerned, any discussion of gender quotas needs to be prefaced with a brief outline of general attitudes towards quotas. Throughout the region, quotas are a distinctly double-edged sword. On the one hand, they have long been associated with communist-era policies, so that they carry particularly negative connotations. On the other hand, attitudes in the former state socialist countries have been changing. For example, a Eurobarometer survey published in 2009 showed that support for gender quotas is nonetheless present in the region. On the question 'if we were to increase the proportion of women MEPs, what would be the most effective way?', 12.2 per cent of Czech women, 11.1 per cent of Hungarian women, 11.4 per cent of Polish women and 10.7 per cent of Slovak women chose the option 'by mandatory quotas', against an EU-27 average of 9.8 per cent (Flash Eurobarometer 266, February 2009). Only in Romania, where the leadership of Nicolae and Elena Ceausescu during the communist regime cast a long shadow over the representation of women in politics after 1990, only 3.6 per cent of women respondents and 5.1 per cent of male respondents chose the option of mandatory quotas. At the time, none of the countries covered in this chapter with the exception of Slovenia had implemented gender quotas for national parliamentary or European elections. Thus, it is unlikely that responses to the questions on women's political representation were shaped by a negative assessment of existing quota systems at the national level.

Within this context, the second vote examined here concerns the introduction of quotas for women on the corporate boards of companies in the EU Member States. On 6 July 2011, the EP adopted a motion for a resolution on women and business leadership, exhorting the Member States to act in order to redress the gender imbalance in positions of leadership on company boards. The resolution passed

**Table 11.3 Vote on the EP Resolution on Extending Maternity Leave, 2010**

| | | *EU-15* | | | *NMS-10* | | |
|---|---|---|---|---|---|---|---|
| | | Men | Women | Total | Men | Women | Total |
| **For** | N | 136 | 88 | 224 | 59 | 37 | 96 |
| | % | 44.3% | 47.6% | 45.5% | 49.6% | 67.3% | 55.2% |
| **Against** | N | 159 | 86 | 245 | 55 | 17 | 72 |
| | % | 51.8% | 46.5% | 49.8% | 46.2% | 30.9% | 41.4% |
| **Abstentions** | N | 12 | 11 | 23 | 5 | 1 | 6 |
| | % | 3.9% | 5.9% | 4.7% | 4.2% | 1.8% | 3.4% |
| **Total** | N | 307 | 185 | 492 | 119 | 55 | 174 |
| | % | 100.0% | 100.0% | 100.0% | 100.0% | 100.0% | 100.0% |

Note: Vote on amendment 12 to the Estrela Report, 20 October 2010.

Source: Own dataset, compiled from Votewatch data (www.votewatch.eu).

comfortably, with 424 votes for, 205 against and 49 abstentions. In the resolution as adopted, paragraph 16b states that the EP

> calls on the European Commission to propose legislation, including quotas, by 2012 to increase female representation in corporate management bodies to 30 per cent by 2015 and to 40% by 2020, while taking account of the Member States' responsibilities and of their economic, structural (i.e. company-size related), legal and regional specificities. (Procedure File 2010/2115(INI))

The Commission's proposal for a directive, which was published in 2012, endorsed a 40 per cent quota for non-executive director positions on company boards (COM [2012] 614 final). The proposal was blocked by Council and eventually withdrawn by Vice-Chair of the Commission Frans Timmermans in 2015 (Euractiv, 2 July 2015).

Table 11.4 summarises how male and female MEPs from the EU-15 and the postcommunist Member States, respectively, voted on paragraph 16b on corporate gender quotas. Overall, 75.7 per cent of women MEPs from the EU-15 Member States, and 74.1 per cent of women MEPs from the new Member States voted in favour of a mandatory quota. Thus, there appears to be no significant opposition the idea of quotas from women MEPs from the former state socialist countries by comparison to the EU-15 Member States. Interestingly, in both groups of countries men were much less likely than women to support the notion of quotas, although we should also note that, while three quarters of the women across the continent agreed on the desirability of quotas, the proportion of men from the Central and East European delegations voting in favour was nearly 18 percentage points below the proportion of men from the EU-15 voting in favour (42.0 per cent and 60.4 per cent, respectively). In both the EU-15 and the postcommunist delegations, the correlation between an MEP's gender and their vote is statistically significant ($p <$ .005). However, as shown in table 11.4, there is a sizeable gender gap in how the

**Table 11.4 EP Vote on Quotas for Women on Corporate Boards, 2011**

|  |  | EU-15 | | | NMS-10 | | |
|---|---|---|---|---|---|---|---|
|  |  | *Men* | *Women* | *Total* | *Men* | *Women* | *Total* |
| **For** | N | 189 | 137 | 326 | 50 | 40 | 90 |
|  | % | 60.4% | 75.7% | 66.0% | 42.0% | 74.1% | 52.0% |
| **Against** | N | 116 | 36 | 152 | 43 | 7 | 50 |
|  | % | 37.1% | 19.9% | 30.8% | 36.1% | 13.0% | 28.9% |
| **Abstentions** | N | 8 | 8 | 16 | 26 | 7 | 33 |
|  | % | 2.6% | 4.4% | 3.2% | 21.8% | 13.0% | 19.1% |
| **Total** | N | 313 | 181 | 494 | 119 | 54 | 173 |
|  | % | 100.0% | 100.0% | 100.0% | 100.0% | 100.0% | 100.0% |

Note: Vote on paragraph 16b of the report, 6 July 2011.

Source: Own dataset, compiled from Votewatch data (www.votewatch.eu).

delegations from Central and Eastern Europe voted, with only 42 per cent of men voting in favour of the proposal, by comparison to 74.1 per cent of women. Finally, it should be noted that, as in the case of the vote on maternity leave, it was a split within the EPP group that made a significant difference to the outcome, with 104 MEPs voting in favour and 106 voting against. This time, however, the position of the EPP was to vote in favour, and the rebels decided to vote against.

Women MEPs from Central and Eastern Europe provided two sets of justifications for their vote. On the one hand, in line with the S&D position, whose group voted overwhelmingly in favour, socialist women such as Vilija **Blinkevičiūtė** (Lithuania), Monika **Beňová** (Slovakia) and Corina **Crețu** (Romania) were in favour of the proposal, emphasising the need for equality of outcome in leadership positions in both the economic and the political realm (European Parliament Plenary, 6 July 2011). On the other hand, conservative women voting against the motion invoked subsidiarity or, alternatively, the historical legacies of state socialism. For instance, Andrea Češková (ECR, Czech Republic) argued that these measures are best achieved at the national, rather than the European, level (the subsidiarity argument), while, in what was perhaps a wilful misunderstanding of the issue and certainly a reference to the communist era, Anna Záborská (EPP, Slovakia) stated 'I experienced an attempt to emancipate the working class through quotas. I firmly believe that quotas constitute positive discrimination, and women do not deserve any type of discrimination' (the historical legacy argument) (European Parliament Plenary, 6 July 2011). Overall, however, neither the vote itself nor the debates suggest that there were significant differences between the women MEPs from the EU-15 and the postcommunist Member States, respectively, certainly not to the extent that women MEPs from Central and Eastern Europe rejected quotas wholesale.

The third vote examined here also concerns measures to increase women's political representation, this time in relation to political representation. On 13 March 2012, the EP passed a resolution entitled 'Women in Political Decision-Making: Quality and Equality', which, similarly to the 2011 resolution on women and business leadership, called on the Member States, the Council, and the Commission 'to design and implement effective gender equality policies and multifaceted strategies for achieving parity in participation in political decision-making and leadership at all levels' (Procedure File 2011/2295 (INI)). Quotas were mentioned numerous times as an example of good (if occasionally ineffective) practice, but there was no explicit proposal for mandatory gender quotas. The motion passed comfortably, with 508 votes for, 124 against and 49 abstentions. Unlike in the case of quotas for women on corporate boards, the Commission did not issue a related legislative proposal, possibly because, in the case of political gender quotas, it was considerably more difficult to argue that measures not involving an economic dimension complied with the principles of subsidiarity and proportionality at the EU level.

Table 11.5 summarises how male and female MEPs from the EU-15 and the EU-10 voted on the motion for a resolution on women in political decision-making.

**Table 11.5  EP Vote on Gender Quotas and Political Representation, 2012**

|            |     | EU-15 | | | NMS-10 | | |
|------------|-----|-------|-------|-------|-------|-------|-------|
|            |     | Men   | Women | Total | Men   | Women | Total |
| **For**         | N | 213    | 148    | 361    | 86     | 52     | 138    |
|                 | % | 67.8%  | 82.2%  | 73.1%  | 72.3%  | 89.7%  | 78.0%  |
| **Against**     | N | 74     | 17     | 91     | 28     | 5      | 33     |
|                 | % | 23.6%  | 9.4%   | 18.4%  | 23.5%  | 8.6%   | 18.6%  |
| **Abstentions** | N | 27     | 15     | 42     | 5      | 1      | 6      |
|                 | % | 8.6%   | 8.3%   | 8.5%   | 4.2%   | 1.7%   | 3.4%   |
| **Total**       | N | 314    | 180    | 494    | 119    | 58     | 177    |
|                 | % | 100.0% | 100.0% | 100.0% | 100.0% | 100.0% | 100.0% |

Note: Vote in the FEMM Committee Report, 13 March 2012.

Source: Own dataset, compiled from Votewatch data (www.votewatch.eu).

Overall, 82.2 per cent of women MEPs from the EU-15 and 89.7 per cent of women MEPs from the EU-10 Member States voted in favour of the motion. Somewhat surprisingly, given the discussion of the vote on gender quotas for corporate boards above, this time the gap between male MEPs from the EU-15 and the EU-10, respectively, was in the opposite direction, with male MEPs from the postcommunist Member States being more inclined to vote in favour than male MEPs from the EU-15 (72.3 per cent and 67.8 per cent, respectively). Once again, the correlation between gender and the vote is strongly statistically significant ($p < .005$). Opposition to the proposal came almost exclusively from the ECR group (forty-seven votes against and 0 in favour) and the EFD group (twenty-one votes against and two in favour). Within the EPP group, the twenty-eight votes against were almost exclusively from male MEPs, both from the EU-15 and from the EU-10. In the debates in the EP plenary, MEPs from the EU-15 and the EU-10 alike used the same type of arguments for and against the proposal identified above. The appropriateness of taking these measures at the European rather than the national level emerged repeatedly in the explanations of the vote by MEPs opposing the measure (European Parliament Plenary Session, 13 March 2012). This is surprisingly and may indicate a certain degree of misunderstanding of the aims of the resolution, which did not actually propose any specific measures to be taken at the EU level, but simply called on the Member States to pay particular attention to a series of measures for improving women's participation in political decision-making. Overall, once again there is no evidence that women MEPs from the postcommunist Member States are significantly opposed to the idea of gender quotas in political decision-making or that there are significant differences between the EU-15 and the EU-10 Member States in this regard.

The fourth and final vote examined here concerns an issue that resonates deeply in the domestic political arena of many EU Member States: reproductive rights. On 9 March 2015, the EP debated the regular report on progress on equality between men and women in the European Union in 2013. Paragraph 45 of the motion for the resolution to adopt the report tackled the sensitive issue of reproductive rights, stating, among others, that the EP 'maintains that women must have control over their sexual and reproductive health and rights, not least by having ready access to contraception and abortion' (procedure 2014/2217(INI)). In the event, paragraph 45 passed with 413 votes for, 232 against and 39 abstentions. However, the overall resolution was amended to include a statement to the effect that 'the formulation and implementation of policies on sexual and reproductive health and rights is a competence of the Member States' (point AF of the Recital).

Table 11.6 summarises how male and female MEPs from the EU-15 and the EU-11 Member States voted on paragraph 45 of the resolution. Overall, there is a clear difference between how women MEPs in the two groups of countries voted: while 74.2 per cent of women MEPs from the EU-15 Member States were in favour of the idea that women should have control over their reproductive health and rights, only 58 per cent of women MEPs from the EU-11 voted for the statement in paragraph 45. Concerning the votes against, the difference is even clearer: 21.2 per cent of women MEPs from the EU-15 Member States voted against paragraph 45, while 40 per cent of the women from the EU-11 voted against it. Thus, women from Central and Eastern Europe were approximately twice as likely to vote against the statement on control over reproductive rights than women from the EU-15.

Have we finally found proof that women in Central and Eastern Europe are more traditionalist than their counterparts in the EU-15? Closer analysis of the vote reveals that, as always, the picture is much more mixed than the overall numbers suggest. If we look at how the national delegations of the postcommunist countries voted, we see that a majority of the EU-11 actually voted in favour of paragraph 45. In Bulgaria (fifteen votes for and zero against), the Czech Republic (sixteen votes for and three against), Estonia (five votes for, one against), Lithuania (seven for, two against), Latvia (six votes for, zero against), Romania (twenty-two votes for, seven against)

**Table 11.6 EP Vote on Reproductive Rights, 2015**

|  |  | *EU-15* | | | *NMS-11* | | |
|---|---|---|---|---|---|---|---|
|  |  | Men | Women | Total | Men | Women | Total |
| **For** | N | 166 | 147 | 313 | 68 | 29 | 97 |
|  | % | 56.1% | 74.2% | 63.4% | 52.7% | 58.0% | 54.2% |
| **Against** | N | 105 | 42 | 147 | 57 | 20 | 77 |
|  | % | 35.5% | 21.2% | 29.8% | 44.2% | 40.0% | 43.0% |
| **Abstentions** | N | 25 | 9 | 34 | 4 | 1 | 5 |
|  | % | 8.4% | 4.5% | 6.9% | 3.1% | 2.0% | 2.8% |
| **Total** | N | 296 | 198 | 494 | 129 | 50 | 179 |
|  | % | 100.0% | 100.0% | 100.0% | 100.0% | 100.0% | 100.0% |

Note: Vote on the report on progress on equality between men and women, 9 March 2015.

Source: Own dataset, compiled from Votewatch data (www.votewatch.eu).

and Slovenia (four votes for and two against), the overwhelming majority of MEPs, whether male or female, support the principle that women should have access to contraception and abortion. In fact, the overwhelming majority of the 77 EU-11 votes against paragraph 45 came from only two countries: Poland (thirty-eight votes against and five in favour) and Hungary (twelve votes against and six in favour). Additionally, the Croatian delegation (six votes against and four in favour) and the Slovak delegation (six votes against and seven in favour) were split on the issue. The pattern for the EU-15 is fairly similar, in that some Member States are decidedly against (Ireland with seven votes against and one in favour; outside the EU-15, Malta with six votes against and zero in favour), while others were split (Germany, with forty-six votes in favour and forty-one against, and Austria with nine votes for and nine votes against). Large numbers of MEPs in France, Italy and Spain also voted against paragraph 45, although the majority of MEPs in these delegations were in favour.

In sum, although clearly very contentious, the vote on paragraph 45 of the report on equality between men and women in the European Union 2013 does not reflect a gender divide as much as it reflects the salience of the issue of reproductive rights at the domestic level. In fact, the countries that were most opposed to the adoption of the principle of access to abortion and contraception were in fact those where access to abortion was restricted at the time of the vote: Poland, Hungary, Ireland and Malta. All four are Catholic countries with powerful national-conservative movements (it should be noted that, at the time of the vote, Ireland had not yet held the referendum on legalising abortion). Additionally, countries such as Croatia were in the process of having a heated national debate on abortion at the time of the vote; in a judgement delivered in March 2017, the Croatian Constitutional Court upheld the 1978 law legalising abortion, which had been challenged by conservative groups, and called for new abortion legislation within two years after the judgement (Centre for Reproductive Rights, 2 March 2017). Overall, the gender gap in the vote on paragraph 45 of the report thus reflects domestic political debates, and the different ways in which these issues shape party stances at the domestic level.

As this section has shown, there are very few differences in the legislative activity of women MEPs from the EU-10/EU-11 and the EU-15 Member States as far as engagement with the policy area of gender equality is concerned. Even in the area of reproductive rights, where women MEPs postcommunist Europe appear at first sight to be more traditionalist than their counterparts in the EU-15, it is clear that what really makes a difference is the salience of the issue of abortion for the national political arena, and that this is equally valid for the EU-11 and for the EU-15 alike.

## CONCLUSION

This chapter has sought to expand the scope of enquiry of scholarship on the EP to both descriptive and substantive representation. I have therefore tested a number of hypotheses on the extent to which, when shifting to from the national to the European political arena, party selectorates, women candidates and women MEPs become involved with a wholly different game played by different rules than those pertaining to the national political arena, and the extent to which this alters their behaviour. The case studies were the Central and East European Member States of the EU, where male dominance is deeply entrenched in political life both in the form of the numerical under-representation of women and in terms of the silencing of critical actors' voices when it comes to the substantive representation of women.

Overall, European-level representation not only leads to changes in existing norms on descriptive male over-representation in politics, but also gives rise to enduring patterns of behaviour with respect to substantive representation, with women MEPs from the postcommunist countries as likely to engage with gender equality norms as their counterparts in the EU-15. There is therefore little evidence to suggest that the EP has become more conservative after the eastern enlargement. Instead, there is substantial evidence of what could be hypothesised to be a 'socialisation effect' for the postcommunist Member States. In terms of descriptive representation, postcommunist parties tend to respond European-level expectations in terms of gender equality by recruiting more women candidates and eventually electing a greater proportion of female MEPs by comparison to the proportion of women in national legislatures. In terms of substantive representation, postcommunist MEPs are by no means particularly reluctant to engage with gender equality, nor are they more likely to vote against gender equality policies than MEPs from the EU-15 Member States. Further research as to the causes and consequences of this 'socialisation effect' hypothesis is certainly necessary and may well advance the research agenda on the EP further.

# 12

## *Gender*Power*?

### On the Multiple Relations between
### Gender and Power in the European Parliament

*Petra Meier, Petra Ahrens[1] and Lise Rolandsen Agustín*

Not only are power relations key to policy-making, but we can even conceive of the policy-making process 'as [the] ultimate arena of power on all societies' (Richardson and Mazey 2015, xiii). In this final chapter, we start from this premise and take a step back to develop an overarching analysis of relations between gender and power in the European Parliament (EP). With the help of the analyses offered in the previous chapters, we reflect on the following questions: What has been achieved as regards gendering the EP? What do we know about the relations between gender and power in the EP? How are power relations gendered, and what do the different contributions teach us in this respect? Were gender relations affected or changed in a way that empowered particular actors, groups, or structures vis-à-vis others? And if so, how, why, and with what consequences? What is the limit of what European Union (EU) institutions, and more specifically the EP, can do to promote gender equality? What, more broadly, can a gender perspective on the EP add to our general understanding of EU integration on the one hand and gender equality policy on the other? What kind of change or continuity can we expect from the current crises, whether economic and financial, democratic, refugee, or Brexit? And how will anti-EU right-wing parties, populism, and conservatism affect gender equality as a goal and in terms of policies?

Discussions of power in the EP context tend to focus on its lack of, or limited, power compared to legislative bodies of democratic nation states. As the only directly elected supranational body, the EP is unique but – still – not a full-fledged legislative body, even though its powers increased over time, putting it on almost equal footing with the Council of the EU. Enlargements resulted in a bigger union and triggered important institutional (treaty) changes, modifying decision-making procedures and reshuffling responsibilities for policy fields. The various crises and recent EP elections have transformed its (ideological) landscape and political priorities quite drastically. Political parties peddling an anti-EU discourse, targeting supranational power, and prizing national sovereignty have gained territory, often hand in hand with conservative voices putting forward a traditional interpretation of gender roles and equality. In general, the EP – erstwhile rather progressive when it came to gender equality issues – has turned into a more political institution, with the election of the President of the Commission as one of the latest innovations in supranational institutional power relations.

Studying gender and power in the EP often meant focusing on the power that women – as a socio-demographic category – acquired over time. From analysing the (increasing) descriptive representation of women as an issue of numerical power, interest extended to substantive representation as an issue of power to promote women's needs and interests, then to empowering women, to gender, and lastly beyond, including an intersectional approach across Europe by furthering gender equality through, for instance, social policies (Hoskyns 1996). Other scholars looked into the symbolic dimension of political representation, and how power and gender interplay at that level (Lombardo and Meier 2016). In sum, we are speaking of power in relation to the descriptive, substantive and symbolic representation of women (Pitkin 1967) or eventually gender and sometimes intersectional aspects.

Nonetheless, the question remains what we are actually talking about when we speak of power: powerful asymmetric gender relations, empowering social groups, their gendered nature or the gendering of power? Power is one of these concepts we – as (feminist) political scientists – tend to use without thinking of the numerous nuances in its existing definitions. And interestingly, while it is a key concept in understanding gender inequality in politics or in general, it is rarely explicitly defined in feminist writings (Allen 1999, 7). In the following, we will explain how we deal with the concept of power and then discuss which of its articulations we found in the different contributions to this volume. We hope to do justice to the multitude of relations between gender and power we found. This multitude might be frustrating from a synthesising point of view, but power is not unidimensional. We do not aim to develop a comprehensive model or theory of the different articulations of power and how they relate to each other, but rather to show the richness and complexity of how gender and power interact in the EP. The asterisks added to both gender and power in the title imply possible suffixes and prefixes, turning these concepts into institutions in themselves but also making it possible to attribute ways of acting – or triggers to act – contexts, and impacts to them that can passively affect us all or be actively stimulated.

## *GENDER*POWER* AS CONCEPT

In political settings, we often think of power in the three dimensions put forward by Lukes (2005). The first dimension of power is very straightforward as it defines power as the capacity to win the vote, to achieve the intended outcome. Speaking of women, this would mean that they manage to win a vote on an issue that is important to them, like promoting gender equality. The second dimension of power that Lukes distinguishes relates not to the outcome of the vote or the power of persuasion that requires, but to the agenda-setting preceding it. Power here means having the capacity to set and dominate the political agenda so as to make sure that only your favoured issues manage to reach the political agenda. When it comes to women, this would not only involve managing to only have favourable issues reach the political but also blocking issues that would harm them, such as the recent bills popping up across Europe attempting to cut down women's rights. The third dimension of power is considered to be the trickiest one, as it refers to the capacity to influence public opinion and thinking at large so as to achieve a hegemony that makes other types of interventions near needless. This would be a setting in which – from the perspective put forward in this book – gender equality would be considered the norm and everything else as deviant.

Yet Lukes' three dimensions are insufficient to capture the relation between gender and power. Power is more than different degrees of domination. It can be creative and constructive, and need not by definition be conceived as a zero-sum game. This chapter thus explores the concept of power and its many faces using Amy Allen's theoretical framework (1998, 1999). Allen also works with a threefold definition, building and reflecting on the three main conceptualisations of power discussed in the literature. These are *power over*, *power to*, and *power with*. Starting from a feminist perspective, she explores what constitutes power. Her comprehensive account includes Arendt's concept of power as well as Lukes' (2005), and Foucault's (1995, 1980) ideas about the normalisation of power through everyday discourses and practices, and about the possibility of resistance that is inherent to power relations. All of them see power as a relationship, but each stresses different aspects, be they the ways to exercise power, levels of manifestation, or actions and practices. Allen tries to bring these different elements together.

According to Allen, *power over* is broadly defined as 'the ability of an actor or set of actors to constrain choices available to another actor or set of actors in a nontrivial way' (Allen 1999, 123). In this 'way of exercising power' (ibid.), *power over* is (in a variety of definitions) the most common variety of power that we encounter in politics. Power is seen as a relationship between subordinated and dominant actors in which the latter are able to constrain the choices or behaviour of the former against their will or preference. As Allen argues, if we add to this definition of *power over* the constraining of choices 'in a way that works to the other's disadvantage' (ibid., 125), this corresponds to domination. For Allen, domination thus is not synonymous with *power over*, but rather a specific form of it. From a feminist perspective, power as domination refers to the 'particular kinds of power that men are able to exercise *over* women' (ibid., 123; emphasis in original) so that they keep women in a subordinate position.

*Power to* for Allen means 'the ability of an individual actor to attain an end or series of ends' (ibid., 126). Lukes (2005, 34) argues that this *power to* 'indicates a "capacity", a "facility", an "ability", not a relationship' and certainly not a relationship between subordinated and dominant groups, as in the case of *power over*. From a feminist approach, *power to* comes closer to the concept of individual empowerment, as it is the power to act that subordinated groups retain even though they are subordinated and, from the perspective of women, it refers to 'our ability to attain certain ends in spite of the subordination of women' (Allen 1999, 126). As Allen puts it, empowerment or *power to* thus is 'the power that women can wield to oppose male domination', or, as she also articulates it, 'the power that women have *in spite* of the power that men exercise over us' (ibid., 122; italics in the original). A particular way of exercising *power to* is resistance, which includes individual actions challenging domination (ibid., 126). Resistance, from a feminist perspective, then is 'the power that women exercise specifically *as a response* to such [male] domination' (ibid., 122; italics in the original). In this conceptualisation, the possibility to find empowerment opportunities within contexts of domination, which is what characterises Allen's concept of power applied to feminist thinking, is particularly evident.

If *power to* has a more individual empowerment dimension, for Allen *power with* highlights the collective dimension of power or the 'ability of a group to act together for the attainment of an agreed-upon end or series of ends' (ibid., 127). Though both conceptualisations of power as an ability or capacity to act, *power to* and *power with*, derive from Arendt's theorisation of power; Allen's conception of *power with* is particularly inspired by Arendt. Arendt did not conceive of power as control over others, but as something that 'springs up whenever people get together and act in concert' (1969, 52) to discuss and address matters of public-political concern; a person has power because they are empowered by a group, so this power emanates from the mutual action of the group (ibid.). Sites of power then are common actions coordinated through speech and persuasion. Arendt's idea of power inspires transformative notions of political power that involve processes of collective empowerment while acting to achieve a common political goal. Her vision emphasises the agency that comes from collective action: 'Power is never the property of an individual; it belongs to a group and remains in existence only so long as the group keeps together' (ibid., 44). When women feel more empowered in politics thanks to the strengthening of women's networks, solidarity, and alliances, this is a great examples of Arendt's notion of power.

Allen applies Arendt's notion of *power with* to understand the collective power that feminists exercise when they 'build coalitions with other social movements, such as the racial equality movement, the gay rights movement, and/or new labor movements' to achieve feminist aims (Allen 1999, 123). Through her feminist articulation of *power with*, Allen is interested in theorising the concept of solidarity to understand the 'collective power that can bridge the diversity of individuals who make up the feminist movement' (ibid., 122) and that can stimulate coalition building among social movements. This concept of solidarity is not exclusionary or based on given, fixed identities, but rather on the collective ability to act together with the aim of 'challenging, subverting, and, ultimately, overturning a system of domination' (ibid., 127). Allen sees in Arendt's concept of power as concerted action the basis for potential intersectional alliances and solidarity: 'Arendt helps us to think about how members of oppositional social movements can be united in a way that, far from excluding or repressing difference, embraces and protects it' (ibid., 104). Velvet triangles (Woodward 2004) and the political discourses articulating such alliances are all examples of this collective empowerment expressed by the notion of *power with*.

Allen's framework conceptualising *power over*, *power to* and *power with* can help us to unpack in what ways power and gender work and interplay at the level of the EP. Simplistically speaking, we can say that gender relations are always also power relations. Starting from this premise, all chapters in this volume analysed power relations. Some chapters focus on who possesses *power over* or *to* and where they are located, while others emphasise the distinction between formal/de jure power and de facto power, and/or between substantial and procedural power. The question then is how this relates to gender, particularly what the power at stake does to gender (relations) and how gender (relations) affect power (im)balances.

This brings two further concepts into the equation: gendered and gendering. Again, these concepts are often used, but seldom precisely defined (Bacchi 2017). Bacchi distinguishes three purposes that the term gendering serves: (1) it indicates 'that some entity needs to be examined through a gender lens', either signalling 'a desire to bring an awareness of gender to a particular topic' (ibid., 23) or looking at it from a gender perspective; (2) it describes the way in which a subject or object becomes ' "gendered", that is, marked as masculine or feminine' (ibid., 23); or (3) it describes 'the active shaping of the categories of "woman" and "man" as kinds of being in a relation of inequality, [. . .]. Gendering practices in this instance constitute "men" and "women' (ibid., 23). The importance of the shift from gender as a category to gendering as a practice lies in its potential to underline that (and how) inequality is created and not simply a static position or status. Bacchi further underlines that gendering as a constituting process never happens alone, rather it exists in parallel to and in interaction with other processes constituting sexuality, ability, class and so on.

For the purpose of the current chapter, we rely on a mixture of the second and third purpose of using the term gendering. Power gives shape to gender, which in turn gives shape to power. We will analyse what the different chapters found in terms of fields, policies, institutions, rules, or practices being marked masculine or feminine – not arguing of what these dimensions consist but simply following the authors' distinctions. We will also look at the way they address gendering as the constitution of men and women. Gendering power relations means that processes of power are marked as masculine or feminine, and that the definition of men and women, and of how processes of power are marked as masculine or feminine, can change.

# *GENDER*POWER WITHIN
# THE EUROPEAN PARLIAMENT

The different analyses of the gendering of structures, policies and practices throughout this book point to the ways in which *power over* and *power to* are intertwined. They also show that *power to* can occur without *power over*, thus confirming Allen's argument of resistance despite subordination (in numerical or structural terms). *Power with* especially exists in the form of alliances and coalitions, not least within the FEMM Committee. However, we also find these forms of power being challenged, for instance, by the rise of right-wing parties and their questioning of gender equality and reconfiguration of gendered power relations.

## *Power Over* and *Power To*

A couple of chapters start by looking into the issue of *power over*, in a first instance referring to men's *power over* women. An example of *power over* in politics is the over-representation of men in parliaments around the world, allowing them to dominate the decisions being taken. Abels' contribution in this volume walks down that line at the outset, analysing the link between *power over* women in relation to the power of the EP, but argues in a different direction than usual. For starters, while the percentage of women in the EP (40.5 per cent) is way above the world average, there is still a vast majority of men, and in that sense the latter have *power over* women, as they can outvote them easily (not even taking into account all the other dimensions of the power over women they dispose of). In this respect, women are a structural minority that cannot turn into a majority unless their number increases. The overall argument tends to be that women are not to be found in high numbers in institutions that have a lot of decision-making power, and that they tend to enter into institutions just as those are losing power. *Power over* for women then goes hand in hand with the absence of much decision-making power, as the institution in which they might have *power over* lacks decision-making power. Abels rightly points out that in the first study ever on women in the EP back in 1986, Vallance and Davies explained the relatively high number of women – compared to their numbers in other legislative bodies – by the fact that European elections are second-order elections and thus of less importance than, for instance, national elections; this is among other issues related to the EP's lack of legislative powers (1986, 6). Abels adds that as the EU polity was 'long perceived as a weak arena for politics, it was initially less interesting for male politicians' (Abels in this volume).

However, Abels then convincingly shows that, in the case of the EP, the more than doubling of the share of women since this legislative body's first election back in 1979 was accompanied by an increase in the institution's powers. She shows how the descriptive representation of women can spill over into their substantive representation because of the increasing legislative powers the EP has acquired. The EP disposes of budgetary and legislative powers, participates in the nomination of Commissioners, and has scrutiny powers vis-à-vis the Commission and, albeit to a lesser extent, the Council. Though the EP's power to legislate is hampered as it lacks the formal right to initiate legislation, has no legislative powers regarding all fields of society, and lacks control over an executive as national parliaments formally do, Abels shows that it has managed to increase its legislating powers over time in a number of fields particularly relevant for gender equality, such as social and employment policy, judicial affairs, migration/asylum, research, and citizenship policy. In her contribution to this volume, van der Vleuten (in this volume) sums this up by stating that the EP has played an agenda-setting role and simultaneously broadened the scope of gender equality-related action from the labour market to other areas such as education and gender-based violence. The FEMM Committee has been proactive, but in plenary 'proposals concerning gender equality have been and continue to be supported by large majorities' too (ibid.).

Mushaben also highlights the *power over* women in the EP, thereby reflecting on the question of critical mass. Throughout her contribution, she convincingly shows how, during the 1980s and 1990s women, MEPs disposed of the power to act and carried out numerous critical acts, although they had not yet reached a critical mass. Intuitively, their low number would have allowed for *power over* women to be exercised, but they seemed to have been able to not be subjected to it. So even at a time when women had not yet reached a critical mass and men could thus easily dominate the EP's debates and policies, women managed to secure some power to act. Mushaben especially refers to the period of the 1980s and 1990s, when the EU produced a more gender-equal frame than compared to subsequent periods and what many of the Member States managed to do in the same period. Mushaben also underlines the capacity of the women of that time to generate *power with* through the impressive bonds, networks and velvet triangles – or pentagons – they managed to establish. Her argument in this contribution is that the fuzziness of those years, the fact that so much was still under construction, and especially the absence of 'rigidly codified procedures' or hierarchical structures left room for women to develop their *power to*, which, in the end, made it possible for them to give shape and contribute to 'EU problem definition and policy formulation regarding gender issues' (Mushaben in this volume). Similarly to Abels, Mushaben thus refers to the relation between *power over* and *power to*. She agrees that there is no linear relation between the two in the sense that men's decreasing *power over* women does not necessarily go hand in hand with an increasing female *power to*. On the contrary, she demonstrates how women's power to act led to what she calls critical acts, which then allowed for furthering their *power to*, not least by breaking the *power over* women.

In her contribution, Zimmermann argues that, compared to other fields, there are not many high-level debates and initiatives on the promotion of gender equality. As van der Vleuten puts it: 'most MEPs continue to see gender equality as a niche affair which does not regard other policy domains' (van der Vleuten in this volume). Abels also points out that most of the debates on matters of gender equality are dominated by women. Women's *power over* a discourse actually carves out their power to act. Zimmermann's chapter discusses the fake nature of *power over* and how it spills over in a limited *power to*. While scholars like Abels and Cengiz show how *power over* and *power to* intertwine in the case of the EP as an increasingly empowered institution, Zimmermann shows how discursive gendering processes feed into *power over* while undermining *power to* and *with*. Zimmermann's chapter focuses on the gendered character of equality debates in the EP and on the gendering processes taking place within them through the social construction of citizens, their relations, and interdependences. Two issues are of relevance here. First, she confirms the well-known fact that debates on equality issues tend to be women-only events, as the vast majority of MEPs attending and participating in these debates are women. In this respect, women do have full control over these debates and thus *power over* the issue. However, as Zimmermann rightly underlines, it is not so much the dominance of women in these debates that is telling, but the absence of men that reflects a certain power position, 'the power of retiring oneself from the discursive visibility', as Zimmermann puts it (Zimmermann in this volume). This is not a forced absence due to women's real dominance or *power over*. It is a voluntary retirement from the discourse and its governance. Power over the debate in terms of dominating it, as Allen would say, here actually reflects a lack of power to act, as the vast majority required to act does not deem it necessary to engage.

Although coming from a totally different perspective, Nugent confirms Zimmermann's analysis of the complex relationship between *power over* and lacking *power to*. Using the concept of a gendered division of labour – here understood as men and women each taking up different aspects of political life and work – Nugent investigates the development and history of the FEMM Committee and its place and role within the EP. Her point is that, when it comes to who deals with gender issues and how, the mostly unchanged and thus stable gendered division of labour shows 'how deeply embedded the gendered order of power is within the FEMM Committee, the EP, and politics' (Nugent in this volume). First of all, though it is a long-standing committee within the EP and has a broad remit, the FEMM Committee is one of the least powerful committees in terms of its neutralised status and the tools it has, making membership an issue of personal interest and willingness to engage. Given the EP's institutional design, the power to act is thus limited. Secondly, membership of FEMM is mainly taken up by women MEPs, and gender issues are mainly put forward, defended, and supported by women MEPs – a phenomenon not exclusive to the EP. It is as if the power to act on behalf of women or gender issues rests solely on the shoulders of women MEPs. It is this division of policy topics, or rather approaches to policy topics, that Nugent calls the gendered division of – in this case – political labour. Interesting in Nugent's analysis is the persistence of this gendered division of political labour over time.

### Power With

While the increase of the EP's power to act did not decrease women's power to act, neither did it necessarily increase their *power with*. Contrary to other EP committees, for instance, the FEMM Committee is only exceptionally assigned the role of competent committee and thus rarely able to take the lead in legislative processes. Its role is rather of a consultative nature. The FEMM Committee would thus be a better forum for *power with* as understood by Allen, though this also largely depends on the political composition of the EP and accordingly of FEMM. Notwithstanding this lack of recognition, it remains an important player. While it often lacks formal *power to*, it remains an important watchdog, pointing out the European institutions' shortcomings in living up to their gender equality commitments. The EP's increased power to act and legislate has thus facilitated, not hampered, the gendering of the Parliament and its policies.

Cengiz' analysis is useful at this point, as she looks into the EP's potential role as a gender budgeting advocate. As taxation and budget policies have a fundamental impact on equality within society, the same goes for the EP. Even in the absence of proper revenue-collecting powers, its spending policies are likely to affect citizens' level of equality. Gender budgeting would be an interesting and justifiable approach for the EP. All the more so, Cengiz argues, given the EU's high-level political and legal commitment to gender equality. Finally, out of all European institutions, the EP would also be best suited to pursue such an approach, given its role of representing the people and advocating the interests of all its citizens, especially in the light of the Council's and Commission's other priorities as, respectively, the budget's providers and spenders. While theoretically the potential exists, as Cengiz convincingly demonstrates, it remains only hypothetical. The EP is politically and ideologically fragmented, and MEPs might also be tempted to toe the line of their country in such matters. The EP has limited veto powers within the budgetary process vis-à-vis the national governments, and there are no incentives to use it. Finally, the FEMM Committee, all in all the main actor in matters of gender equality advocacy, does not have any formal standing to act when it comes to budgetary processes and policies. Though not using this particular language, Cengiz actually suggests adopting a *power with* strategy when she recommends seeking of strategic internal and external networks and alliances, so that members of the FEMM and of the Budget and Budgetary Control Committees can act in concert with other interested stakeholders within the EP and with actors who have influence over the members states' budgetary positions, for instance, in the national parliaments. While this strategy is interesting on paper, in light of the conclusions to be drawn from Abels' chapter, it is unlikely to materialise. In the current climate, such alliances would probably either not emerge or turn out too weak to allow for the power to act. It would also require reframing the current dominant neoliberal discourse limiting the scope of the debate.

Ahrens' analysis of gender mainstreaming in the EP is somewhat positive. Looking into discursive constructions and dynamics, Ahrens analyses how the FEMM Committee managed to keep gender mainstreaming on the EP agenda and even institutionalised it. It is particularly interesting how she shows that the FEMM Committee not only focused on gender mainstreaming in itself, but also on its own role, making it impossible to forget about not just gender mainstreaming but FEMM as well. While not stating it explicitly, Ahrens' contribution underlines the importance of committed actors within the FEMM Committee and of it as a hub or space for concerted feminist action in order to push *power to* and *power with*.

## National and European Power Dynamics

Chiva's and Cullen's contributions to this volume take a different approach, looking at the power dynamics, including gender relations, in national politics and those at the level of the EP. They show how *power over* women at the national level spills over into the EP and partly hampers MEPs' *power to* and especially *power with*. For the case of the South-East European countries, Chiva asks whether the representation of women in the EU's postcommunist Member States' EP delegations helps to overcome male dominance. She argues that these countries constitute a distinctive group within the EU, which, in the context of this volume, is to be understood as being due to women's descriptive underrepresentation in their national parliaments (*power over* women), but also due to the 'marginalisation of women's voices in political debate and policy-making, and perpetuation of gender stereotypes concerning women's roles within the traditional family unit in political debate' (Chiva in this volume). These forms of *power over* women at different levels of the political system strongly hamper their *power to*, as Chiva underlines that descriptive underrepresentation thus spills over into limited substantive representation: 'it is not simply that women are numerically a minority in national legislatures; it is also the case that critical actors' ability to "act for" women is also constrained by a heavily male-dominated environment' (ibid.).

Looking into the Irish case, Cullen asks a similar question. Throughout these two chapters, both authors show how nationally prevailing frames on gender relations in South-Eastern Europe and Ireland dominate the respective women MEPs' projections of their work and priorities in the EP. Cullen argues, for instance, that most female Irish MEPs did not demonstrate a high level of commitment to address gender equality when they were MEPs. Chiva shows how South East European women MEPs do partly display a more conservative voting pattern on women's issues than other female MEPs. Both argue that the women MEPs they studied voted along similar lines as they would have done in their national parliament, thereby actually not differing from (women) MEPs from other Member States. Political positions at the national level overall are a solid predictor of voting positions within the EP.

Cullen also demonstrates how nationally prevailing gender frames prevent Irish women MEPs from, for instance, serving on the FEMM Committee, given the dominant Irish position on abortion. Yet this does not mean that some of these women MEPs would not have liked to take a more progressive position on a number of matters. They felt committed to the line their national party drew in these matters and thus refrained from serving on the FEMM Committee, as it might have put them in a difficult position when their party line proved incompatible with FEMM's. While in other cases MEPs might consciously opt to join FEMM so as to defend conservative positions traditionally not defended in the FEMM Committee, these women chose not to. They would not have liked to defend the conservative positions of their national party's line and dominant national gender frames, which they did not necessarily share. In this respect, the national political context and its *power over* women hampered them in their leeway to develop power to act within the EP, nor did they have *power with*, as they saw limited to no options to join FEMM so as to develop concerted action with other feminist MEPs.

However, both scholars underline that this does not mean that the national context dominated the entire action radius of (women) MEPs from Ireland or the South-East European Member States. Cullen shows that the EU had an important influence on the development and evolution of gender equality legislation in Ireland. It contributed to breaking up the very conservative Irish gender regime, making Irish policies less patriarchal and familial, as she calls it. And as their time and work in the EP shaped their feminist consciousness and attitudes, it also made Irish MEPs take up more progressive positions back home. Chiva shows how the EP managed to crack the *power over* women in the sense that the mainstream parties active in South-Eastern Europe that belong to the three main European party groups tend to have more women MEPs elected than their proportion of women MPs in the national parliaments would suggest. While others in this volume join a general argument that this might have to do with the EP's limited amount of power compared to other parliaments, in the South-East European context it is nonetheless a politically interesting institution. Chiva calls this a socialisation effect for the parties from the South-East European Member States, whereby the latter tend to respond to EU-level expectations in terms of descriptive gender equality.

## The Challenges of Opposing Power(s)

As van der Vleuten underlines, there are also clear patterns of opposition. The opposing voices come from right-wing nationalists, conservatives and Eurosceptics; these party groups have increased in numbers and are supported by some Christian Democrats. van der Vleuten shows how these arguments are similar to those found in national politics: 'liberals will criticize costs of regulation and claim respect for individual choices; conservative Christians defend essentialist positions, the family as composed of man–woman–children and special treatment for mothers; national-ist conservatives and Eurosceptics oppose every regulation or budget line for gender equality policies as an attack on state sovereignty' (van der Vleuten in this volume). Parallel to the rise of these parties, their arguments have also grown stronger over the past years. Warasin, Kantola, Rolandsen Agustín and Coughlan confirm these find-ings. They look into the ways in which gender equality is politicised within the EP and point to an increasing politicisation of gender equality issues. They further show that debates around gender equality are particularly polarising compared to other debates. This dynamic is to be found within the FEMM Committee as well as in the EP plenary, both seeing an increase in conflictual inter-group relations. The grand coalition of centre-right and centre-left political groups is less strong when it comes to gender equality issues than when it comes to other issues. Though cross-group alliances do still exist, they are issue-specific, and this is especially the case within the FEMM Committee.

Without dealing with the issue in depth, Mushaben also evokes the rise of Euro-phobic parties within the EP and how they counter a feminist gendering of policy issues, as do Ahrens, Cengiz and Zimmermann. These chapters show that there now is more of a counter-discourse than used to be the case in the past. Furthermore, it is often intermingled with anti-immigrant (mainly anti-Muslim) discourse. While this opens up the debate, it does not necessarily broaden it to an extent that takes the needs, interests, and contexts of diverse groups of citizens into account, in fact, it is thus not allowing for *power with* to develop.

Unpacking what she calls the European discourse community, Zimmermann shows how it presents a certain social reality by foregrounding particular gender positions and relations, more precisely binary, elitist and neoliberal ones, as she describes them. In this discourse community, gender quasi-exclusively refers to het-erosexual cis-gendered men and women and considers them homogenous groups. Intersectional or gender-critical positions are mostly absent, not only making the gender discourse presented in the EP old-fashioned, but equally turning it, due to the homogeneous presentation, into what she calls an unobjectionable norm. As Zimmermann underlines, this particular gendering or social construction of men and women is relevant, as it is not only an issue of political-discourse production, but it may also literally normalise certain presentations over others. Since debates are characterised by the dominance of binary, cis-gendered, and heteronormative concepts and articulations, 'the gender discourse in the EP is revealed as precarious, turning a blind eye on intersectional realities, and finally running a risk to enhance some of these social inequalities it ignores' (Zimmerman in this volume). It is the last point that is key. A narrow gendering of men and women in all their dimen-sions strongly reduces the power to act, as the framing of gender relations provides little space to present what could be labelled non-normalised presentations. This last dynamic also undermines the possibility of *power with*, as broader alliances allowing for the empowerment of larger groups of citizens are strongly hampered. A small group is dominating the process of gendering social relations, presenting them in a narrow way. All in all, this leaves little room for gender equality debates to come up with innovative or far-reaching analyses of gender positions and relations, or of subsequent policies. To the contrary, Zimmermann shows how all of this shuts down any options for moving forward.

## LESSONS TO DRAW?

Reading the different contributions within this volume from a power perspective allowed us to not only connect them beyond their individual contributions, but also to show how complex relations between gender and power are, also within the EP. This book convincingly shows that the EP is not such a unified actor for gender equality as generally tends to be assumed. A first explanation for this is the fact that the EP is a highly gendered institution in itself, as many of the contributions in this volume show. Referring back to Bacchi's (2017) distinction, this means that institutions are marked as either masculine or feminine, and that gendered practices constitute the idea of men and women as well as their unequal relation. The genderedness of the EP thus refers to the presence of men and women MEPs and the division of labour within the institution. It also refers to the gendered dominant discourses, including the ways in which these articulate ideas of heteronormativity and generally lack concern for intersectional demands, for example.

Looking at its genderedness through power lenses shows us that in the EP *power over* does not necessarily involve *power to*, and that it is precisely its genderedness that hampers *power with*. *Power over* (as the ability to constrain the choices of others) and *power to* (the individual ability to achieve an end) are intertwined. But this book's contributions do not confirm conventional expectations in several ways: firstly, though men still have power over women in numerical terms, it is decreasing, this despite the fact that the EP has simultaneously gained power. Secondly, *power to*, in the form of critical acts, has preceded critical mass (which is meant to enable *power over*), since women used existing opportunities for potential resistance despite numerical, discursive, and/or structural domination. Expectations are confirmed, however, in the sense that gender equality within the EP as an institution is characterised by a lack of power: men are absent in the debates, and the FEMM Committee lacks power. In other words, women hold *power over* in terms of the debate but lack *power to* due to a general lack of interest in the policy field gender equality; this is nevertheless partly contested by the fact that gender equality is an increasingly politicised area where symbolic stakes are getting higher, also in light of the rise of right-wing parties. And finally, looking at the national/transnational dynamic, national frames tend to dominate work in the EP, thus affecting and constraining *power to* and *power with* at the European level.

The collective ability to achieve ends through alliances and coalitions, defined as *power with*, is somewhat challenged in the context of the EP. While the FEMM Committee acts as the main space for developing *power with* through alliances of committed actors and has the important role of initiator and watchdog, it also lacks recognition, and in some policy areas the necessary alliances with other stakeholders that feminist policy change requires do not materialise. We could thus argue that there is engagement for *power to* within the EP, but not necessarily for *power over* or *with*. What has been promoted as gender equality fluctuates strongly over time, and the EP has not always been very effective in promoting gender equality. This fluctuating and varying engagement for *power to* can be explained by the varying presence and absence over time of individual actors committed to the cause of gender equality, some organised in velvet triangles. This chapter's theorisations of power show that power in feminist analyses is never just domination or empowerment – as

Allen would say – but always a mix of the two. Empirically grasping this interplay inherent to the concept of power is very important for feminist analyses of political institutions and processes. There is thus much more at stake than the fact that the EP is an institution lacking power compared to many other legislatures and other European institutions.

# NOTE

1  Petra Ahrens' work received funding from the European Research Council (ERC) under grant agreement No. 771676 of the European Union's Horizon 2020 research and innovation programme.

# References

Abels, Gabriele, and Joyce Marie Mushaben. 2012. "Conclusion: Rethinking the Double Democratic Deficit of the EU." In *Gendering the European Union: New Approaches to Old Democratic Deficits,* edited by Gabriele Abels and Joyce Marie Mushaben, 228–47. London: Palgrave Macmillan.

Abels, Gabriele, and Joyce Marie Mushaben. 2014. " 'Dieses Mal ist es anders' – oder doch nicht? Eine genderpolitische Analyse der Europawahl 2014 und ihrer Folgen." *Femina Politica* 23(2): 138–50.

Abels, Gabriele. 2011. "Gender Equality Policy." In *Policies within the EU Multi-Level System. Instruments and Strategies of European Governance,* edited by Hubert Heinelt and Michèle Knodt, 325–48. Baden-Baden: Nomos.

Abels, Gabriele. 2012. "Research by, for and about Women: Gendering Science and Research Policy." In *Gendering the European Union: New Approaches to Old Democratic Deficits,* edited by Gabriele Abels and Joyce Marie Mushaben, 187–207. New York: Palgrave Macmillan.

Abels, Gabriele. 2013. "Parlamentarische Kontrolle im Mehrebenensystem der EU – ein unmögliches Unterfangen?" In *Parlamentarische Kontrolle und Europäische Union,* edited by Birgit Eberbach-Born, Sabine Kropp, Andrej Stuchlik, and Wolfgang Zeh, 79–102. Baden-Baden: Nomos-Verlag.

Abels, Gabriele. 2015. "Where Women Stand: Descriptive vs. Substantive Representation in the European Parliament Since the 2014 Election." Paper presented to the European Consortium for Political Research (ECPR) Gender and Politics Conference, University of Montreal, August 2015.

Acker, Joan. 1992. "From Sex Roles to Gendered Institutions." *Contemporary Sociology* 21(5): 565–69.

Addabo, Tindara, Lanzi, Diego, and Picchio, Antonella. 2010. "Gender Budgets: A Capability Approach." *Journal of Human Development and Capabilities* 11(4): 479–501.

Ahrens, Petra, and Anne-Charlott Callerstig. 2017. "The European Social Fund and the Institutionalisation of Gender Mainstreaming in Sweden and Germany." In *Towards Gendering*

*Institutionalism,* edited by Heather MacRae, and Elaine Weiner. New York: Rowman & Littlefield.

Ahrens, Petra, and Anna van der Vleuten. (2019). "Fish Fingers and Measles? Assessing Complex Gender Equality in the Scenarios for the Future of Europe." *Journal of Common Market Studies* https://doi.org/10.1111/jcms.12922.

Ahrens, Petra. 2016. "The Committee on Women's Rights and Gender Equality in the European Parliament: Taking Advantage of Institutional Power Play." *Parliamentary Affairs* 69(4): 778–93.

Ahrens, Petra. 2018a. *Actors, Institutions and the Making of EU Gender Equality Programs.* Basingstoke: Palgrave Macmillan.

Ahrens, Petra. 2018b. "Anti-feministische Politiker*innen im Frauenrechtsausschuss des Europäischen Parlaments – Wendepunkt oder Resilienz in der EU Gleichstellungspolitik?" *Feministische Studien* 36(2): 403–16.

Allegretti, Giovanni, and Roberto Falanga. 2016. "Women in Budgeting: A Critical Assessment of Participatory Budgeting and Experiences." In *Gender Responsive and Participatory Budgeting,* edited by Cecilia Ng. New York: Springer.

Allen, Amy. 1998. "Rethinking Power." *Hypatia* 13(1): 21–40.

Allen, Amy. 1999. *The Power of Feminist Theory: Domination, Resistance, Solidarity.* New York: Westview.

Anosovs, Evarts, Eva-Maria A. Poptcheva, and Giulio Sabbati. 2014. "Women in Parliaments." *At a Glance,* 27 April 2014 https://www.europarl.europa.eu/RegData/bibliotheque/briefing/2014/140765/LDM_BRI(2014)140765_REV2_EN.pdf.

Arendt, Hannah. 1969. *On Violence.* New York: Harcourt, Brace, Jovanovich.

Arnold, Laura W., and Barbara M. King. 2003. "Women, Committees, and Institutional Change." In *Women Transforming Congress,* edited by Cindy Simon Rosenthal, 284–315. Norman, OK: University of Oklahoma Press.

Bacchi, Carol Lee. 1999. *Women, Policy, and Politics: The Construction of Policy Problems.* London: Sage.

Bacchi, Carol Lee. 2009. "The Issue of Intentionality in Frame Theory: The Need for Reflexive Framing." In *The Discursive Politics of Gender Equality. Stretching, Bending and Policymaking,* edited by Emanuela Lombardo, Petra Meier and Mieke Verloo, 19–35. London: Routledge.

Bacchi, Carol. 2017. "Policies as Gendering Practices: Re-Viewing Categorical Distinctions." *Journal of Women, Politics & Policy* 38(1): 20–41. doi: 10.1080/1554477X.2016.1198207.

Baekgaard, Martin, and Ulrik Kjaer. 2012. "The Gendered Division of Labor in Assignments to Political Committees: Discrimination or Self-Selection in Danish Local Politics?" *Politics & Gender* 8(04): 465–82. https://doi.org/10.1017/S1743923X12000499.

Barnes, Tiffany. 2014. "Women's Representation and Legislative Committee Appointments: The Case of the Argentine Provinces." *Revista Uruguaya de Ciencia Política* 23(2): 135–63.

Bassel, Leah, and Akwugo Emejulu. 2017. *Minority Women and Austerity: Survival and Resistance in France and Britain.* Bristol: Policy Press.

Beaudoin, Steven. 2013. "Microhistoire, performance et étude de débats parlementaires: le 'Thermidor'de Victorien Sardou e tle Théâtre de la politique." In *Faire parler le parlement. Méthodes et enjeux de l'analyse des débats parlementaires pour les sciences sociales,* edited by Claire de Galembert, Olivier Rozenberg and Cécile Vigour, 109–25. Paris: Réseau Européen Droit et Société.

Behning, Ute, and Birgit Sauer, eds. 2005. *Was bewirkt Gender Mainstreaming? Evaluierung durch Policy-Analysen.* Frankfurt am Main: Campus-Verlag.

Bekkengen, Lisbeth. 2002. "Man Får Välja: Om Föräldraskap Och Föräldraledighet i Arbetsliv Och Familjeliv [You May Choose – Parenting and Parental Leave in Working Life and Family]." Karlstad: University, Institutionen för ekonomi.

Beloff, Max, and Gillian Peele. 1985. *The Government of the UK: Political Authority in a Changing Society.* New York: Norton.

Benedetto, Giacomo. 2005. "Rapporteurs as Legislative Entrepreneurs: The Dynamics of the Codecision Procedure in Europe's Parliament." *Journal of European Public Policy* 12(2): 67–88.

Benedetto, Giacomo. 2012. "Budget Reform and the Lisbon Treaty." In *European Union Budget Reform,* edited by Giacomo Benedetto, 40–58. London: Palgrave Macmillan.

Bennett, Andrew, and Jeffrey T. Checkel. 2015. *Process Tracing: From Metaphor to Analytic Tool.* Cambridge: Cambridge University Press.

Berger, Peter, and Thomas Luckmann. 1980. *Die gesellschaftliche Konstruktion der Wirklichkeit: Eine Theorie der Wissenssoziologie.* Frankfurt/Main: Fischer-Taschenbuch-Verlag.

Bergqvist, Christina, Elin Bjarnegård, and Pär Zetterberg. 2016. "The Gendered Leeway: Male Privilege, Internal and External Mandates, and Gender equality Policy Change." *Politics, Groups, and Identities* 0(0): 1–17. https://doi.org/10.1080/21565503.2016.1229627.

Beveridge, Fiona, and Samantha Velluti. 2008. *Gender and the Open Method of Coordination: Perspectives on Law, Governance and Equality in the EU.* Aldershot, UK: Ashgate.

Beveridge, Fiona, Sue Nott, and Kylie Stephen. 2000. "Mainstreaming and the Engendering of Policy-Making: A Means to an End?" *Journal of European Public Policy* 7(3): 385–405.

Birchfield, Vicki, and Geoffrey Harris. March 2015. "European Parliamentary Elections: Global Lessons from a Regional Political Crisis." Paper presented at the European Union Studies Association Biennial Conference, Boston, MA.

Bird, Karen. 2005. "Gendering Parliamentary Questions." *British Journal of Politics and International Relations* 7: 353–70.

Bjarnegård, Elin, and Rainbow Murray. 2015. "The Causes and Consequences of Male Over-Representation: A Research Agenda." Paper presented at the ECPR Joint Sessions Workshop on *The Causes and Consequences of Male Over-representation,* Warsaw, April 2015.

Bjarnegård, Elin. 2013. *Gender, Informal Institutions and Political Recruitment: Explaining Male Dominance in Parliamentary Representation.* Basingstoke: Palgrave Macmillan.

Blomgren, Magnus. 2003. *Cross-Pressure and Political Representation in Europe: A Comparative Study of MEPs and the Intra-Party Arena.* Statsvetenskapliga institutionens skriftserie, Umeå universitet. https://www.diva-portal.org/smash/get/diva2:140194/FULLTEXT01.pdf.

Boltanski, Luc, and Eve Chiapello. 2005. *The New Spirit of Capitalism.* London/New York: Verso.

Bolzendahl, Catherine I., and Daniel J. Myers. 2004. "Feminist Attitudes and Support for Gender Equality: Opinion Change in Women and Men, 1974–1998." *Social Forces* 83(2): 759–89. https://doi.org/10.2307/3598347.

Bolzendahl, Catherine I. 2014. "Opportunities and Expectations: The Gendered Organisation of Legislative Committees in Germany, Sweden, and the United States." *Gender & Society* 28(6): 847–76. https://doi.org/10.1177/0891243214542429.

Brazier, Alex, and Ruth Fox. 2011. "Reviewing Select Committee Tasks and Modes of Operation." *Parliamentary Affairs* 64(2): 354–69. https://doi.org/10.1093/pa/gsr007.

Brunn, Gerhard. 2012. *Die europäische Einigung.* Stuttgart: Reclam.

Buckley, Fiona, and Yvonne Galligan. 2013. "Politics and Gender on the Island of Ireland: The Quest for Political Agency." *Irish Political Studies* 28(3): 315–21.

Buckley, Fiona, Yvonne Galligan, and Claire McGing. 2016. "Women and the Election: Assessing the Impact of Gender Quotas." In *How Ireland Voted 2016: The Election That Nobody Won,* edited by Michael Gallagher and Michael Marsh, 185–205. Basingstoke: Palgrave Macmillan.

Buckley, Fiona. 2013. "Women and Politics in Ireland: The Road to Sex Quotas." *Irish Political Studies* 28(3): 341–59.

Budlender, Debbie, ed. 2010. *Gender Budgeting in South Eastern Europe: UNIFEM Experiences.* Bratislava: UNIFEM.

Budlender, Debbie, Elson, Diane, Hewitt, Guy, and Mukhopadhyay, Tani, eds. 2002. *Gender Budgets Make Cents: Understanding Gender-Responsive Budgets.* London: Commonwealth Secretariat.

Burns, Charlotte, Anna Rasmussen, and Christine Reh, 2013. "Legislative Codecision and Its Impact on the Political System of the European Union." *Journal of European Public Policy* 20(7): 941–52.

Burns, Charlotte. 2013. "Consensus and Compromise Become Ordinary – But at What Cost? A Critical Analysis of the Impact of the Changing Norms of Codecision upon European Parliament Committees." *Journal of European Public Policy* 20(7): 988–1005.

Buzogány, Aaron. 2013. "Learning from the Best? Interparliamentary Networks and the Parliamentary Scrutiny of EU Decision-Making." In *Practices of Inter-Parliamentary Coordination in International Politics – The European Union and Beyond,* edited by Ben Crum, and John Erik Fossum, 17–32. Colchester: ECPR Press.

Carroll, Susan J. 2008. "Committee Assignments: Discrimination or Choice?" In *Legislative Women: Getting Elected, Getting Ahead,* edited by Beth Reingold. Boulder, CO: Lynne Rienner Publishers.

Celis, Karen, and Joni Lovenduski. 2018. "Power Struggles: Gender Equality in Political Representation." *European Journal of Politics and Gender* 1(1–2): 149–66.

Celis, Karen, and Sarah Childs. 2012. "The Substantive Representation of Women: What to Do with Conservative Claims?" *Political Studies* 60(2): 213–25.

Celis, Karen, and Sarah Childs. 2018. "Conservatism and Women's Political Representation." *Politics & Gender* 14(1): 5–26.

Celis, Karen, Sarah Childs, Johanna Kantola, and Mona Lena Krook. 2008. "Rethinking Women's Substantive Representation." *Representation* 44(2): 99–110.

Celis, Karen, Sarah Childs, Johanna Kantola, and Mona Lena Krook. 2014. "Constituting Women's Interests through Representative Claims." *Politics and Gender* 10(2): 149–74.

Celis, Karen. 2009. "Substantive Representation of Women (and Improving It): What It is and Should Be About?" *Comparative European Politics* 7(1): 95–113.

Chappell, Louise, and Georgina Waylen. 2013. "Gender and the Hidden Life of Institutions." *Public Administration* 91(3): 599–615.

Childs, Sarah, and Mona Lena Krook. 2006. "Critical Perspectives: Do Women Represent Women? Rethinking the 'Critical Mass' Debate." *Politics & Gender* 2: 491–530. https://doi.org/10.1017/S1743923X06061149.

Childs, Sarah, and Mona Lena Krook. 2009. "Analysing Women's Substantive Representation: From Critical Mass to Critical Actors." *Government and Opposition* 44(2): 125–45.

Childs, Sarah, and Julie Withey. 2004. "Women Representatives Acting for Women: Sex and the Signing of Early Day Motions in the 1997 British Parliament." *Political Studies* 52(3): 552–64. https://doi.org/10.1111/j.1467-9248.2004.00495.x.

Childs, Sarah. 2001. "'Attitudinally Feminist'? The New Labour Women MPs and the Substantive Representation of Women." *Politics* 21(3): 178–85. https://doi.org/10.1111/1467-9256.00149.

Childs, Sarah. 2016. *The Good Parliament*. Bristol: BUP.

Chiva, Cristina. 2014. "Gender, European Integration and Candidate Recruitment: The European Parliament Elections in the New EU Member States." *Parliamentary Affairs* 67(2): 458–94.

Chiva, Cristina. 2017. *Gender, Institutions and Political Representation: Reproducing Male Dominance in Europe's New Democracies*. Basingstoke: Palgrave Macmillan.

Cicchi, Lorenzo. 2016. *Is Euro-Voting Truly Supranational? National affiliation and political group membership in European Parliament*. Pisa: Pisa University Press.

Cicchi, Lorenzo. 2017. "The European Parliament's Political Groups: Between High Cohesion and Recurrent Breakdowns." In *PADEMIA Research Notes on Parliamentary Democracy*, 2017/03.

Coffe, Hilde, and Katia Schnellecke. 2013. "Female Representation in German Parliamentary Committees: 1972–2009." In *ECPR General Conference*. Bordeaux, France, 4–7 September 2013. https://doi.org/10.1017/CBO9781107415324.004.

Collins, Ken, Charlotte Burns, and Alex Warleigh. 1998. "Policy Entrepreneurs: The Role of European Parliament Committees in the Making of EU Policy." *State Law Review* 19(1): 1–11.

Committee on Women's Right and Gender Equality. 2010. Report on Gender Aspects of the Economic Downturn and Financial Crisis. (2009/2204 (INI)). Rapporteur Raúl Romeva i Rueda (Greens/EFA). Brussels: European Parliament.

Committee on Women's Right and Gender Equality. 2013a. Report on the Impact of the Economic Crisis on Gender Equality and Women's Rights (2012/2301 (INI)). Rapporteur Elisabeth Morin-Chartier (EPP). Brussels: European Parliament.

Committee on Women's Right and Gender Equality. 2013b. Report on Sexual and Reproductive Health and Rights – 2013 (2013/2040 (INI)). Rapporteur Edite Estrela (S&D). Brussels: European Parliament.

Committee on Women's Right and Gender Equality. 2014. Report on Equality between Women and Men in the European Union – 2012 (2013/2156 (INI)). Rapporteur Inés Cristina Zuber (GUE/NGL). Brussels: European Parliament.

Corbett, Richard, Francis Jacobs, and Darren Neville. 2016. *The European Parliament*. 9th ed. London: John Harper Publishing.

Costello, Rory, and Robert Thomson. 2010. "The Policy Impact of Leadership in Committees: Rapporteurs' Influence on the European Parliament's Opinions." *European Union Politics* 11(2): 219–40.

Council of Europe. 1998. *Conceptual Framework, Methodology and Presentation of Good Practices: Final Report of Activities of the Group of Specialists on Mainstreaming*. Strasbourg: EG-S-MS. Strasbourg: Council of Europe.

Council of Europe. 2005. *Gender Budgeting: Final Report of the Group of Specialists on Gender Budgeting*. Strasbourg: Council of Europe.

Crawford, Mary, and Barbara Pini. 2011. "The Australian Parliament: A Gendered Organisation." *Parliamentary Affairs* 64(1): 82–105. https://doi.org/10.1093/pa/gsq047.

Crenshaw, Kimberlé. 1989. "Demarginalizing the Intersection of Race and Sex: A Black Feminist Critique of Antidiscrimination Doctrine, Feminist Theory and Antiracist Politics." *The University of Chicago Legal Forum* 1989: 139–67.

Crenshaw, Kimberlé. 1991. "Mapping the Margins: Intersectionality, Identity Politics and Violence against Women of Colour." *Stanford Law Review* 43(6): 1241–99.

Crum, Ben, and John Erik Fossum, eds. 2013. *Practices of Interparliamentary Coordination in International Politics: The European Union and Beyond*. Colchester: ECPR Press.

Culhane, Leah. 2017. "Local Heroes and 'cute hoors': Informal Institutions, Male Over-representation and Candidate Selection in the Republic of Ireland." In *The Irish Legislative*

*Gender Quota: The First Election in G. Waylen: Gender and Informal Institutions*, 45–66. London: Rowman & Littlefield International.

Cullen, Pauline, and Mary Murphy. 2016. "Gendered Mobilisations against Austerity in Ireland." *Gender, Work & Organisation* 24(1): 83–97.

Cullen, Pauline, and Mary P. Murphy. 2018. "Irish Feminist Approaches against Austerity Regimes. Austerity, Gender Inequality and Feminism after the Crisis in Ireland." *Rosa Luxemburg Foundation.* https://www.rosalux.eu/publications/irish-feminist-approaches-against-austerity-regimes/.

Cullen, Pauline. 2015. "Feminist NGOs and the European Union: Contracting Opportunities and Strategic Response." *Social Movement Studies* 14(4): 410–426.

Cullen, Pauline. 2018. "Irish Female Members of the European Parliament: Critical Actors for Women's Interests?" *Politics & Gender* 14(3): 483–511.

Dahlerup, Drude, and Monique Leyenaar. 2013a. *Breaking Male Dominance in Old Democracies*. Oxford: Oxford University Press.

Dahlerup, Drude, and Monique Leyenaar. 2013b. "Introduction." In *Breaking Male Dominance in Old Democracies*, edited by Drude Dahlerup and Monique Leyenaar, 1–19. Oxford: Oxford University Press.

Dahlerup, Drude. 2006. "The Story of the Theory of Critical Mass." *Politics & Gender* 2(4): 511–22.

De Wilde, Pieter. 2011. "No Polity for Old Politics? A Framework for Analyzing the Politicization of European Integration." *Journal of European Integration* 33(5): 559–75.

Debusscher, Petra, and Anna van der Vleuten. 2017. "Equality Policies in the EU through a Feminist Historical Institutionalist Lens." In *Towards Gendering Institutionalism Equality in Europe,* edited by Heather MacRae and Elaine Weiner, 3–24. London: Rowman & Littlefield.

Della Porta, Donatella, and Dieter Rucht, eds. 2013. *Meeting Democracy*. New York: Cambridge University Press.

Devitt, Camilla. 2015. "Mothers or Migrants? Labour Supply Policies in Ireland 1997–2007." *Social Politics* 23(2): 214–38.

Diamond, Irene. 1977. *Sex Roles in the State House*. New Haven, CT: Yale University Press.

Diaz, Mercedes Mateo. 2005. *Representing Women? Female Legislators in West European Parliaments*. Colchester: ECPR Press.

Dodson, Debra L. 2006. *The Impact of Women in Congress*. Oxford: Oxford University Press.

Dovi, Suzanne. 2015. "The Politics of Non-Presence" Paper prepared for presentation at the ECPG Conference. Uppsala, 11–13 June 2015.

Dustin, Moira, Ferreira, Nuno, and Susan Millns, eds. 2019. *Gender and Queer Perspectives on Brexit*. Basingstoke: Palgrave Macmillan.

Eder, Klaus. 2010. "Europe as a Narrative Network. Taking the Social Embeddedness of Identity constructions seriously." In *Debating Political Identity and Legitimacy in the European Union. Interdisciplinary Views,* edited by Sonia Lucarelli, Furio Cerutti, and Vivien A. Schmidt, 38–55. London; New York: Routledge/GARNET.

Edwards, Alice. 2010. "Transitioning Gender: Feminist Engagement with International Refugee Law and Policy 1950–2010." *Refugee Survey Quarterly* 29(2): 21–45.

Einhorn, Barbara. 1993. *Cinderella Goes to Market: Citizenship, Gender and Women's Movements in East Central Europe*. London: Verso.

Einhorn, Barbara. 2006. *Citizenship in an Enlarging Europe: From Dream to Awakening*. Basingstoke: Palgrave Macmillan.

Elgström, Ole. 2005. "Consolidating 'Unobjectionable' Norms: Negotiating Norm Spread in the European Union." In *European Union Negotiations: Processes, Networks and Institutions*, edited by Ole Elgström and Christer Jönsson, 29–44. London/New York: Routledge.

Elomäki, Anna, and Kantola Johanna. 2018. "Theorizing Feminist Struggles in the Triangle of Neoliberalism, Conservatism and Nationalism." *Social Politics* 25(3): 337–60.

Elomäki, Anna. 2015. "The Economic Case for Gender Equality in the European Union: Selling Equality to Decision-Makers and Neoliberalism to Women's Organisations." *European Journal of Women's Studies* 22(3): 288–302.

Elomäki, Anna. 2018. "Gender Quotas for Corporate Boards: Depoliticising Gender and the Economy." *NORA Nordic Journal of Women s Studies* 26(1): 53–68.

Erzeel, Sylvia, and Karen Celis. 2016. "Political Parties, Ideology and the Substantive Representation of Women." *Party Politics* 22(5): 576–86.

Erzeel, Silvia. 2015. "Explaining Legislators' Actions on Behalf of Women in the Parliamentary Party Group: The Role of Attitudes, Resources, and Opportunities." *Journal of Women, Politics & Policy* 36(4): 440–63.

Euractiv. 2015. "MEPs Fuming Over Commission's Abandonment of Maternity Leave Directive." 2 July 2015. https://www.euractiv.com/section/justice-home-affairs/news/meps-fuming-over-commission-s-abandonment-of-maternity-leave-directive/ (last accessed on 20 November 2018).

Eurofound. 2014. *Social Partners and Gender Equality in Europe*. Luxemburg: Publications Office of the European Union.

European Commission. 2012. "Proposal for a Directive of the European Parliament and of the Council on Improving the Gender Balance Among Non-Executive Directors of Companies Listed on Stock Exchange and Related Measures." COM(2012) 614 final. Brussels, 14 November 2012.

European Commission. 2014. "Gender Equality: EU Action Triggers STeady Progress." Press Release, Brussels, 14 April 2014.

European Commission. 2015. "Delivering for Parents: Commission Withdraws Stalled Maternity Leave Proposal and Paves the Way for a Fresh Approach." Press Release, Brussels, 1 July 2015.

European Institute for Gender Equality. 2015. *Gender Equality Index 2015 – Measuring Gender Equality in the European Union 2005–2012*. Vilnius: EIGE. https://eige.europa.eu/gender-equality-index/2012.

European Institute for Gender Equality. 2017. *Gender Equality Index 2017 – Measuring gender equality in the European Union 2005–2015*. Vilnius. https://eige.europa.eu/gender-equality-index/2015.

European Parliament – Legislative Observatory. 2008. *Health and Safety at Work: Workers Who Are Pregnant, Have Recently Given Birth or Are Breastfeeding*. Procedure File 2008/0193(COD).

European Parliament – Legislative Observatory. 2010. *Women and Business Leadership*. Procedure File 2010/2115 (INI).

European Parliament – Legislative Observatory. 2011. *Women in Political Decision Making – Quality and Equality*. Procedure File 2011/2295 (INI).

European Parliament – Legislative Observatory. 2014. *Progress on Equality between Women and Men in the European Union in 2013*. Procedure File 2014/2217 (INI).

European Parliament News. 2011. "Women's Rights Committee's New Chair 'Feminist to His Fingertips'. " http://www.europarl.europa.eu/news/en/news-room/20111014STO29303/Women's-Rights-committee's-new-chair-feminist-to-his-fingertips.

European Parliament. 1984. "Report Drawn Up on Behalf of the Committee on Social Affairs and Employment on the Proposal from the Commission of the European Communities to the Council for a Directive on Parental Leave and Leave for Family Reasons." http://aei.pitt.edu/61767/1/B1843.pdf.

European Parliament. 2003a. "Resolution on Gender Mainstreaming in the European Parliament (2002/2025 (INI))."

European Parliament. 2003b. "Report on Gender Mainstreaming in the European Parliament (2002/2025 (INI))."

European Parliament. 2006a. "Report on Gender Mainstreaming in the Work of the Committees (2005/2149 (INI))."

European Parliament. 2006b. "Debates. Thursday, 1 June 2006 – Brussels." http://www.europarl.europa.eu/sides/getDoc.do?pubRef=-//EP//TEXT+CRE+20060601+ITEM-008+DOC+XML+V0//EN&language=EN&query=INTERV&detail=4-155.

European Parliament. 2006c. "Working Document on the Integrated Approach to Equality between Men and Women in the Work of the Committees (INI/2005/2149)." Rapporteur: Anna Záborská. http://www.europarl.europa.eu/sides/getDoc.do?pubRef=//EP//NONSGML+COMPARL+PE378.717 + 01+DOC+PDF+V0 //EN&language=EN.

European Parliament. 2009a. "Report on the Gender Mainstreaming in the Work of Its Committees and Delegations (short presentation) (2008)/2245 (INI))." Rapporteur: Anna Záborská. http://www.europarl.europa.eu/sides/getDoc.do?pubRef=-//EP//TEXT+CRE+20090421+ITEM-028+DOC+XML+V0//EN.

European Parliament. 2009b. "Report on Gender Mainstreaming in the Work of Its Committees and Delegations (2008/2245 (INI))."

European Parliament. 2009c. "Amendments 1–16 to the Draft Report on Gender Mainstreaming in the Work of its Committees and Delegations (2008/2245 (INI))." PE 421.194v01–00.

European Parliament. 2010. "Debates. 18 October 2010." http://www.europarl.europa.eu/sides/getDoc.do?type=CRE&reference=20101018&secondRef=ITEM-013&language=EN&ring=A7-2010-0032.

European Parliament. 2014a. *Gender Mainstreaming in Committees and Delegations of the European Parliament*. Study Commissioned by the European Parliament, Directorate-General for Internal Policies. doi: 10.2861/55611.

European Parliament. 2014b. *Post-Election Survey 2014: European Elections 2014 – Socio-Demographic Annex*. Brussels: EP, Directorate-General for Communication. http://www.europarl.europa.eu/pdf/eurobarometre/2014/post/post_ee2014_sociodemographic_annex_en.pdf.

European Parliament. 2014c. *Women in the European Parliament*. Brussels: European Parliament.

European Parliament. 2014d. Committee Statistical Report for the 7th Legislature – 2009–2014, Brussels.

European Parliament. 2015. *The EU Budget for Gender Equality: Analytical Study. Study for the FEMM Committee*. Brussels: EP Directorate-General for Internal Policies. http://www.europarl.europa.eu/RegData/etudes/STUD/2015/490708/IPOL_STU(2015)490708_EN.pdf.

European Parliament. 2016a. "Resolution of 8 March 2016 on Gender Mainstreaming in the Work of the European Parliament (2015/2230 (INI))."

European Parliament. 2016. *Women in the European Parliament*. Brussels: European Parliament.

European Parliament. 2017a. *Gender Equality in the European Parliament Secretariat – State of Play and the Way Forward 2017–2019*. Brussels: European Parliament.

European Parliament. 2017b. Handbook on the Ordinary Legislative Procedure, Brussels.

European Parliament. 2017c. Women in the European Parliament, Brussels, 8 March 2017.

European Parliament. 2018a. "Updating of the Study on Gender Mainstreaming in Committees and Delegations of the European Parliament. Policy Department for Citizens' Rights and Constitutional Affairs." Study. http://www.europarl.europa.eu/RegData/etudes/STUD/2018/608850/IPOL_STU(2018)608850_EN.pdf.

European Parliament. 2018b. *Women in the European Parliament*. Brussels: European Parliament.

European Parliament. 2018c. *Legislative Powers*. http://www.europarl.europa.eu/aboutparliament/en/20150201PVL00004/Powers-and-procedures (last accessed on 27 May 2018).

European Parliament. 2019a. "European Parliament resolution of 15 January 2019 on gender mainstreaming in the European Parliament (2018/2162 (INI))."

European Parliament. 2019b. "Legislative Train Schedule. Maternity Leave Directive." http://www.europarl.europa.eu/legislative-train/theme-deeper-and-fairer-internal-market-with-a-strengthened-industrial-base-labour/file-maternity-leave-directive.

European Parliament. 2019c. "Legislative Train Schedule. Gender Balance on Boards." http://www.europarl.europa.eu/legislative-train/theme-area-of-justice-and-fundamental-rights/file-gender-balance-on-boards.

European Parliament. 2019d. "Text Adopted by Parliament, Partial Vote at 1st Reading/Single Reading." https://oeil.secure.europarl.europa.eu/oeil/popups/summary.do?id=1569677&t=d&l=en.

European Parliament. 2019e. "Amendments 1–159. Draft report Angelika Mlinar. Gender mainstreaming in the European Parliament (2018/2162 (INI))." http://www.europarl.europa.eu/sides/getDoc.do?pubRef=//EP//NONSGML+COMPARL+PE-629.466+01+DOC+PDF+V0//EN&language=EN https://www.europarl.europa.eu/doceo/document/FEMM-AM-629466_EN.pdf?redirect.

European Parliament. Directorate General for Internal Policies. 2014. *Gender Mainstreaming in Committees and Delegations of the European Parliament*. (PE 493.051): 15, 13. http://www.europarl.europa.eu/RegData/etudes/etudes/join/2014/493051/IPOL-FEMM_ET(2014)493051_EN.pdf.

European Parliamentary Research Service. 2014. "Europe's First Women." *European Parliament Research Service Blog*, 5 March 2014. https://epthinktank.eu/2014/03/05/europes-first-women/.

Europees Parlement. 1981. *De positie van de vrouw in de Europese Gemeenschap*. Luxembourg: Bureau voor Officiële Publikaties van de Europese Gemeenschappen.

Farrel, Henry, and Adrienne Héritier. 2003. "The Invisible Transformation of Codecision: Problems of Democratic Legitimacy." *Swedish Institute for European Policy Studies* no. 7 (June): 1–33.

Ferree, Myra Marx. 2012. *Varieties of Feminism. German Gender Politics in Global Perspective*. Stanford: Stanford University Press.

Finnemore, Martha, and Kathryn Sikkink. 1998. "International Norm Dynamics and Political Change." *International Organisation* 52(4): 887–917.

Fitzi, Gregor, Juergen Mackert, and Bryan S. Turner. 2018. *Populism and the Crisis of Democracy*. London: Routledge.

Fortin-Rittberger, Jessica, and Berthold Rittberger. 2014. "Do Electoral Rules Matter? Explaining National Differences in Women's Representation in the European Parliament." *European Union Politics* 15(4): 496–520.

Fortin-Rittberger, Jessica, and Berthold Rittberger. 2015. "Nominating Women for Europe: Exploring the Role of Political Parties' Recruitment Procedures for European Parliament Elections." *European Journal of Political Research* 54(4): 767–83.

Fortin-Rittberger, Jessica. 2016. "Cross-National Gender-Gaps in Political Knowledge: How Much is Due to Context?" *Political Research Quarterly* 69(3): 391–402.

Foucault, Michel. 1980. *Power/Knowledge: Selected Interviews and Other Writings 1972–1977*. New York: Panteon Books.

Foucault, Michel. 1995. *Discipline and Punish. The Birth of the Prison*. New York: Vintage.

Franceschet, Susan, and Jennifer Piscopo. 2018. "Gender Quotas and Women's Substantive Representation: Lessons from Argentina." *Politics & Gender* 4(3): 393–425.

Fraser, Nancy. 2013. *Fortunes of Feminism: From State-Managed Capitalism to Neoliberal Crisis*. London/New York: Verso.

Frederick, Brian. 2009. "Are Female House Members Still More Liberal in a Polarized Era? The Conditional Nature of the Relationship between Descriptive and Substantive Representation." *Congress & the Presidency* 36(2): 181–202. https://doi.org/10.1080/07343460902948097.

Friedman, Sally. 1996. "House Committee Assignments of Women and Minority Newcomers, 1965–1994." *Legislative Studies Quarterly* 21(1): 73–81.

Frisch, Scott A, and Sean Q Kelly. 2003. "A Place at the Table." *Women and Politics* 25(3): 1–26. https://doi.org/10.1300/J014v25n03.

Funkel, Manuel, and Christoph Trebesch. 2017. *Financial Crises and the Populist Right*. München: ifo Institut – Leibniz-Institut für Wirtschaftsforschung an der Universität München.

Gadinger, Frank, Sebastian Jarzebski, and Taylan Yildiz. 2014. "Vom Diskurs zur Erzählung. Möglichkeiten einer politikwissenschaftlichen Politikanalyse." *Politische Vierteljahresschrift* 55(1): 67–93.

Galligan, Yvonne, and Sara Clavero. 2008. "Prospects for Women's Legislative Representation in Post-Socialist Europe: The Views of Female Politicians." *Gender and Society* 22(2): 149–71.

Galligan, Yvonne, and Sara Clavero. 2012. "Gendering Enlargement of the European Union." In *Gendering the European Union: New Approaches to Old Democratic Deficits*, edited by Gabriele Abels and Joyce Marie Mushaben, 104–23. Basingstoke: Palgrave Macmillan.

Gattermann, Katjana, and Sofia Vasilopoulou. 2015. "Absent Yet Popular? Explaining News Visibility of Members of the European Parliament." *European Journal of Political Research* 54(1): 121–40.

Gertzog, Irwin Norman. 1995. *Congressional Women: Their Recruitment, Integration, and Behaviour*. 2nd ed. Westport, CT: Praeger.

Grace, Joan. 2016. "Presence and Purpose in the Canadian House of Commons: The Standing Committee on the Status of Women." *Parliamentary Affairs* 69(4): 830–44. https://doi.org/10.1093/pa/gsw008.

Guerrina, Roberta, and Annick Masselot. 2018. "Walking into the Footprint of EU Law: Unpacking the Gendered Consequences of Brexit." *Social Policy & Society* 17(2): 319–30.

Guerrina, Roberta. 2017. Gendering European Economic Narratives: Assessing the Costs of the Crisis to Gender Equality. In *Gender and the Economic Crisis in Europe*, edited by Johanna Kantola and Emanuela Lombardo, 95–115. London: Palgrave Macmillan.

Gustafsson, Michael. 2011a. "Notes From the Chair." *FEMM Newsletter*, 2011.

Gustafsson, Michael. 2011b. "Report on Gender Mainstreaming in the Work of the European Parliament." 2011/2151 (INI). Committee on Women's Rights and Gender Equality.

Haastrup, Toni, and Meryl Kenny. 2016. "Gendering Institutionalism: A Feminist Institutionalist Approach to EU Integration Theory." In *Gendering European Integration Theory*, edited by Gabriele Abels and Heather MacRae, 197–216. Berlin/Toronto: Barbara Budrich.

Häge, Frank M., and Daniel Naurin. 2013. "The Effect of Codecision on Council Decision-Making: Informalization, Politicization and Power." *Journal of European Public Policy* 20(7): 953–71.

Häge, Frank M., and Nils Ringe. 2016. "Rapporteur-Shadow Rapporteur Networks and Policy-Making in the European Parliament." Paper presented at the Midwest Political Science Association Meeting, Chicago, IL, April 2016 and at the 2016 Meeting of the American Political Science Association, Philadelphia, PA, September 2016.

Hageman, Sara. 2012. "Negotiations of the European Union Budget: How Decision Processes Constrain Policy Ambitions." In *European Union Budget Reform,* edited by Giacomo Benedetto, 23–39. London: Palgrave Macmillan.

Hausemer, Pierre. 2006. "Participation and Political Competition in Committee Report Allocation: Under What Conditions Do MEPs Represent Their Constituents?" *European Union Politics* 7(4): 505–30. https://doi.org/10.1177/1465116506069441.

Heath, Roseanna Michelle, Leslie A. Schwindt-Bayer, and Michelle M. Taylor-Robinson. 2005. "Women on the Sidelines: Women's Representation on Committees in Latin American Legislatures." *American Journal of Political Science* 49(2): 420–36. https://doi.org/10.1111/j.0092-5853.2005.00132.x.

Hefftler, Claudia, Christine Neuhold, Olivier Rozenberg, and Juli Smith, eds. 2015. *The Palgrave Handbook of National Parliaments and the European Union*. Basingstoke: Palgrave Macmillan.

Helfferich, Barbara, and Felix Kolb. 2001. "Multilevel Action Coordination in European Contentious Politics: The Case of the European Women's Lobby." In *Contentious Europeans: Protest and Politics in an Emerging Polity*, edited by Douglas Imig and Sydney Tarrow, 143–162 Washington DC: Rowman & Littlefield.

Hentges, Gudrun, and Kristina Nottbohm. 2017. "Die Verbindung von Antifeminismus und Europakritik. Positionen der Parteien 'Alternative für Deutschland' und 'Front National'." In *Europäische Identität in der Krise? Europäische Identitätsforschung und Rechtspopulismusforschung im Dialog*, edited by Gudrun Hentges, Kristina Nottbohm, and Hans-Wolfgang Platzer, 167–208. Wiesbaden: Springer VS.

Héritier, Adrienne. 2013. "Twenty Years of Legislative Co-decision in the European Union: Experiences and Implications." *Journal of European Public Policy* 20(7): 1074–82.

Hix, Simon, Bjørn Høyland. 2013. "Empowerment of the European Parliament." *Annual Review of Political Science* 16: 171–89.

Hix, Simon. 2008. "Towards a Partisan Theory of EU Politics." *Journal of European Public Policy* 15(8): 1254–65.

Hobolt, Sara Binzer. 2014. "A Vote for the President? The Role of *Spitzenkandidaten* in the 2014 European Parliament elections." *Journal of European Public Policy* 21(10): 1528–40.

Holst, Cathrine, and Helena Seibicke. 2018. "Unpacking Gender Expertise: The Case of the European Women's Lobby." In *Expertisation and Democracy in Europe* edited by Magdalena Góra, Cathrine Holst, and Marta Warat. New Work: Routledge.

Hooghe, Lisbeth, and Gary Marks. 2009. "A Postfunctionalist Theory of European Integration: From Permissive Consensus to Constraining Dissensus." *British Journal of Political Science* 39(1): 1–23.

Hooghe, Lisbeth, and Gary Marks. 2012. "Politicization." In *The Oxford Handbook of the European Union,* edited by Erik Jones, Anand Menon, and Stephen Weatherill, 840–53. Oxford: Oxford University Press.

Hoskyns, Catherine. 1996. *Integrating Gender: Women, Law and Politics in the European Union.* London: Verso.

Huber, Katrin, and Michael Shackleton. 2013. "Codecision: A Practitioner's View from Inside the Parliament." *Journal of European Public Policy* 20(7): 1040–55.

Hubert, Agnès, and Maria Stratigaki. 2016. "Twenty Years of EU Gender Mainstreaming: Rebirth Out of the Ashes?" *Femina Politica* 25(2): 21–36.

Hubert, Agnès. 2012. "Gendering Employment Policy: From Equal Pay to Work-Life Balance." In *Gendering the European Union: New Approaches to Old Democratic Deficits,* edited by Gabriele Abels and Joyce Marie Mushaben, 146–68. Basingstoke: Palgrave Macmillan.

Hughes, Melanie M., and Pamela Paxton. 2008. "Continuous Change, Episodes, and Critical Periods: A Framework for Understanding Women's Political Representation over Time." *Politics & Gender* 4(2): 233–64. https://doi.org/10.1017/S1743923X08000329.

Ilonszki, Gabriella. 2004. *Women in Decision-Making: CEE Experiences.* Budapest: Open Society Institute.

Jacobs, Francis. 2015. "Handling of European Union Legislation since the Treaty of Lisbon." Paper presented at the 14th Biennial Conference of the European Union Studies, Boston, MA, March 2015.

Jacquot, Sophie. 2015. *Transformations in EU Gender Equality: From Emergence to Dismantling.* Houndmills; Basingstoke Hampshire; New York: Palgrave Macmillan.

Jacquot, Sophie. 2017. A Policy in Crisis. The Dismantling of the EU Gender Equality Policy. In *Gender and the Crisis in Europe,* edited by Johanna Kantola and Emanuela Lombardo, 27–48. London: Palgrave Macmillan.

Janssen, Thilo. 2013. *Die Europäisierung der rechten EU-Gegner. Rechte europäische Parteien und rechte Fraktionen im Europäischen Parlament vor den Europawahlen 2014.* Berlin: Rosa-Luxemburg-Stiftung.

Jogerst, Michael A. 1993. *Reform in the House of Commons: The Select Committee System.* Lexington: The University Press of Kentucky.

Kaeding, Michael, and Alan Hardacre. 2013. "The European Parliament and the Future of Comitology after Lisbon." *European Law Journal* 19(3): 382–40.

Kanter, Rosabeth Moss. 1977. *Men and Women of the Corporation.* New York: Basic Books.

Kantola, Johanna, and Lise Rolandsen Agustín. 2019. "Gendering the representative work of the European Parliament: A political analysis of women MEP's perceptions of gender equality in party groups." *Journal of Common Market Studies* 57(4): 768–786.

Kantola, Johanna, and Lise Rolandsen Agustín. 2016. "Gendering Transnational Party Politics: The Case of European Union." *Party Politics* 22(5): 641–51.

Kantola, Johanna, and Emanuela Lombardo, eds. 2017. *Gender and the Economic Crisis in Europe. Politics, Institutions and Intersectionality.* Basingstoke: Palgrave Macmillan.

Kantola, Johanna, and Emanuela Lombardo. 2018. "EU Gender Equality Policies." In *Handbook of European Policies. Interpretive Approaches to the EU,* edited by Hubert Heinelt and Sybille Münch, 331–49. Cheltenham: Edward Elgar.

Kantola, Johanna, and Kevät Nousiainen. 2009. "Institutionalizing Intersectionality in Europe: Introducing the Theme." *International Feminist Journal of Politics* 11(4): 459–78.

Kantola, Johanna, and Mieke Verloo. 2018. "Revisiting Gender Equality at Times of Recession: a Discussion of the Strategies of Gender and Politics Scholarship Dealing with Equality." *European Journal of Politics and Gender* 1(1–2): 205–22.

Kantola, Johanna. 2006. *Feminists Theorize the State*. Basingstoke: Palgrave Macmillan.

Kantola, Johanna. 2009. "Women's Political Representation in the European Union." *The Journal of Legislative Studies* 15: 379–400.

Kantola, Johanna. 2010. *Gender and the European Union*. Basingstoke: Palgrave Macmillan.

Karamessini, Maria, and Jill Rubery, eds. 2014. *Women and Austerity: The Economic Crisis and the Future for Gender Equality*. London; New York: Routledge.

Kemper, Andreas. 2014. *Keimzelle der Nation, Teil 2. Wie sich in Europa Parteien und Bewegungen für konservative Familienwerte, gegen Toleranz und Vielfalt und gegen eine progressive Geschlechterpolitik radikalisieren*. Berlin: Friedrich-Ebert-Stiftung.

Kenney, Sally J. 2002. "Breaking the Silence: Gender Mainstreaming and the Composition of the European Court of Justice." *Feminist Legal Studies* 10(3): 257–70.

Kiianmaa, Nelli (ed.). 2013. *Gender Equality Barometer 2012*. Helsinki: Finnish Ministry of Social Affairs and Health.

Klatzer, Elisabeth, and Christa Schlager. 2017. "The Gendered Nature of Economic Governance in the EU: A Key Battleground for Gender Equality." In *Towards Gendering Institutionalism: Equality in Europe*, edited by Heather MacRae, and Elaine Weiner, 165–82. Lanham MD: Rowman & Littlefield.

Kohn, Walter S. G. 1981. "Women in the European Parliament." *Parliamentary Affairs* 34(2): 210–20. https://doi.org/10.1093/oxfordjournals.pa.a054198.

König, Thomas. 2008. "Why Do Member States Empower The European Parliament?" *Journal of European Public Policy* 15(2): 167–88.

Korolczuk, Elżbieta, and Agnieszka Graff. 2018. "Gender as 'Ebola from Brussels': The Anticolonial Frame and the Rise of Illiberal Populism." *Signs: Journal of Women in Culture and Society* 43(4): 797–821.

Köttig, Michaela, Petö, Andrea, and Renate Bitzan, eds. 2017. *Gender and Far Right Politics in Europe*. Basingstoke: Palgrave Macmillan.

Kováts, Eszter. 2018. "Questioning Consensuses: Right-Wing Populism, Anti-Populism, and the Threat of 'Gender Ideology'." *Sociological Research Online* 528–38.

Kreppel, Amie. 2010. "Necessary But Not Sufficient: Understanding the Impact of Treaty Reform on the Internal Development of the European Parliament" *Journal of European Public Policy* 10(6): 884–911.

Kriesi, Hanspeter, and Takis S. Pappas. 2015. *European Populism in the Shadow of the Great Recession*. Colchester: ECPR Press.

Krizsan, Andrea, and Raluca Maria Popa. 2015. "Women's Movements Challenging Gender-Based Violence in the Countries of Central and Eastern Europe." In *Mobilising for Policy Change: Women's Movements in Central and Eastern European Domestic Violence Policy Struggles*, edited by Andrea Krizsan, 1–44. Budapest: CEU Press.

Krizsan, Andrea, and Birte Siim. 2018. "Gender Equality and Family in Populist Radical-Right Agendas: European Parliamentary Debates 2014." In *Gender and Generational Division in EU Citizenship*, edited by Trudie Knijn and Manuela Naldini. Cheltenham: Edward Elgar, 39–59.

Krizsan, Andrea. 2015. *Mobilising for Policy Change: Women's Movements in Central and Eastern European Domestic Violence Policy Struggles*. Budapest: CEU Press.

Kucklick, Christoph. 2008. *Das unmoralische Geschlecht. Zur Geburt einer negativen Andrologie*. Frankfurt/Main: Suhrkamp.

Kuhar, Roman, and David Paternotte. 2017. *Anti-Gender Campaigns. Mobilising Against Equality*. London; New York: Rowman & Littlefield.

Kulawik, Teresa. 2009. "Staking the Frame of a Feminist Discursive Institutionalism." *Politics & Gender* 5(2): 262–71.

Landorff, Laura. 2019. *Inside European Parliament Politics: Informality, Information and Intergroups*. Basingstoke: Palgrave Macmillan.

Lazaridis, Gabriella, Giovanna Campani, and Annie Benveniste. 2016. *The Rise of the Far Right in Europe. Populist Shifts and 'Othering'*. London: Palgrave MacMillan.

Locher, Birgit. 2007. *Trafficking in the European Union. Norms, Advocacy-Networks and Policy-Change*. Wiesbaden: VS Verlag für Sozialwissenschaften.

Locher, Birgit. 2012. "Gendering the EU Policy Process." In *Gendering the European Union. New Approaches to Old Democratic Deficits*, edited by Gabriele Abels and Joyce Mushaben, 63–84. Houndmills: Palgrave Macmillan.

Lombardo, Emanuela, and Lise Rolandsen Agustín. 2011. "Framing Gender Intersections in the European Union: What Implications for the Quality of Intersectionality in Policies?" *Social Politics* 19(4): 482–512.

Lombardo, Emanuela, and Maxime Forest. 2012. *The Europeanization of Gender Equality Policies: A Discursive-Sociological Approach*. New York: Palgrave Macmillan.

Lombardo, Emanuela, and Petra Meier. 2008. "Framing Gender Equality in the European Union Political Discourse." *Social Politics* 15(1): 101–29.

Lombardo, Emanuela, and Petra Meier. 2016. *The Symbolic Representation of Gender: A Discursive Approach*. New York: Routledge.

Lombardo, Emanuela, Petra Meier, and Mieke Verloo, eds. 2009. *The Discursive Politics of Gender Equality: Stretching, Bending and Policymaking*. London: Routledge.

Lombardo, Emanuela. 2005. "Integrating or Setting the Agenda? Gender Mainstreaming in the European Constitution-Making Process." *Social Politics* 12(3): 412–32.

Lombardo, Emanuela. 2016. "Social Constructivism in European Integration Theories: Gender and Intersectionality Perspectives." In *Gendering European Integration Theory. Engaging new Dialogues*, edited by Heather MacRae and Gabriele Abels, 123–46. Berlin; Toronto: Barbara Budrich Publishers.

Lovecy, Jill. 2002. "Gender Mainstreaming and the Framing of Women's Rights in Europe: The Contribution of the Council of Europe." *Feminist Legal Studies* 10(3): 271–83.

Lühiste, Maarja, and Meryl Kenny. 2016. "Pathways to Power: Women's Representation in the 2014 European Parliament Elections." *European Journal of Political Research* 55(3): 626–41.

Lukes, Steven. 2005. *Power: A Radical View*. New York: Palgrave Macmillan.

Lum Kathryn, and Géraldine Renaudière. 2014. "The Rise of the Extreme Right in Europe: The Gender and Sexuality Dimensions of Anti-Immigrant Discourse." http://critcom.councilforeuropeanstudies.org/the-rise-of-the-extreme-right-in-europe-the-gender-and-sexuality-dimensions-of-anti-immigrant-discourse/.

Mackay, Fiona, and Petra Meier. 2003. "Institutions, Change, and Gender Relations: Towards a Feminist New Institutionalism?" Paper presented at the European Consortium for Political Research Joint Sessions of Workshops. Edinburgh, 28 March–2 April 2003.

Mackay, Fiona, Meryl Kenny, and Louise Chappell. 2010. "New Institutionalism through a Gender Lens: Towards a Feminist Institutionalism?" *International Political Science Review* 31(5): 573–88.

Mackay, Fiona. 2009. "Travelling the Distance? Equal Opportunities in the Scottish Parliament." In *The Scottish Parliament 1999–2009: The First Decade*, edited by Charlie Jeffrey and James Mitchell, 48–55. Edinburgh: Luath Press/Hansard Society.

Mackay, Fiona. 2014. "Nested Newness, Institutional Innovation, and the Gendered Limits of Change." *Politics and Gender* 10(14): 549–71.

MacRae, Heather, and Elaine Weiner, eds. 2017. *Towards Gendering Institutionalism Equality in Europe*. London: Rowman & Littlefield.

MacRae, Heather, and Gabriele Abels. 2016. "Why and How to Gender European Integration Theory? Introduction." In *Gendering European Integration Theory: Engaging new Dialogues*, edited by Gabriele Abels and Heather MacRae, 9–37. Leverkusen: Barbara Budrich Publishers.

Macrae, Heather. 2010. "The EU as a Gender Equal Polity: Myths and Realities." *Journal of Common Market Studies* 48(1): 155–74.

MacRae, Heather. 2012. "Double-Speak: The European Union and Gender Parity." *West European Politics* 35(2): 301–318.

Mahoney, James, and Kathleen Thelen. 2010. "A Theory of Gradual Institutional Change." In *Explaining Institutional Change: Ambiguity, Agency and Power*, edited by James Mahoney and Kathleen Thelen. Cambridge: Cambridge University Press.

Mamadouh, Virginie, and Tapio Raunio. 2003. "The Committee System: Powers, Appointments and Report Allocation." *Journal of Common Market Studies* 41(2): 333–51.

Mansbridge, Jane. 1999. "Should Blacks Represent Blacks and Women Represent Women? A Contingent 'Yes'." *The Journal of Politics* 61(03): 628–57.

Marx, Karl. 1887/1999. *Capital: A Critique of Political Economy. Volume One*. Marx/Engels Internet Archive (marxists.org). https://www.marxists.org/archive/marx/works/download/pdf/Capital-Volume-I.pdf (last accessed on 30 October 2018).

Matland, Richard E., and Kathleen A. Montgomery, eds. 2003. *Women's Access to Political Power in Postcommunist Europe*. Oxford: Oxford University Press.

Mazey, Sonia. 1998. "The European Union and Women's Rights: From the Europeanization of National Agendas to the Nationalization of a European Agenda?" *Journal of European Public Policy* 5(1): 131–52.

Mazey, Sonia. 2001. *Gender Mainstreaming in the EU: Principles and Practice*. London: Kogan Page.

McElroy, Gail, and Kenneth Benoit. 2010. "Party Policy and Group Affiliation in the European Parliament." *British Journal of Political Science* 40(2): 377–98.

McElroy, Gail, and Kenneth Benoit. 2012. "Policy Positioning in the European Parliament." *European Union Politics* 13(1): 150–67.

McElroy, Gail. 2006. "Committee Representation in the European Parliament." *European Union Politics* 7(1): 5–29. https://doi.org/10.1177/1465116506060910.

McEvoy, Caroline. 2016. "Does the Descriptive Representation of Women Matter? A Comparison of Gendered Differences in Political Attitudes between Voters and Representatives in the European Parliament." *Politics and Gender* 12(4): 754–80. https://doi.org/10.1017/S1743923X16000118

Meier, Petra, and Karen Celis. 2011. "Sowing the Seeds of Its Own Failure: Implementing the Concept of Gender Mainstreaming." *Social Politics* 18(4): 469–89.

Milevska, Tanja. 2014. "Left Parties Win Gender Parity Contest in New EU Parliament." *EurActive*, 5 June 2014. https://www.euractiv.com/section/future-eu/news/left-parties-win-gender-parity-contest-in-new-eu-parliament/.

Millard, Frances. 2014. "Not Much Happened: The Impact of Gender Quotas in Poland." *Communist and Postcommunist Studies* 47(1): 1–11.

Mlinar, Angelika. 2016. "Report on Gender Mainstreaming in the Work of the European Parliament" (2015/2230 (INI)). Brussels: Committee on Women's Rights and Gender Equality. 23 February 2016. http://www.europarl.europa.eu/doceo/document/A-8-2016-0034_EN.html?redirect.

Moir, Eilidh and Michael Leyshon. 2013. "The Design of Decision-Making: Participatory Budgeting and the Production of Localism." *Local Environment* 18(9): 1002–23.

Momsen, Janet. 2010. *Gender and Development.* Abington: Routledge.

Mudde, Cas. 2007. *Populist Radical Right Parties in Europe.* Cambridge: Cambridge University Press.

Murphy, Mary C., and John O'Brennan. 2014. "Reflections on Forty Years of Irish Membership of the European Union." Special issue, *Administration* 62(3).

Murphy, Mary P. 2015. "Forty Years of the EU Influencing Social Policy in Ireland – A Glass Half Full?" *Administration* 62: 69–86.

Murray, Rainbow, and Réjane Sénac. 2018. "Explaining Gender Gaps in Legislative Committees." *Journal of Women, Politics & Policy* 39(3): 310–35. https://doi.org/10.1080/1554477X.2018 1477397.

Mushaben, Joyce Marie, and Gabriele Abels. 2015. "The Lack of Gender Equality in EU Decision Making Means Citizens Are Still Suffering from a 'Double Democratic' Deficit." *EUROPP: European Politics and Policy.* https://blogs.lse.ac.uk/europpblog/2014/08/28/the-lack-of-gender equality-in-eu-decision-making-means-eu-citizens-are-still-suffering-from-a-double-democratic-deficit/.

Mushaben, Joyce Marie. 1985. "Innocence Lost: Environmental Images and Political Experiences among the West German Greens." *New Political Science* 6(1): 39–66. https://doi.org/10.1080/07393148508429599.

Mushaben, Joyce Marie. 1994. "The Other *Democratic Deficit.* Women in the European Community Before and After Maastricht." In *Europe after Maastricht: American and European Perspectives,* edited by Paul Michael Lützeler, 251–75. Providence: Berghahn.

Mushaben, Joyce Marie. 1999. "The Politics of Critical Acts: Women and Leadership in the European Union." *European Studies Journal* 15(2): 51–91.

Mushaben, Joyce Marie. 2017. *Becoming Madam Chancellor: Angela Merkel and the Berlin Republic.* Cambridge: Cambridge University Press.

Nelsen, Brent F., and James L. Guth. 2015. *Religion and the Struggle for European Union: Confessional Culture and the Limits of Integration.* Washington D.C.: Georgetown University Press.

Neunreither, Karlheinz. 1994. "The Democratic Deficit of the European Union: Towards Closer Cooperation between the European Parliament and the National Parliaments." *Government and Opposition* 29(3): 299–314.

Nitoiu, Christian. 2015. "The Politicisation of the Neighbourhood in the European Parliament: From 2009 to 2014." Paper presented at the ECPR Joint Sessions, University of Warsaw, 29 March–2 April 2015. https://ecpr.eu/Filestore/PaperProposal/6e89fa03-a655-4be6-bb65-e399b47ea830.pdf.

Norris, Pippa, and Ronald Inglehart. 2003. *Rising Tide: Gender Equality and Cultural Change Around the World.* New York: Cambridge University Press.

Norris, Pippa. 1997. "Introduction: Theories of Recruitment." In *Passages to Power: Legislative Recruitment in Advanced Democracies,* edited by Pippa Norris, 1–14. Cambridge: Cambridge University Press.

Nussbaum, Martha. 2003. "Capabilities as Fundamental Entitlements: Sen and Social Justice." *Feminist Economics* 9(2–3): 33–59.

O'Brien, Diana Z. 2012. "Gender and Select Committee Elections in the British House of Commons." *Politics & Gender* 8(2): 178–204. https://doi.org/10.1017/S1743923X12000153.

Osborn, Tracy L. 2012. *How Women Represent Women: Political Parties, Gender, and Representation in the State Legislatures.* Oxford: Oxford University Press.

Pajnik, Mojca, and Birgit Sauer, eds. 2017. *Populism and the Web: Communicative Practices of Parties and Movements in Europe.* New York: Routledge.

Palmieri, Sonia. 2011. *Gender-Sensitive Parliaments: A Global Review of Good Practice.* Geneva: Inter-parliamentary Union. http://archive.ipu.org/pdf/publications/gsp11-e.pdf (last accessed on 1 March 2019).

Panitch, Leo, and Greg Albo, eds. 2017. *Rethinking Democracy, Socialist Register 2018.* New York: Monthly Review Press.

Patzelt, Werner J., ed. 2003. *Parlamente und ihre Funktionen. Institutionelle Mechanismen und institutionelles Lernen im Vergleich.* Wiesbaden: Springer VS.

Pearce, Andrew. 2013. *My Personal Story: In and out of Europe.* Kibworth: Matador.

Phillips, Anne. 1995. *The Politics of Presence.* Oxford: Oxford University Press.

Pimminger, Irene. 2015. "Sag beim Abschied leise Servus? Aktuelle Entwicklungen in der EU-Gleichstellungspolitik." *Friedrich Ebert Stiftung* (October): 1–8.

Piscopo, Jennifer M. 2014. "Inclusive Institutions versus Feminist Advocacy: Women's Legislative Committees and Caucuses in Latin America." Paper presented at the International Political Science Association World Congress, Montreal, Canada, July 2014.

Pitkin, Hanna. 1967. *The Concept of Representation.* Berkeley and Los Angeles, CA: University of California Press.

Pollack, Mark, and Emilie Hafner-Burton. 2000. "Mainstreaming Gender in the European Union." *Journal of European Public Policy* 7(3): 432–56.

Praud, Jocelyne. 2012. "Introduction: Gender Parity and Quotas in European Politics." *West European Politics* 35(2): 286–300.

Pristed Nielsen, Helene, and Lise Rolandsen Agustín. 2013. "Women, Participation and the European Parliament." In *Negotiating Gender and Diversity in an Emergent European Public Sphere,* edited by Birte Siim and Monika Mokre, 201–22. Basingstoke: Palgrave Macmillan.

Prügl, Elisabeth. 2012. "'If Lehman Brothers Had Been Lehman Sisters. . .': Gender and Myth in the Aftermath of the Financial Crisis." *International Political Sociology* 6(1): 21–35.

Puwar, Nirmal. 2004. *Space Invaders: Race, Gender and Bodies Out of Place.* New York: Berg.

Quinlan, Stephen, and Martin Okolikj. 2016 "This Time It's Different But Not Really! The 2014 European Parliament Elections in Ireland." *Irish Political Studies* 31(2): 1–15.

Rai, Shirin M. 2010. "Analysing Ceremony and Ritual in Parliament." *The Journal of Legislative Studies* 16(3): 284–97.

Rai, Shirin M. 2012. "Political Performance: Reading Parliamentary Politics." *Warwick Performance and Politics Network. Working Papers* 1(1): 3–27. http://www2.warwick.ac.uk/fac/cross\_fac/wppn/publications/workingpapers/vol\_1\_issue\_1\_shirin\_rai.pdf (last accessed on 22 June 2018).

Rai, Shirin M. 2014. "Political Performance: A Framework for Analysing Democratic Politics." *Political Studies* 63(5): 1179–97.

Rankin, Jennifer. 2018. "The EU Is Too White – and Brexit Likely to Make it Worse, MEPs and Staff Say." *The Guardian online*, 29 August 2018. https://www.theguardian.com/world/2018/aug/29/eu-is-too-white-brexit-likely-to-make-it-worse (last accessed on 1 March 2019).

Rauh, Christian. 2018. "EU Politicization and Policy Initiatives of the European Commission: The Case of Consumer Policy." *Journal of European Public Policy* 26(3): 344–65. https://doi.org/10.1080/13501763.2018.1453528.

Raunio, Tapio, and Wolfgang M. Wagner. 2017. "Ideology or National Interest? External Relations Votes in the European Parliament." *The Amsterdam Centre for Contemporary European Studies Research Paper/ACCESS EUROPE Research Paper* 2017 (1): 1–32.

Rees, Teresa L. 1998. *Mainstreaming Equality in the European Union: Education, Training and Labour Market Policies.* London: Routledge.

Rees, Teresa L. 2002. *National Policies on Women and Science in Europe.* Brussels: Office for Official Publications of the European Union.

Renman, Vilde, and Caroline Conroy. 2014. "Advances in EU Gender Equality: Missing the Mark?" *European Policy Institutes Network* 41: 1–12.

Richardson, Jeremy, and Sonia Mazey, ed. 2015. *European Union: Power and policy-making.* London; New York: Routledge.

Ripoll Servent, Ariadna. 2018. *The European Parliament.* London: Palgrave Macmillan.

Rittberger, Berthold, and Phillipp Schroeder. 2016. "The Legitimacy of Regional Institutions." In *The Oxford Handbook of Comparative Regionalism*, edited by Tanja Boerzel and Thomas Risse. Oxford: Oxford University Press.

Rittberger, Berthold. 2005. *Building Europe's Parliament: Democratic Representation Beyond the Nation State.* Oxford: Oxford University Press.

Rittberger, Berthold. 2012. "Institutionalizing Representative Democracy in the European Union: The Case of the European Parliament." *JCMS – Journal of Common Market Studies* 50(1): 18–37.

Robeyns, Ingrid. 2003. "Sen's Capability Approach and Gender Inequality: Selecting Relevant Capabilities." *Feminist Economics* 9(2): 61–92.

Roederer-Rynning, Christilla, and Justin Greenwood. 2015. "The Culture of Trilogues." *Journal of European Public Policy* 22(8): 1148–65.

Roger, Léa, and Thomas Winzen. 2015. "Party Groups and Committee Negotiations in the European Parliament: Outside Attentions and the Anticipation of Plenary Conflict." *Journal of European Public Policy* 22(3): 391–408.

Roger, Léa. 2016. *Voice(s) in the European Parliament: Deliberation and Negotiation in EP Committees.* Baden-Baden: Nomos.

Roggeband, Conny, and Andrea Krizsan. 2018. "Reversing Gender Policy Progress: Patterns of Backsliding in Central and Eastern European New Democracies." *European Journal of Politics and Gender* 1(3): 367–85.

Rolandsen Agustín, Lise. 2012. "(Re)defining Women's Interests? Political Struggles over Women's Collective Representation in the Context of the European Parliament." *European Journal of Women's Studies* 19(1): 23–40.

Rolandsen Agustín, Lise. 2013. *Gender Equality, Intersectionality, and Diversity in Europe.* New York: Palgrave Macmillan.

Roth, Silke. 2007. "Sisterhood and Solidarity? Women's Organisations in the Expanded European Union." *Social Politics* 14(4): 460–87.

Roth, Silke. 2008. *Gender Politics in the Expanding European Union: Mobilisation, Inclusion, Exclusion.* Oxford: Berghahn.

Rowley, Michelle V. 2006. Review of *Book Reviews*, by Ronald Inglehart, Pippa Norris, V. Spike Peterson, Marianne Braig, and Sonja Wölte. *Signs: Journal of Women and Culture Society* 31(2): 560–65. https://doi.org/10.1086/491678.

Rueschemeyer, Marilyn, and Sharon L. Wolchik. 2009. *Women in Power in Postcommunist Parliaments*. Bloomingdale: Indiana University Press.

Rueschemeyer, Marilyn. 1998. *Women in the Politics of Postcommunist Europe*. London: M.E. Sharpe.

Russell, Meg, and Meghan Benton. 2011. *Selective Influence: The Policy Impact of House of Commons Select Committees*. The Constitution Unit, University College London. https://www.ucl.ac.uk/constitution-unit/sites/constitution-unit/files/153.pdf.

Saxonberg, Steven. 2000. "Women in East European Parliaments." *Journal of Democracy* 11(2): 145–58.

Schaffer, Johanna. 2008. *Ambivalenzen der Sichtbarkeit. Über die die visuellen Strukturen der Sichtbarkeit*. Bielefeld: transcript.

Scherpereel, John A., Jerry Wohlgemuth, and Margaret Schmelzinger. 2017. "The Adoption and Use of Twitter as a Representational Tool among Members of the European Parliament." *European Politics and Society* 18(2): 111–27.

Schmidt, Vivien A. 2010. "Taking Ideas and Discourse Seriously: Explaining Change Through Discursive Institutionalism as the Fourth 'New Institutionalism'." *European Political Science Review* 2(1): 1–25.

Schmidt, Vivien A. 2011. "Speaking of Change: Why Discourse Is Key to the Dynamics of Policy Transformation." *Critical Policy Studies* 5(2): 106–26.

Schonard, Martina. 2018. "Equality between men and women." *Fact Sheets on the European Union*. Brussels: European Parliament. http://www.europarl.europa.eu/factsheets/en/sheet/59/equality-between-men-and-women.

Schwindt-Bayer, Leslie A, and Renato Corbetta. 2004. "Gender Turnover and Roll-Call Voting in the U.S. House of Representative." *Legislative Studies Quarterly* 29(2): 215–29.

Sen, Amartya. 1993. "Capability and Well-Being." In *The Quality of Life*, edited by Martha Nussbaum and Amartya Sen, 30–53. New York: Oxford University Press.

Sen, Amartya. 1995. *Inequality Reexamined*. New York: Oxford University Press.

Settembri, Pierpaolo, and Christine Neuhold. 2009. "Achieving Consensus through Committees: Does the European Parliament Manage?" *Journal of Common Market Studies* 47(1): 127–51.

Shackleton, Michael. 1998. "The European Parliament's New Committees of Inquiry: Tiger or Paper Tiger?" *Journal of Common Market Studies* 36(1): 115–30.

Sharp, Rhonda, and Ray Broomhill. 2002. "Budgeting for Equality: The Australian Experience." *Feminist Economics* 8(1): 25–47.

Shreeves, Rosamund, Martina Prpic, and Eulalia Claros, 2019. "Briefing. Women in Politics in the EU. State of Play." EPRS European Parliamentary Research Service. http://www.europarl.europa.eu/RegData/etudes/BRIE/2019/635548/EPRS_BRI(2019)635548_EN.pdf (last accessed on 31 March 2019).

Spierings, Niels and Andrej Zaslove. 2017. "Gender, Populist Attitudes, and Voting: Explaining the Gender Gap in Voting for Populist Radical Right and Populist Radical Left Parties." *West European Politics* 40(4): 821–47.

Spierings, Niels, Andrej Zaslove, Liza M. Mügge, and Sarah L. de Lange. 2015. "Gender and Populist Radical-Right Politics: An Introduction." *Patterns of Prejudice* 49(1–2): 3–15.

Squires, Judith. 2008. "Intersecting Inequalities: Reflecting on the Subjects and Objects of Equality." *Political Quarterly* 79(1): 53–61.

Statham, Paul, and Hans-Jörg Trenz. 2012. "The Politicization of the European Union: From Constitutional Dreams to Euro-Zone crisis Nightmares." Paper presented at the ARENA Conference on Democracy as Idea and Practice, University of Oslo, January 2012.

Steger, Gerhard. 2010. "Austria's Budget Reform: How to Create Consensus for a Decisive Change of Fiscal Rules." *OECD Journal on Budgeting* 2010 (1): 1–14.

Stockemer, Daniel. 2007. "Why Are There Differences in the Political Representation of Women in the 27 Countries of the European Union?" *Perspectives on European Politics and Society* 8(4): 476–93.

Stotsky, Janet. 2007. "Budgeting with Women in Mind." *Finance and Development* 44(2): 12–15.

Stratigaki, Maria. 2005. "Gender Mainstreaming vs. Positive Action. An Ongoing Conflict in EU Gender Equality Policy." *European Journal of Women's Studies* 12(2): 165–86.

Stratigaki, Maria. 2012. "Gendering the Social Policy Agenda: Anti-Discrimination, Social Inclusion and Social Protection." In *Gendering the European Union. New Approaches to Old Democratic Deficits*, edited by Gabriele Abels and Joyce Marie Mushaben, 169–86. Basingstoke: Palgrave Macmillan.

Strid, Sofia. 2009. *Gendered Interests in the EU: The European Women's Lobby and the Organisation and Representation of Women's Interests.* PhD dissertation, Örebro University.

Swers, Michele. 2001. "Understanding the Policy Impact of Electing a Women: Evidence from Research on Congress and State Legislatures." *Political Science & Politics* 34(2): 217–20. https://doi.org/10.1017/S1049096501000348.

Swers, Michele. 2002. *The Difference Women Make: The Policy Impact of Women in Congress.* Chicago: University of Chicago Press.

Swers, Michele. 2013. *Women in the Club: Gender and Policy Making in the Senate.* Chicago, IL: University of Chicago Press.

Teghtsoonian, Katherine. 2016. "Methods, Discourse, Activism: Comparing Institutional Ethnography and Governmentality." *Critical Policy Studies* 10(3): 330–47.

Thelen, Kathleen, and Sven Steinmo. 1992. "Institutionalism in Comparative Politics." In *Structuring Politics: Historical Institutionalism in Comparative Analysis*, edited by Sven Steinmo, Kathleen Thelen, and Frank Longstreth, 1–32. Cambridge: Cambridge University Press.

Thomson, Jennifer. 2017. "Resisting Gendered Change: Feminist Institutionalism and Critical Actors." *International Political Science Review* 39(2): 178–91.

Tömmel, Ingeborg. 2014. *The European Union: What It Is and How It Works.* Houndmills: Palgrave Macmillan.

Treib, Oliver. 2014. "The Voter Says No, But Nobody Listens: Causes and Consequences of the Eurosceptic Vote in the 2014 European Election." *Journal of European Public Policy* 21(10): 1541–54.

Tremblay, Manon. 1998. "Do Female MPs Substantively Represent Women? A Study of Legislative Behaviour in Canada's 35th Parliament." *Canadian Journal of Political Science/Revue Canadienne de Science Politique* 31(3): 435–65.

Vainiomäki, Päivi. 2013. "Equalising Opportunities – The Women's Rights Committees: 1979–1999." Archive and Documentation Centre (CARDOC), Director-General for the Presidency, European Parliament. https://doi.org/10.2861/11114.

Vallance, Elizabeth, and Elizabeth Davies. 1986. *Women of Europe: Women MEPs and Equality Policy.* Cambridge: Cambridge University Press.

van der Vleuten, Anna, and Mieke Verloo. 2012. "Ranking and Benchmarking: The Political Logic of New Regulatory Instruments in the Fields of Gender Equality and Anti-Corruption." *Policy & Politics* 40(1): 71 – 86.

van der Vleuten, Anna, Petra Ahrens, and Alexandra Scheele. 2016. "20 Jahre Vertrag von Amsterdam – reelle Vision oder reale Desillusion europäischer Gleichstellungspolitik?" *Femina Politica* 25(2): 9–21.

van der Vleuten, Anna. 2001. *Dure Vrouwen, Dwarse Staten. Een institutioneel-realistische visie op de totstandkoming en implementatie van Europees beleid*. Nijmegen: Nijmegen University Press.

van der Vleuten, Anna. 2005. "Pincers and Prestige: Explaining the Implementation of EU Gender Equality Legislation." *Comparative European Politics* 3(4): 464–88.

van der Vleuten, Anna. 2007. *The Price of Gender Equality: Member States and Governance in the European Union*. Aldershot, Hampshire: Ashgate.

van der Vleuten, Anna. 2012. "Gendering the Institutions and the Actors of the EU." In *Gendering the European Union. New Approaches to Old Democratic Deficits*, edited by Gabriele Abels, and Joyce Marie Mushaben, 41–62. New York: Palgrave Macmillan.

Vega, Arturo, and Juanita M. Firestone. 1995. "The Effects of Gender on Congressional Behavior and the Substantive Representation of Women." *Legislative Studies Quarterly* 20(2): 213. https://doi.org/10.2307/440448.

Verloo, Mieke, and David Paternotte. 2018. "The Feminist Project under Threat in Europe." *Politics and Governance* 6(3): 1–5.

Verloo, Mieke, ed. 2007. *Multiple Meanings of Gender Equality: A Critical Frame Analysis of Gender Policies in Europe*. Budapest: Central European University Press.

Verloo, Mieke, ed. 2018. *Varieties of Opposition to Gender Equality in Europe: Theory, Evidence and Practice*. New York: Routledge.

Verloo, Mieke. 2005. "Displacement and Empowerment: Reflections on the Concept and Practice of the Council of Europe Approach to Gender Mainstreaming and Gender Equality." *Social Politics* 12(3): 344–65.

Verloo, Mieke. 2006. "Multiple Inequalities, Intersectionality and the European Union." *European Journal of Women's Studies* 13(3): 211–38.

Wainwright, Martin. 2004. "UKIPs Bloomer over Women's Rights." *The Guardian*, 21 July 2004. https://www.theguardian.com/politics/2004/jul/21/uk.gender.

Walby, Sylvia. 2015. *Crisis*. Oxford: Wiley Blackwell.

Wängnerud, Lena. 2002. "Testing the Politics of Presence: Women's Representation in the Swedish Riksdag." *Scandinavian Political Studies* 23(1): 67–91.

Wängnerud, Lena. 2009. "Women in Parliaments: Descriptive and Substantive Representation." *Annual Review of Political Science* 12(1): 51–69. https://doi.org/10.1146/annurev.polisci.11.053106.123839.

Wängnerud, Lena. 2015. *The Principles of Gender-Sensitive Parliaments*. New York: Routledge.

Wiener, Antje, and Thomas Diez. 2004. "Introducing the Mosaic of Integration Theory." In *European Integration Theory*, edited by Thomas Diez and Antje Wiener, 1–21. Oxford: Oxford University Press.

Wobbe, Theresa, and Ingrid Biermann. 2009. *Von Rom nach Amsterdam. Die Metamorphosen des Geschlechts in der Europäischen Union*. Wiesbaden: VS Verlag für Sozialwissenschaften.

Wodak, Ruth. 2015. *The Politics of Fear: What Right-Wing Populist Discourses Mean*. Los Angeles, CA/London/New Delhi/Singapore/Washington, DC: Sage.

Woodward, Alison E. 2004. "Building Velvet Triangles: Gender and Informal Governance." In *Informal Governance and the European Union*, edited by Thomas Christiansen and Simona Piattoni, 76–93. Cheltenham, UK: Edward Elgar.

Woodward, Alison E. 2012. "From Equal Treatment to Gender Mainstreaming and Diversity Management." In *Gendering the European Union*, edited by Gabriele Abels, and Joyce Marie Mushaben, 85–103. New York: Palgrave Macmillan.

Xydias, Christina. 2016. "Discrepancies in Women's Presence between European National Legislatures and the European Parliament: A Contextual Explanation." *Political Research Quarterly* 69(4): 800–12.

Yin, Robert K. 2014. *Case Study Research: Design and Methods*. Thousand Oaks, CA: Sage.

Yordanova, Nikoleta. 2011. "Inter-Institutional Rules and Division of Power in the European Parliament: Allocation of Consultation and Co-Decision Reports." *West European Politics* 34(1): 97–121. https://doi.org/10.1080/01402382.2011.523547.

Yordanova, Nikoleta. 2013. *Organising the European Parliament: The Role of Committees and their Legislative Influence*. Colchester: ECPR Press.

Yule, Jule. 2000. "Women Councillors and Committee Recruitment." *Local Government Studies* 26(3): 31–54. https://doi.org/10.1080/03003930008433998.

Zimmermann, Julia Maria. 2017. *Ko-Konstruktionen von Geschlecht, Sexualität und europäischer Konstruktion im Europäischen Parlament 1999–2014. Diskurse, Narrative, Mythen*. PhD dissertation, University of Luxembourg.

# About the Authors

**Gabriele Abels** is Jean Monnet Chair for comparative politics and European integration at the Institute of Political Science, University of Tuebingen, Germany. She is member of a number of editorial and advisory boards in the field of EU studies and politics. She is a founding member of the journal *Femina Politica*. Her research interests include democratisation and parliamentarisation of the EU system, theorising European integration, gender and EU politics, the role of regions in the EU system, and regulatory policy-making.

**Petra Ahrens** is Senior Researcher in the ERC-funded research project 'Gender, party politics and democracy in Europe: A study of European Parliament's party groups' (EUGenDem) at the University of Tampere, Finland. She works on gender equality policies and politics in the European Union and Germany, gendered power relations and political strategies like gender mainstreaming, and on civil society organisations and participatory democracy. Her work has been published in academic journals such as the *Journal of Common Market Studies*, *Parliamentary Affairs* and *West European Politics*. She is also the author of *Actors, Institutions, and the Making of EU Gender Equality Programs* (2018).

**Firat Cengiz** is Senior Lecturer in Law and a Marie Curie Fellow at the University of Liverpool. She had worked as Assistant Professor at the University of Tilburg and a Max Weber Fellow at the European University Institute before joining the Liverpool University. Her research interests include European citizens' democratic participation to the making of economic policies. Her current research project on this subject benefits from a competitive Marie Curie Career Integration Grant.

**Cristina Chiva** holds a PhD from the University of Manchester, UK. She is currently Lecturer in EU politics at the University of Salford Manchester, UK. Her research focuses on women's representation in Europe's new democracies, on the impact of EU accession on gender equality in the postcommunist, and on gender and European integration. Her most recent work – *Gender, Institutions and Political Representation: Reproducing Male Dominance in Europe's New Democracies* (2018) – explores the causal mechanisms responsible for sustaining male privilege in politics in postcommunist Europe since 1990. Her comparative study of women's representation in the European Parliament delegations of the postcommunist Member States, entitled *Gender, European integration and Candidate Recruitment: The European Parliament Elections in the New EU Member States*, was published in 2014.

**Ciara Coughlan** holds an MA in European political and administrative studies from the College of Europe, Bruges. Her thesis focuses on gender mainstreaming in EU climate change policy. Since completing her studies, she has worked as a graduate trainee with the Committee for Women's Rights and Gender Equality in the European Parliament. Currently, she is working as a UK government policy Advisor, focusing on violence against women and girls in developing countries.

**Pauline Cullen** is Professor of sociology and politics in the Department of Sociology, Maynooth University, National University of Ireland. Her work examines civil society mobilisation on social justice and gender equality at national and European Union levels, women's movements, and gender and political representation. Her work has been published in leading academic journals such as the *Journal of Civil Society*, *Social Movement Studies*, *Gender Work & Organisation*, *Politics & Gender*, and *Policy & Society*.

**Johanna Kantola** is Professor of gender studies at the Faculty of Social Sciences at the Tampere University, Finland. She is the PI of the ERC Consolidator Grant (2018–2023) project 'Gender, party politics and democracy in Europe: A study of European Parliament's party groups' (EUGenDem) and Academy of Finland (2016–2020) project 'Gender and power in reconfigured corporatist Finland' (GePoCo). Her publications include *Gender and Political Analysis* and *Gender and the Economic Crisis in Europe: Politics, Institutions and Intersectionality* (2017, both co-edited with Emanuela Lombardo), *The Oxford Handbook on Gender and Politics* (2013, with Georgina Waylen, Karen Celis and Laurel Weldon) and *Gender and the European Union* (2010). She is also the editor of Palgrave Macmillan's Gender and Politics Book Series with Sarah Childs.

**Petra Meier** is Full Professor in politics at the University of Antwerp, the co-founder of A\*, the Antwerp Gender & Sexuality Studies Network and a member of the Executive Committee of the European Consortium for Political Research. Her research focuses on the representation of gender in politics and policies, more particularly what institutions how (re)produce gender (in)equality, and on what contributes to fostering equality in a more sustainable way. She studies questions of democracy and representation; electoral systems and gender quotas; the concept of representation, especially symbolic representation; the discursive construction and design of public policies; and issues of inequality in multilevel systems.

**Joyce Marie Mushaben** holds a PhD from Indiana University. Currently, she is a Curators' Distinguished Professor of Comparative Politics & Gender Studies at the University of Missouri-St. Louis. Her research focuses on women's leadership, gender policies, citizenship/migration policies, Euro-Islam debates and comparative welfare state reforms. She also serves on editorial boards for journals such as *German Politics & Society*, *German Politics*, *Femina Politica* and the *Journal of Immigrant & Refugee Studies*. Her major publications include: *From Post-War to Post-Wall Generations: Changing Attitudes towards the National Question and NATO in the Federal Republic of Germany, 1949–1995* (1998); *The Changing Faces of Citizenship: Integration and Mobilization among Ethnic Minorities in Germany* (2008); *Gendering the European Union: New Responses to Old Democratic Deficits* (co-edited with Gabriele Abels, 2012); and *Becoming Madam Chancellor: Angela Merkel and the Berlin Republic* (2017). She received the Women's Trailblazer Award in 1999, followed by the Chancellor's Award for Excellence in Research Creativity in 2007, the Governor's Award for Teaching Excellence in 2012 and a Curators' Distinguished Research Professor in 2012. She, commonly known as 'Dr. J.', was named the University's first Professor of Global Studies in 2016.

**Mary Nugent** holds a PhD in political science from Rutgers University, where she studied women and politics. Her thesis examines the role of men in the representation of women in politics, with a focus on the UK Parliament. She is an American Political Science Association Congressional Fellow, working as a policy advisor in the office of Congresswoman Deb Haaland, one of the first Native American women ever elected to the US Congress. Originally from the UK, she did her undergraduation from Cambridge University. Her research interests include gender quotas, youth representation and intersectionality in candidate selection. Her work has been published in leading academic journals such as *Party Politics*, *Parliamentary Affairs* and *Journal of Politics*.

**Lise Rolandsen Agustín** is Associate Professor at the Department of Politics and Society at the University of Aalborg (Denmark). Her research interests include gender equality, social movements, intersectionality and gender-based violence. Her publications include *Gender Equality, Intersectionality and Diversity in Europe* (2013) and *Sexual Harassment in the Work Place* (*Seksuel chikane pa arbejdspladsen. Faglige, politiske og retlige spor*) (with Anette Borchorst, 2017). Together with Petra Ahrens, she has co-edited *Gendering the European Parliament: Structures, Policies and Practices*.

**Anna van der Vleuten** is Professor of Contesting Europeanization at the Institute for Management Research, Radboud University, Netherlands. Her research interests include the intersection of comparative regionalism, EU and gender studies. Her current projects focus on gendering EU external relations, contestation of transgender rights and categories of sex. Her latest publications include 'Fish Fingers and Measles? Assessing Complex Gender Equality in the Scenarios for the Future of Europe' by Petra Ahrens (*Journal of Common Market Studies*, forthcoming); 'Feminist Engagement with Gender Equality in Regional Governance' by Conny Roggeband and Anouka van Eerdewijk (2020); and *Rethinking Gender Equality in Global Governance*, Engberg-Pedersen, Lars, Fejerskov, Adam and Cold-Ravnkilde Signe (eds) (2019).

**Markus Warasin** holds a PhD degree in political theory and history of ideas from the University of Innsbruck and an MA degree in international politics from the Universite Libre de Bruxelles. He joined the European Public Service in 2005, where he served as Head of Unit for the EP Committee on Women's Rights and Gender Equality (2014–2016, and 2019–ongoing), as Cabinet Advisor of the President of the European Parliament (2017–2019), and as Head of the Policy Unit of the EP Communication Service coordinating the concept for the awareness-raising campaign towards the 2014 elections (2010–2014). As a University lecturer, freelance journalist, and book author, Markus focuses on European integration, on communication policy, and on equality and diversity policies.

**Julia Maria Zimmermann** holds an MA in sociology, philosophy and economic and social history from Friedrich-Schiller-University in Jena, Germany. In 2017, she obtained her PhD in sociology from the University of Luxembourg on the discursive co-construction of gender and European identity in the European Parliament.

# Index

Note: Page numbers in *italic* indicate figures and tables in the corresponding page.

www.ingramcontent.com/pod-product-compliance
Lightning Source LLC
Chambersburg PA
CBHW022352280326
41935CB00007B/162

*9781538156865*